Wolfenstein ®

Titan
COMICS

WOLFENSTEIN

TITAN COMICS

EDITOR: JONATHAN STEVENSON

Senior Comics Editor: Andrew James
Art Assistant: Luke Kemp-James
Titan Comics Editorial: Lauren Bowes,
Lauren McPhee, Amoona Saohin
Production Assistant: Natalie Bolger
Production Controller: Peter James
Production Supervisor: Maria Pearson
Senior Production Controller: Jackie Flook
Art Director: Oz Browne
Senior Sales Manager: Steve Tothill
Press Officer: Will O'Mullane
Direct Sales & Marketing Manager: Ricky Claydon
Brand Manager: Chris Thompson
Publishing Manager: Darryl Tothill
Publishing Director: Chris Teather
Operations Director: Leigh Baulch
Executive Director: Vivian Cheung
Publisher: Nick Landau

Published by Titan Comics
A division of Titan Publishing Group Ltd.
144 Southwark St.
London
SE1 0UP

A CIP catalogue record for this title is available from the British Library

First edition: December 2017

ISBN: 9781785863417

10 9 8 7 6 5 4 3 2 1

Printed in Spain.

For rights information contact **jenny.boyce@titanemail.com**

WWW.TITAN-COMICS.COM

Follow us on Twitter @ComicsTitan

Visit us at facebook.com/comicstitan

WRITER
DAN WATTERS

ARTISTS
PIOTR KOWALSKI & RONILSON FREIRE

COLORS
BRAD SIMPSON
GREG MENZIE
THIAGO RIBEIRO

LETTERS
JONATHAN STEVENSON

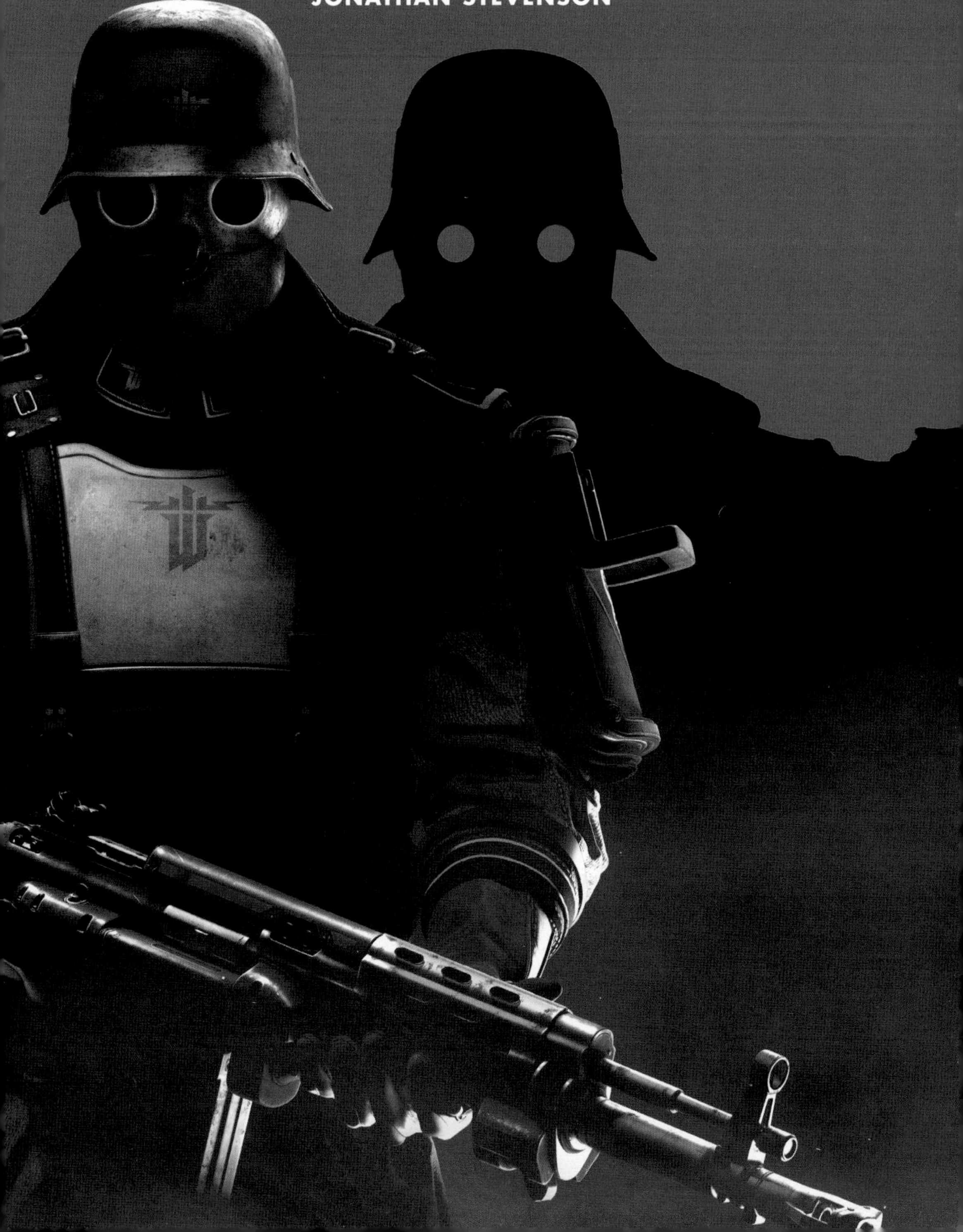

THE STORY SO FAR...

On the morning of July 16, 1946, Allied forces launched a massive offensive against the fortress and weapons laboratory run by General Wilhelm "Deathshead" Strasse. The General, a key figure within the fascist Regime, was instrumental in developing and deploying the advanced technologies that allowed the Regime to turn the tide of the war against the Allies.

US special forces hero, Captain William "B.J." Blazkowicz, was captured during the raid and taken to a laboratory for human experimentation, where he was forced by Deathshead to choose which of his companions would be executed. Left for dead in an incinerator, B.J. managed to escape, but not before suffering a critical head injury in the attempt.

Blazkowicz fell into a coma and was taken to a psychiatric hospital where he remained in a vegetative state for 14 years under the care of Anya Oliwa and her parents, who ran the Polish facility. In 1960, the Regime ordered that the hospital be shut down and commenced killing the patients and Anya's family when they resisted. B.J. awoke in the nick of time and managed to escape the hospital

with Anya after having wiped out the extermination squad.

Hiding out on Anya's grandparents' farm, Blazkowicz learned that the Regime defeated the Allies and now ruled the world with an iron fist. The US surrendered in 1948 when the fascists dropped an atom bomb over Manhattan. With the help of some farm tools, B.J. tortured a captured Regime officer into revealing the whereabouts of a group of detained resistance fighters.

After being smuggled under cover onto a night train to Berlin with Anya, B.J. encountered the nefarious fascist commander Frau Engel and her lover Bubi. Frau Engel subjected B.J. to a nonsense "purity test," toying with him like a cat playing with a mouse. B.J. managed to stay under cover and eventually Frau Engel let him go.

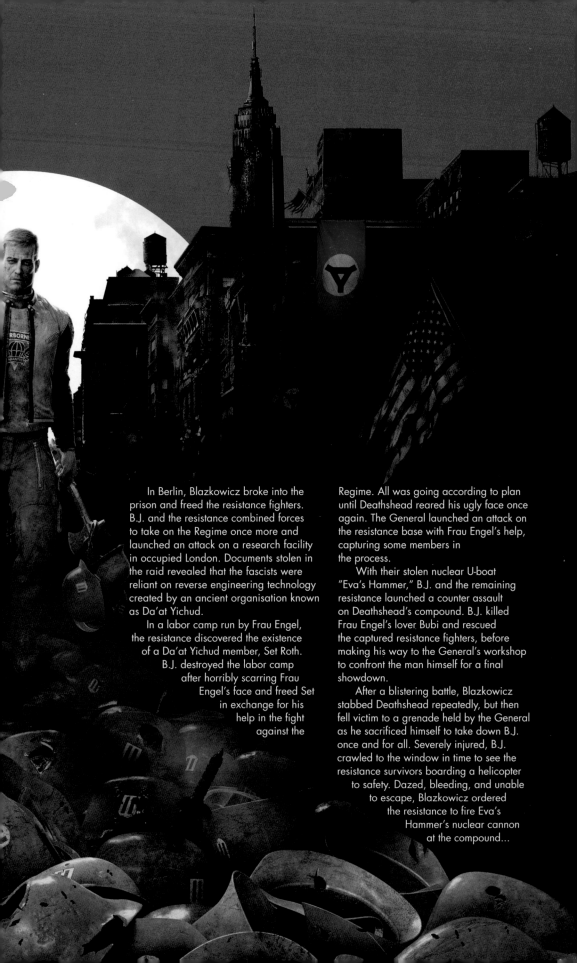

In Berlin, Blazkowicz broke into the prison and freed the resistance fighters. B.J. and the resistance combined forces to take on the Regime once more and launched an attack on a research facility in occupied London. Documents stolen in the raid revealed that the fascists were reliant on reverse engineering technology created by an ancient organisation known as Da'at Yichud.

In a labor camp run by Frau Engel, the resistance discovered the existence of a Da'at Yichud member, Set Roth. B.J. destroyed the labor camp after horribly scarring Frau Engel's face and freed Set in exchange for his help in the fight against the Regime. All was going according to plan until Deathshead reared his ugly face once again. The General launched an attack on the resistance base with Frau Engel's help, capturing some members in the process.

With their stolen nuclear U-boat "Eva's Hammer," B.J. and the remaining resistance launched a counter assault on Deathshead's compound. B.J. killed Frau Engel's lover Bubi and rescued the captured resistance fighters, before making his way to the General's workshop to confront the man himself for a final showdown.

After a blistering battle, Blazkowicz stabbed Deathshead repeatedly, but then fell victim to a grenade held by the General as he sacrificed himself to take down B.J. once and for all. Severely injured, B.J. crawled to the window in time to see the resistance survivors boarding a helicopter to safety. Dazed, bleeding, and unable to escape, Blazkowicz ordered the resistance to fire Eva's Hammer's nuclear cannon at the compound…

CHAPTER 1

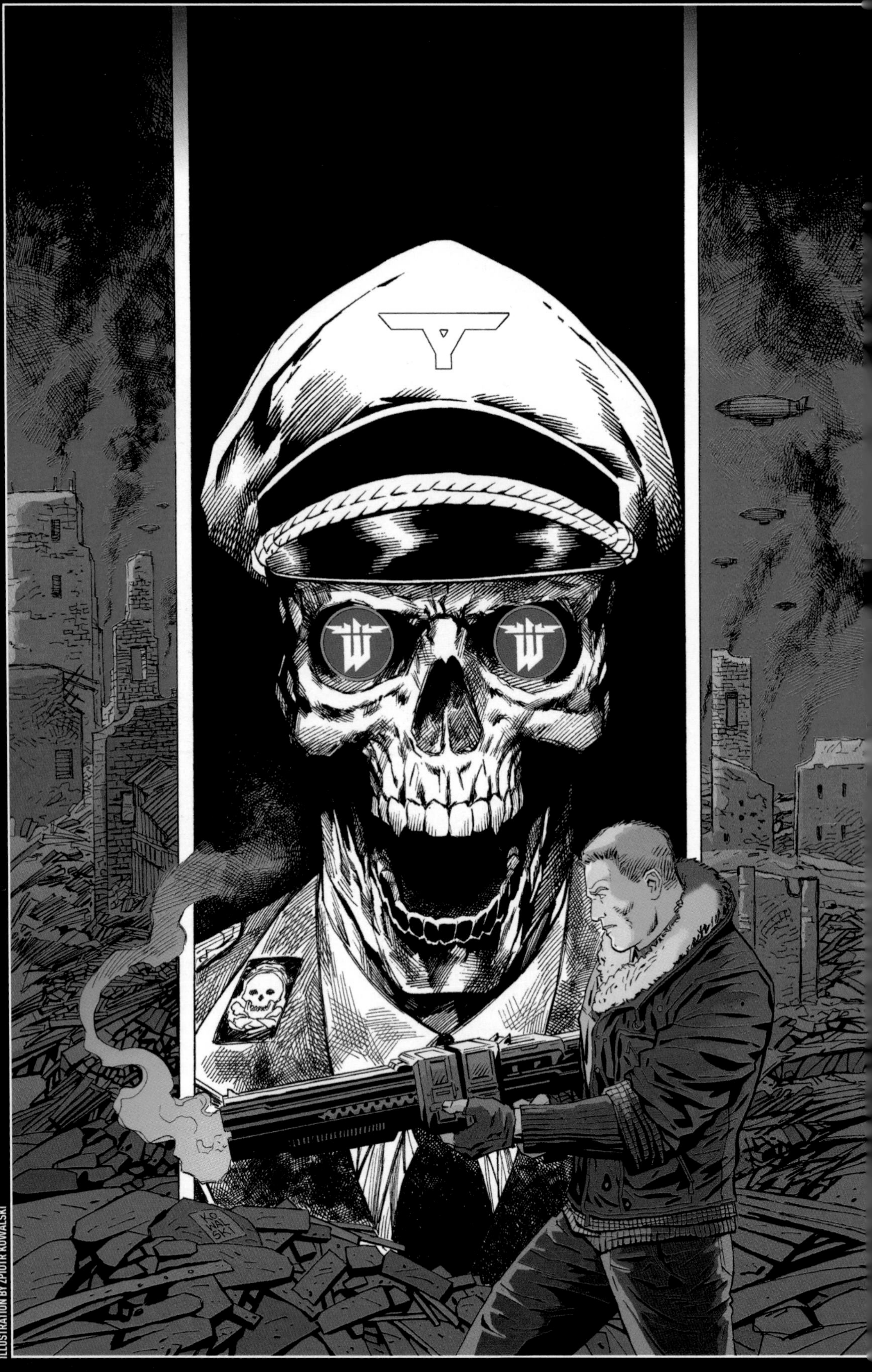
KO WAL SKI

ILLUSTRATION BY ZPIOTR KOWALSKI

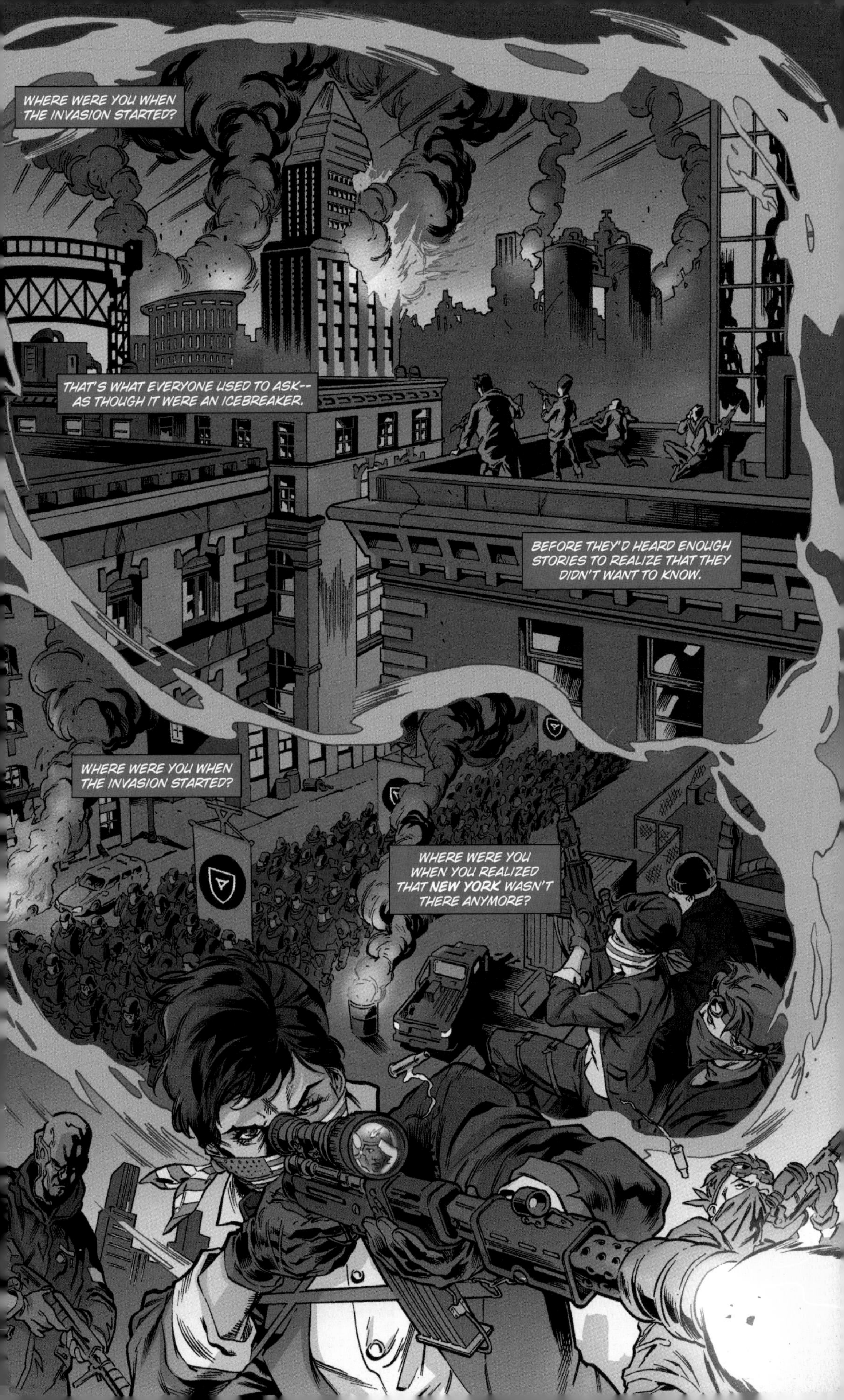
WHERE WERE YOU WHEN THE INVASION STARTED?
THAT'S WHAT EVERYONE USED TO ASK-- AS THOUGH IT WERE AN ICEBREAKER.
BEFORE THEY'D HEARD ENOUGH STORIES TO REALIZE THAT THEY DIDN'T WANT TO KNOW.
WHERE WERE YOU WHEN THE INVASION STARTED?
WHERE WERE YOU WHEN YOU REALIZED THAT **NEW YORK** WASN'T THERE ANYMORE?

JOHN CURRY WAS A TAILOR IN MISSOURI, ONCE UPON A TIME.

HE HAD MARRIED SANDRA AND THEY'D HAD TWO BEAUTIFUL CHILDREN.

HE LOVED HIS FAMILY DEARLY, THOUGH IT WAS PERHAPS HIS SON THAT HE WAS CLOSEST TO.

HE SAW HIMSELF IN THE BOY, AND WANTED TO GIVE HIM THE LIFE HE'D NEVER HAD GROWING UP.

SANDRA HAD TREMBLED IN HIS ARMS AS THE NEWS ON THE RADIO HAD GOTTEN CONSISTENTLY WORSE.

SHE'D WANTED TO UP AND LEAVE. TAKE THE KIDS AND HEAD NORTH.

JOHN TOLD HER SHE WAS DAFT, THAT THE GOOD OL' BOYS IN THE US MILITARY WOULD PULL THROUGH--THAT GOD WOULD NOT ALLOW THE LAND OF THE FREE TO SEE CHAINS AGAIN.

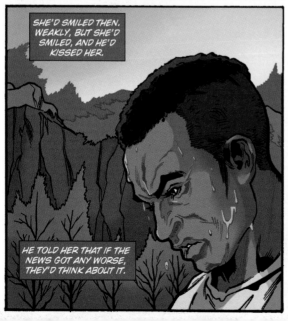

SHE'D SMILED THEN. WEAKLY, BUT SHE'D SMILED, AND HE'D KISSED HER.

HE TOLD HER THAT IF THE NEWS GOT ANY WORSE, THEY'D THINK ABOUT IT.

THE NEXT DAY THE NEWS HAD SIMPLY STOPPED ALTOGETHER.

AND BY THE DAY AFTER THAT, IT WAS FAR TOO LATE.

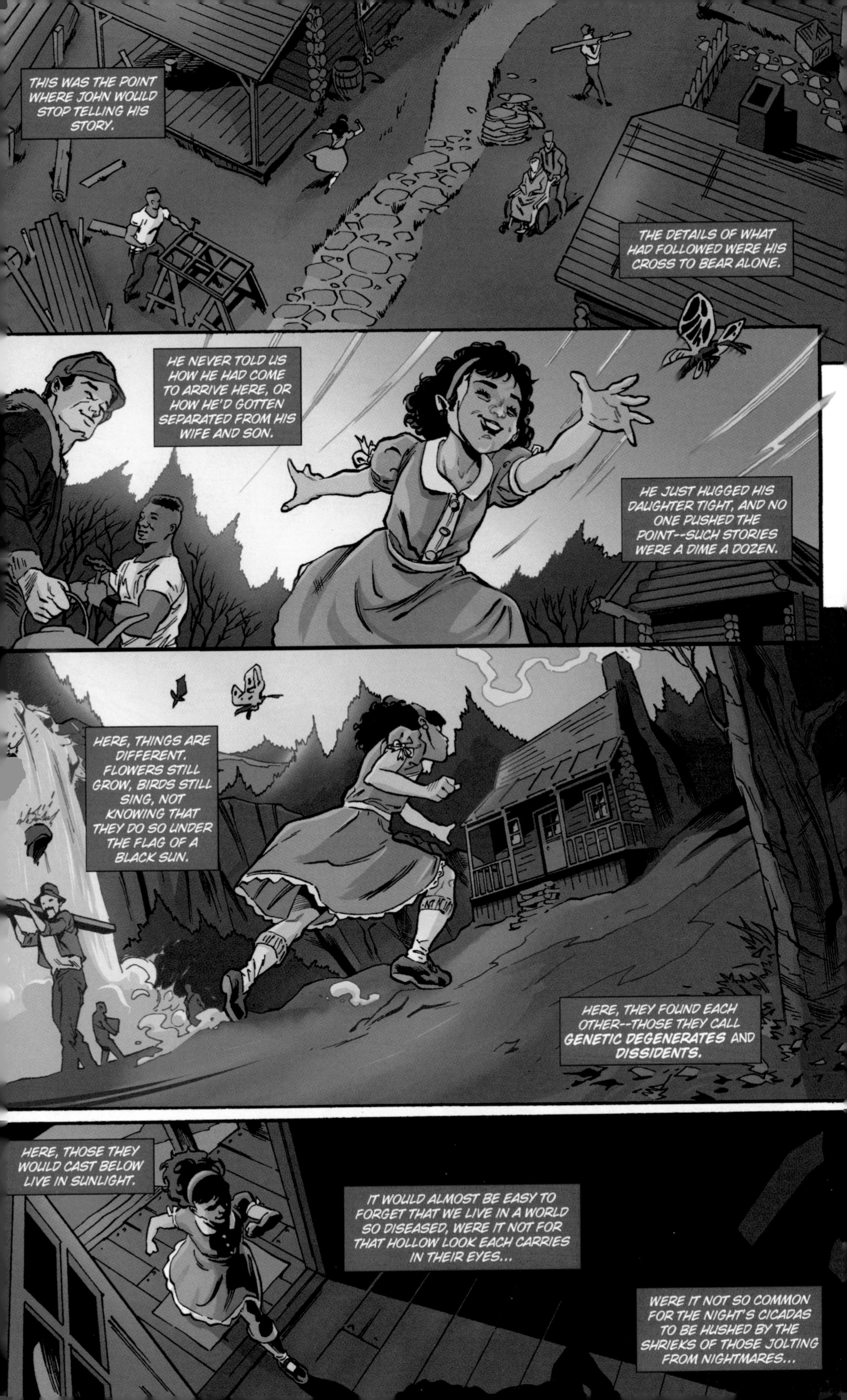
THIS WAS THE POINT WHERE JOHN WOULD STOP TELLING HIS STORY.
THE DETAILS OF WHAT HAD FOLLOWED WERE HIS CROSS TO BEAR ALONE.
HE NEVER TOLD US HOW HE HAD COME TO ARRIVE HERE, OR HOW HE'D GOTTEN SEPARATED FROM HIS WIFE AND SON.
HE JUST HUGGED HIS DAUGHTER TIGHT, AND NO ONE PUSHED THE POINT--SUCH STORIES WERE A DIME A DOZEN.
HERE, THINGS ARE DIFFERENT. FLOWERS STILL GROW, BIRDS STILL SING, NOT KNOWING THAT THEY DO SO UNDER THE FLAG OF A BLACK SUN.
HERE, THEY FOUND EACH OTHER--THOSE THEY CALL GENETIC DEGENERATES AND DISSIDENTS.
HERE, THOSE THEY WOULD CAST BELOW LIVE IN SUNLIGHT.
IT WOULD ALMOST BE EASY TO FORGET THAT WE LIVE IN A WORLD SO DISEASED, WERE IT NOT FOR THAT HOLLOW LOOK EACH CARRIES IN THEIR EYES...
WERE IT NOT SO COMMON FOR THE NIGHT'S CICADAS TO BE HUSHED BY THE SHRIEKS OF THOSE JOLTING FROM NIGHTMARES...

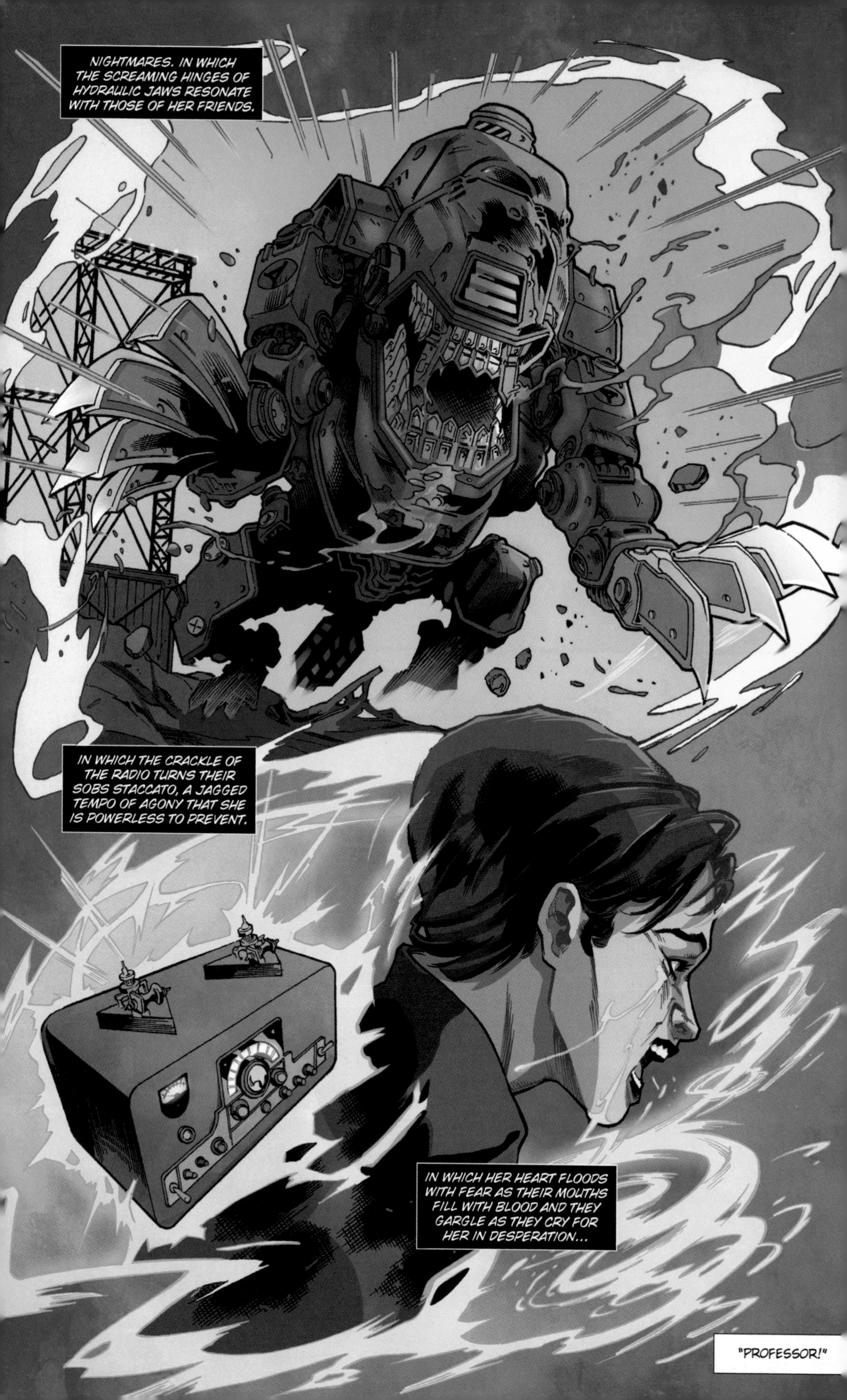
NIGHTMARES. IN WHICH THE SCREAMING HINGES OF HYDRAULIC JAWS RESONATE WITH THOSE OF HER FRIENDS.
IN WHICH THE CRACKLE OF THE RADIO TURNS THEIR SOBS STACCATO, A JAGGED TEMPO OF AGONY THAT SHE IS POWERLESS TO PREVENT.
IN WHICH HER HEART FLOODS WITH FEAR AS THEIR MOUTHS FILL WITH BLOOD AND THEY GARGLE AS THEY CRY FOR HER IN DESPERATION...
"PROFESSOR!"

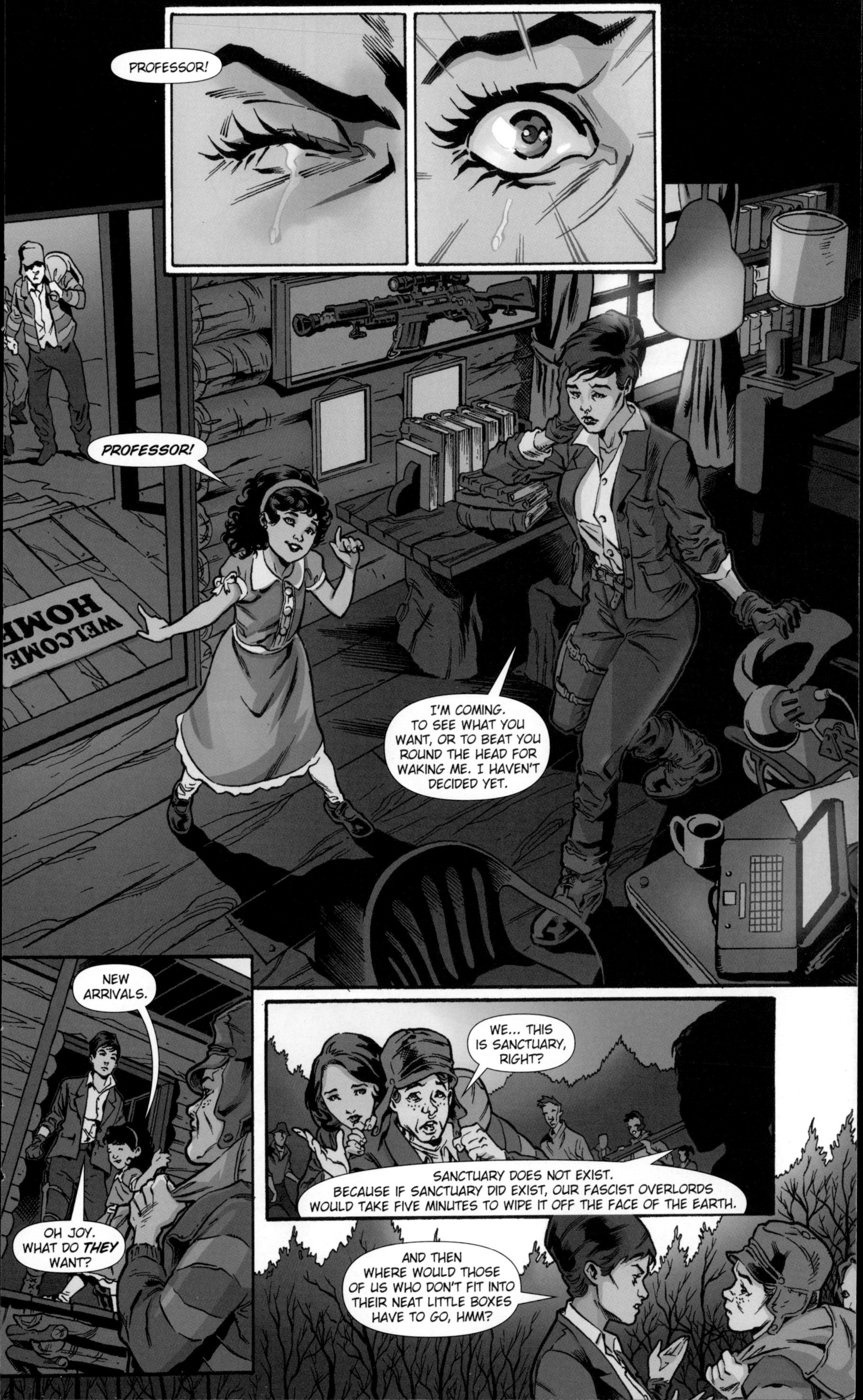
PROFESSOR!
PROFESSOR!
I'M COMING. TO SEE WHAT YOU WANT, OR TO BEAT YOU ROUND THE HEAD FOR WAKING ME. I HAVEN'T DECIDED YET.
WELCOME HOME
NEW ARRIVALS.
OH JOY. WHAT DO THEY WANT?
WE... THIS IS SANCTUARY, RIGHT?
SANCTUARY DOES NOT EXIST. BECAUSE IF SANCTUARY DID EXIST, OUR FASCIST OVERLORDS WOULD TAKE FIVE MINUTES TO WIPE IT OFF THE FACE OF THE EARTH.
AND THEN WHERE WOULD THOSE OF US WHO DON'T FIT INTO THEIR NEAT LITTLE BOXES HAVE TO GO, HMM?

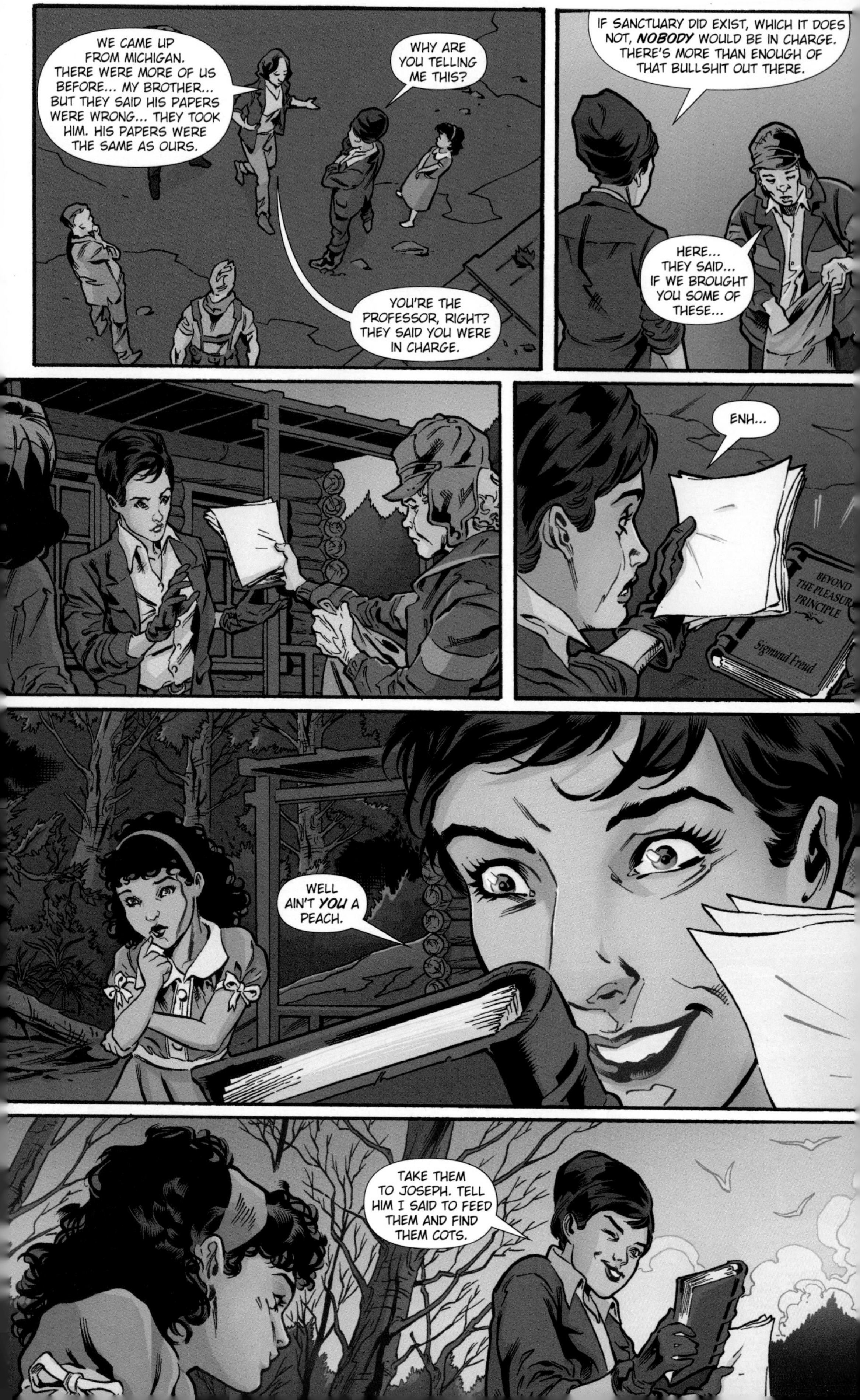

WE CAME UP FROM MICHIGAN. THERE WERE MORE OF US BEFORE... MY BROTHER... BUT THEY SAID HIS PAPERS WERE WRONG... THEY TOOK HIM. HIS PAPERS WERE THE SAME AS OURS.
WHY ARE YOU TELLING ME THIS?
YOU'RE THE PROFESSOR, RIGHT? THEY SAID YOU WERE IN CHARGE.
IF SANCTUARY DID EXIST, WHICH IT DOES NOT, NOBODY WOULD BE IN CHARGE. THERE'S MORE THAN ENOUGH OF THAT BULLSHIT OUT THERE.
HERE... THEY SAID... IF WE BROUGHT YOU SOME OF THESE...
ENH...
BEYOND THE PLEASURE PRINCIPLE
Sigmund Freud
WELL AIN'T YOU A PEACH.
TAKE THEM TO JOSEPH. TELL HIM I SAID TO FEED THEM AND FIND THEM COTS.

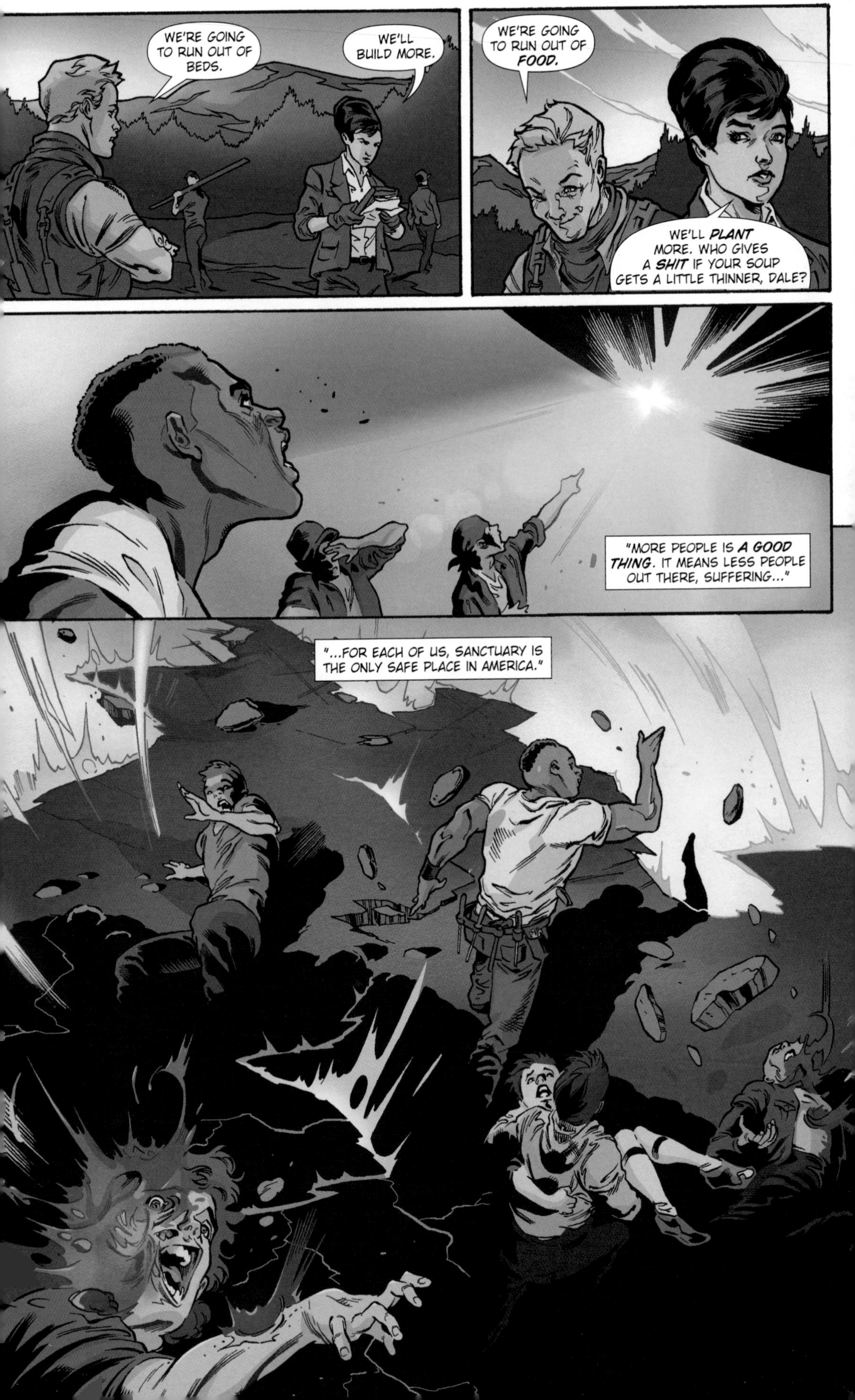
WE'RE GOING TO RUN OUT OF BEDS.
WE'LL BUILD MORE.
WE'RE GOING TO RUN OUT OF FOOD.
WE'LL PLANT MORE. WHO GIVES A SHIT IF YOUR SOUP GETS A LITTLE THINNER, DALE?
"MORE PEOPLE IS A GOOD THING. IT MEANS LESS PEOPLE OUT THERE, SUFFERING..."
"...FOR EACH OF US, SANCTUARY IS THE ONLY SAFE PLACE IN AMERICA."

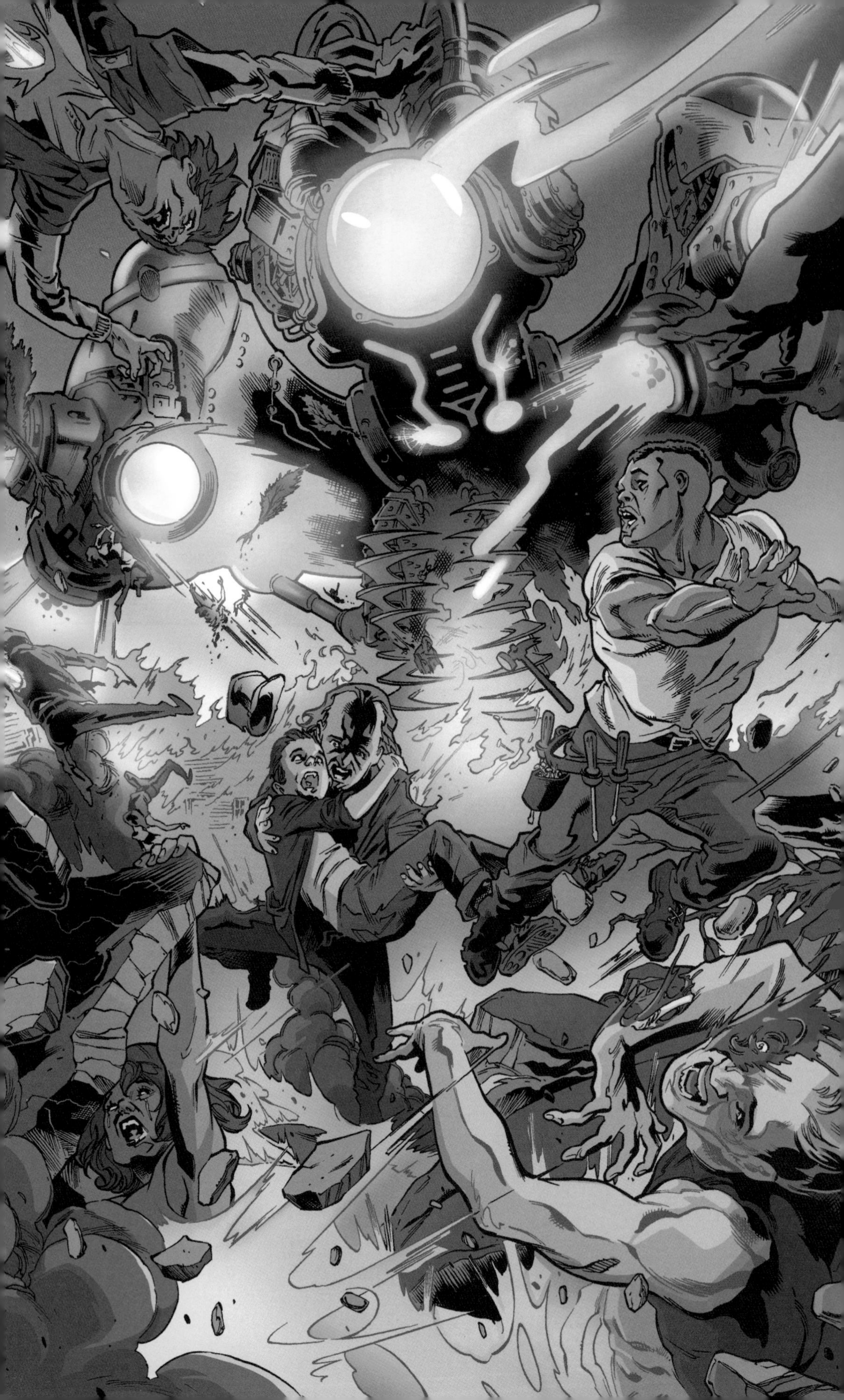

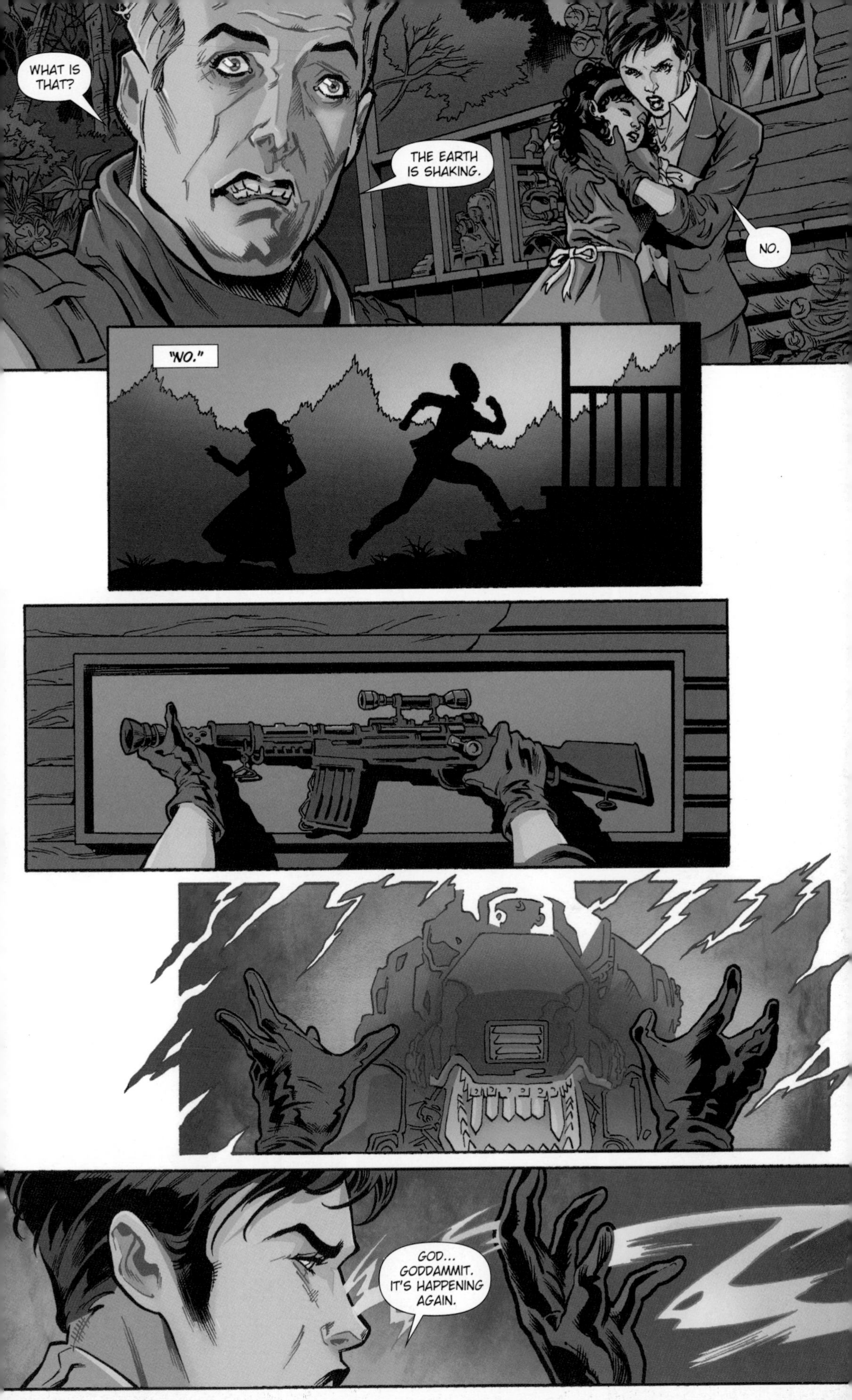
WHAT IS THAT?
THE EARTH IS SHAKING.
NO.
"NO."
GOD... GODDAMMIT. IT'S HAPPENING AGAIN.

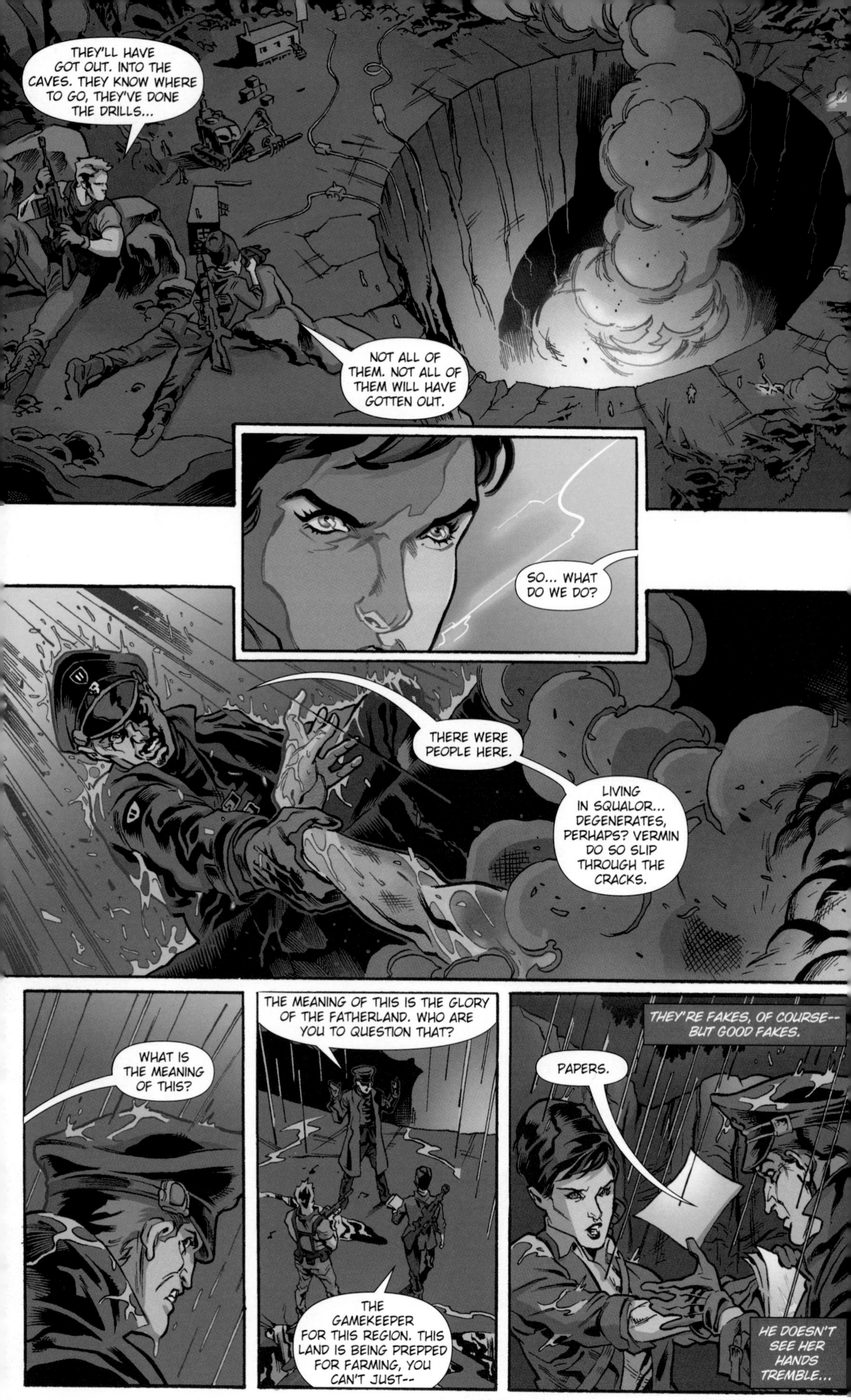
THEY'LL HAVE GOT OUT. INTO THE CAVES. THEY KNOW WHERE TO GO, THEY'VE DONE THE DRILLS...
NOT ALL OF THEM. NOT ALL OF THEM WILL HAVE GOTTEN OUT.
SO... WHAT DO WE DO?
THERE WERE PEOPLE HERE.
LIVING IN SQUALOR... DEGENERATES, PERHAPS? VERMIN DO SO SLIP THROUGH THE CRACKS.
WHAT IS THE MEANING OF THIS?
THE MEANING OF THIS IS THE GLORY OF THE FATHERLAND. WHO ARE YOU TO QUESTION THAT?
THE GAMEKEEPER FOR THIS REGION. THIS LAND IS BEING PREPPED FOR FARMING, YOU CAN'T JUST--
THEY'RE FAKES, OF COURSE-- BUT GOOD FAKES.
PAPERS.
HE DOESN'T SEE HER HANDS TREMBLE...

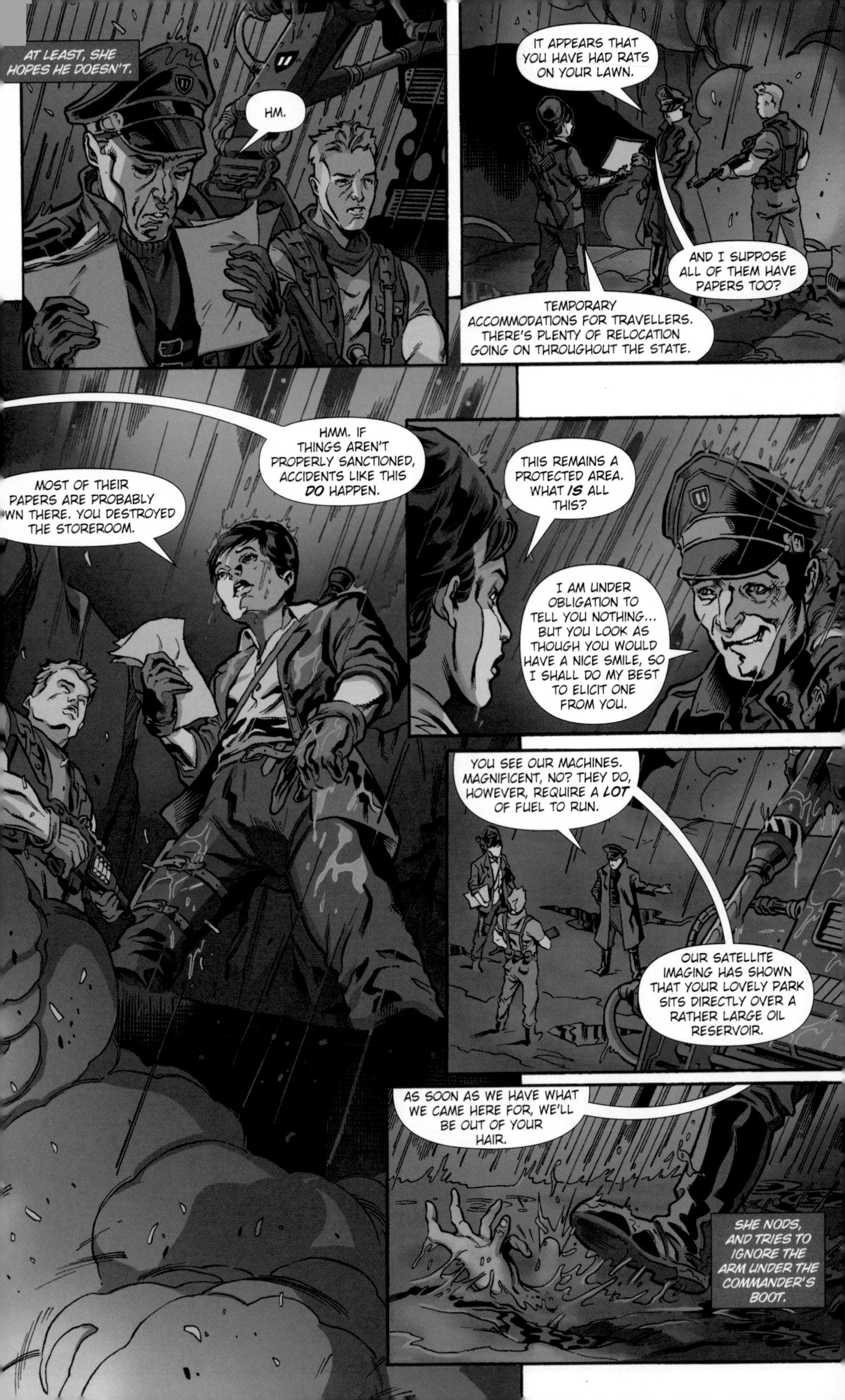
AT LEAST, SHE HOPES HE DOESN'T.
HM.
IT APPEARS THAT YOU HAVE HAD RATS ON YOUR LAWN.
TEMPORARY ACCOMMODATIONS FOR TRAVELLERS. THERE'S PLENTY OF RELOCATION GOING ON THROUGHOUT THE STATE.
AND I SUPPOSE ALL OF THEM HAVE PAPERS TOO?
MOST OF THEIR PAPERS ARE PROBABLY WN THERE. YOU DESTROYED THE STOREROOM.
HMM. IF THINGS AREN'T PROPERLY SANCTIONED, ACCIDENTS LIKE THIS DO HAPPEN.
THIS REMAINS A PROTECTED AREA. WHAT IS ALL THIS?
I AM UNDER OBLIGATION TO TELL YOU NOTHING... BUT YOU LOOK AS THOUGH YOU WOULD HAVE A NICE SMILE, SO I SHALL DO MY BEST TO ELICIT ONE FROM YOU.
YOU SEE OUR MACHINES. MAGNIFICENT, NO? THEY DO, HOWEVER, REQUIRE A LOT OF FUEL TO RUN.
OUR SATELLITE IMAGING HAS SHOWN THAT YOUR LOVELY PARK SITS DIRECTLY OVER A RATHER LARGE OIL RESERVOIR.
AS SOON AS WE HAVE WHAT WE CAME HERE FOR, WE'LL BE OUT OF YOUR HAIR.
SHE NODS, AND TRIES TO IGNORE THE ARM UNDER THE COMMANDER'S BOOT.

AND SO THE PEOPLE OF SANCTUARY WAIT, IN THE POROUS HILLS JUST BEYOND WHERE THEY ONCE CALLED HOME.

AFTER THE FIRST MONTH, SOME BEGIN TO MAKE MURMURS ABOUT LEAVING. BUT NO-ONE DOES.

NOBODY HAS ANYWHERE TO GO.

AND STILL THE MACHINES GO DEEPER, UNTIL THE ENTIRE HILLSIDE REVERBERATES TO THEIR HUM.

TOO DEEP. THEY'RE GOING TOO DEEP FOR OIL.

WHO CARES? HOW DO WE GET THEM TO *LEAVE*?

WE WAIT. THEY LEAVE.

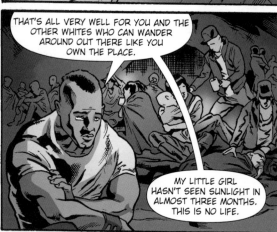

THAT'S ALL VERY WELL FOR YOU AND THE OTHER WHITES WHO CAN WANDER AROUND OUT THERE LIKE YOU OWN THE PLACE.

MY LITTLE GIRL HASN'T SEEN SUNLIGHT IN ALMOST THREE MONTHS. THIS IS NO LIFE.

YOU NEED TO GO TALK TO THEM. FIND OUT WHEN THEY'RE LEAVING.

THERE'S NOTHING I CAN--

DAMMIT.

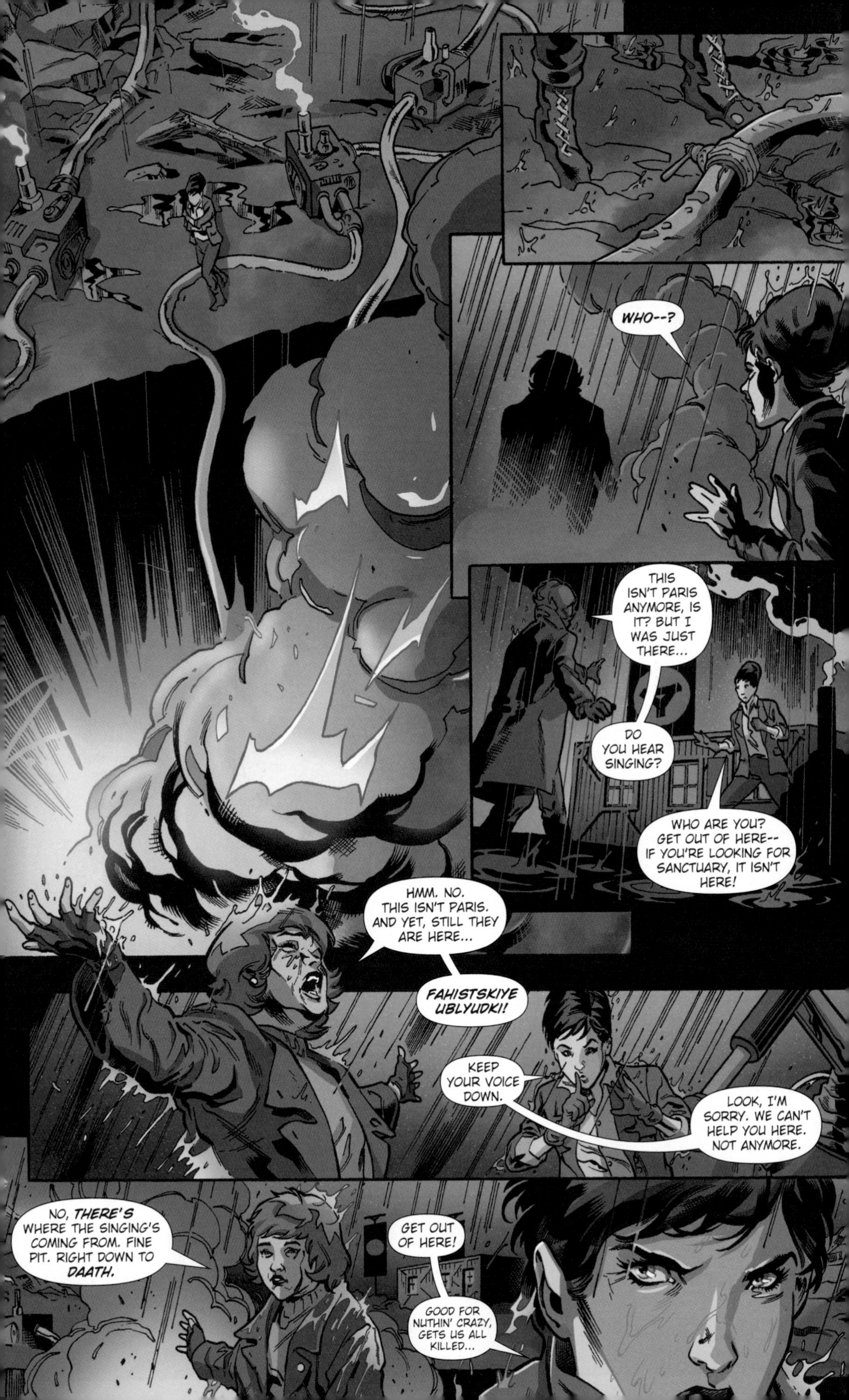
WHO--?
THIS ISN'T PARIS ANYMORE, IS IT? BUT I WAS JUST THERE...
DO YOU HEAR SINGING?
WHO ARE YOU? GET OUT OF HERE-- IF YOU'RE LOOKING FOR SANCTUARY, IT ISN'T HERE!
HMM. NO. THIS ISN'T PARIS. AND YET, STILL THEY ARE HERE...
FAHISTSKIYE UBLYUDKI!
KEEP YOUR VOICE DOWN.
LOOK, I'M SORRY. WE CAN'T HELP YOU HERE. NOT ANYMORE.
NO, THERE'S WHERE THE SINGING'S COMING FROM. FINE PIT. RIGHT DOWN TO DAATH.
GET OUT OF HERE!
GOOD FOR NUTHIN' CRAZY, GETS US ALL KILLED...

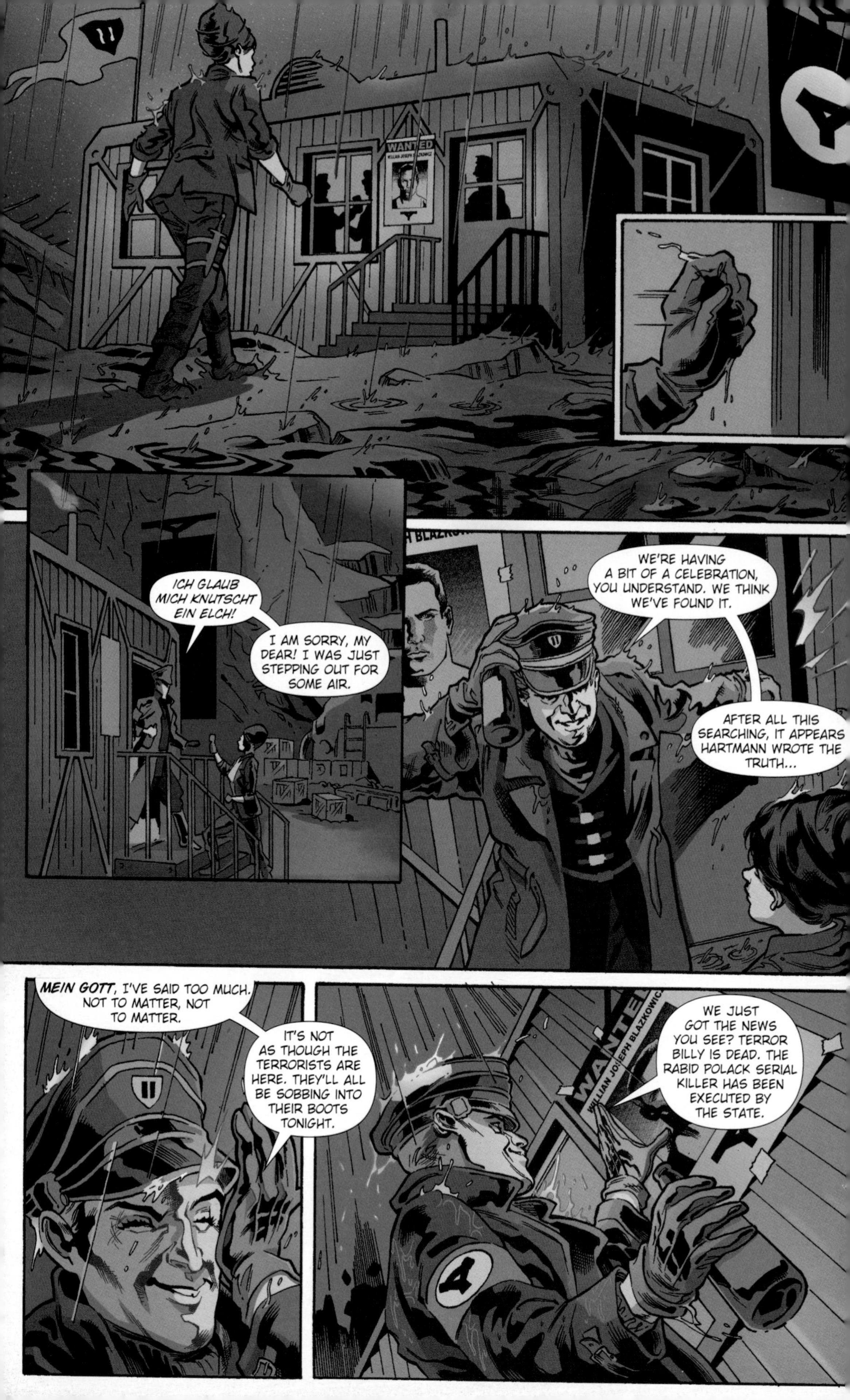
WANTED
ICH GLAUB MICH KNUTSCHT EIN ELCH!
I AM SORRY, MY DEAR! I WAS JUST STEPPING OUT FOR SOME AIR.
WE'RE HAVING A BIT OF A CELEBRATION, YOU UNDERSTAND. WE THINK WE'VE FOUND IT.
AFTER ALL THIS SEARCHING, IT APPEARS HARTMANN WROTE THE TRUTH...
MEIN GOTT, I'VE SAID TOO MUCH. NOT TO MATTER, NOT TO MATTER.
IT'S NOT AS THOUGH THE TERRORISTS ARE HERE. THEY'LL ALL BE SOBBING INTO THEIR BOOTS TONIGHT.
WE JUST GOT THE NEWS YOU SEE? TERROR BILLY IS DEAD. THE RABID POLACK SERIAL KILLER HAS BEEN EXECUTED BY THE STATE.
WANTED
WILLIAM JOSEPH BLAZKOWICZ

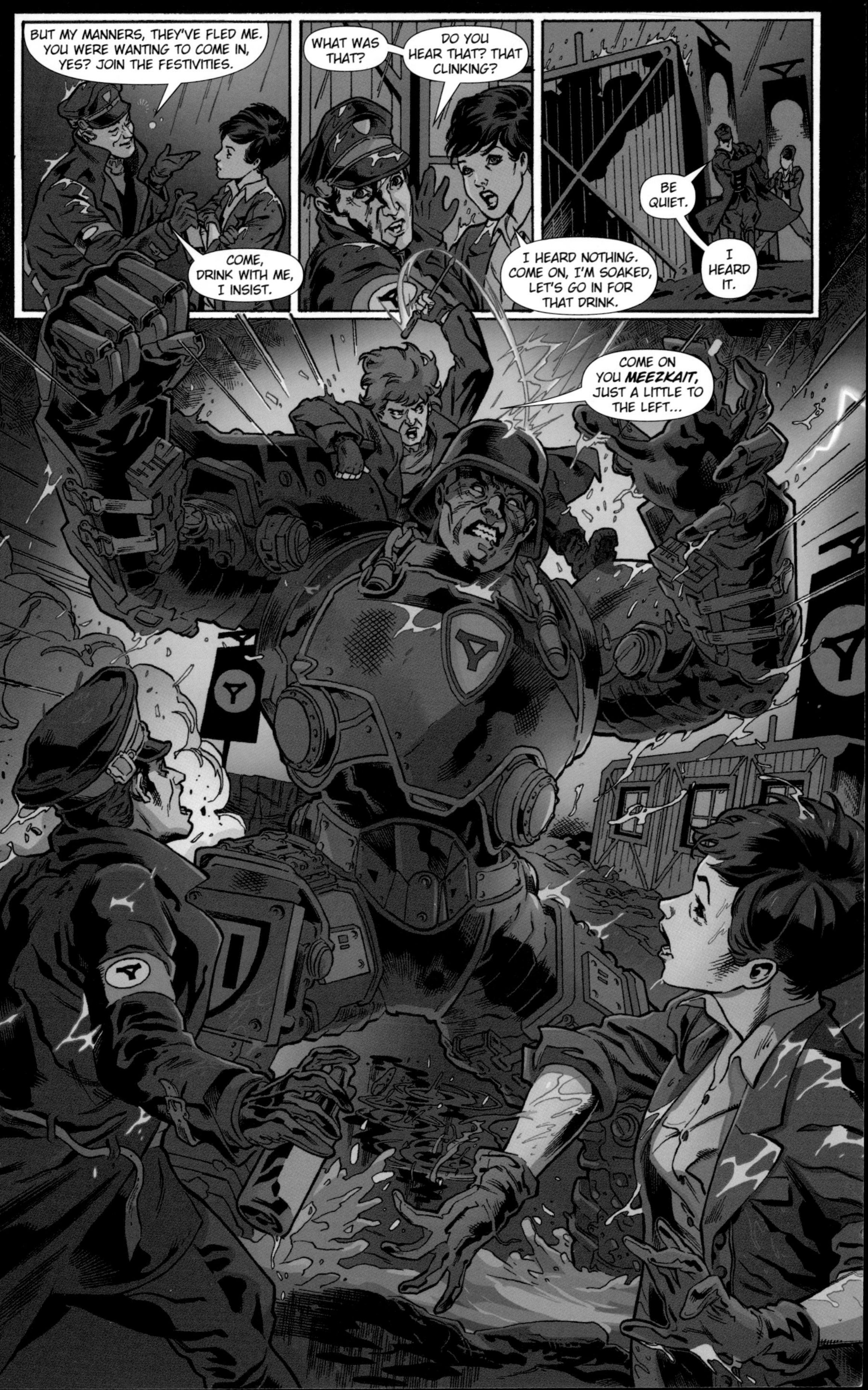

BUT MY MANNERS, THEY'VE FLED ME. YOU WERE WANTING TO COME IN, YES? JOIN THE FESTIVITIES.
COME, DRINK WITH ME, I INSIST.
WHAT WAS THAT?
DO YOU HEAR THAT? THAT CLINKING?
I HEARD NOTHING. COME ON, I'M SOAKED, LET'S GO IN FOR THAT DRINK.
BE QUIET.
I HEARD IT.
COME ON YOU ***MEEZKAIT,*** JUST A LITTLE TO THE LEFT...

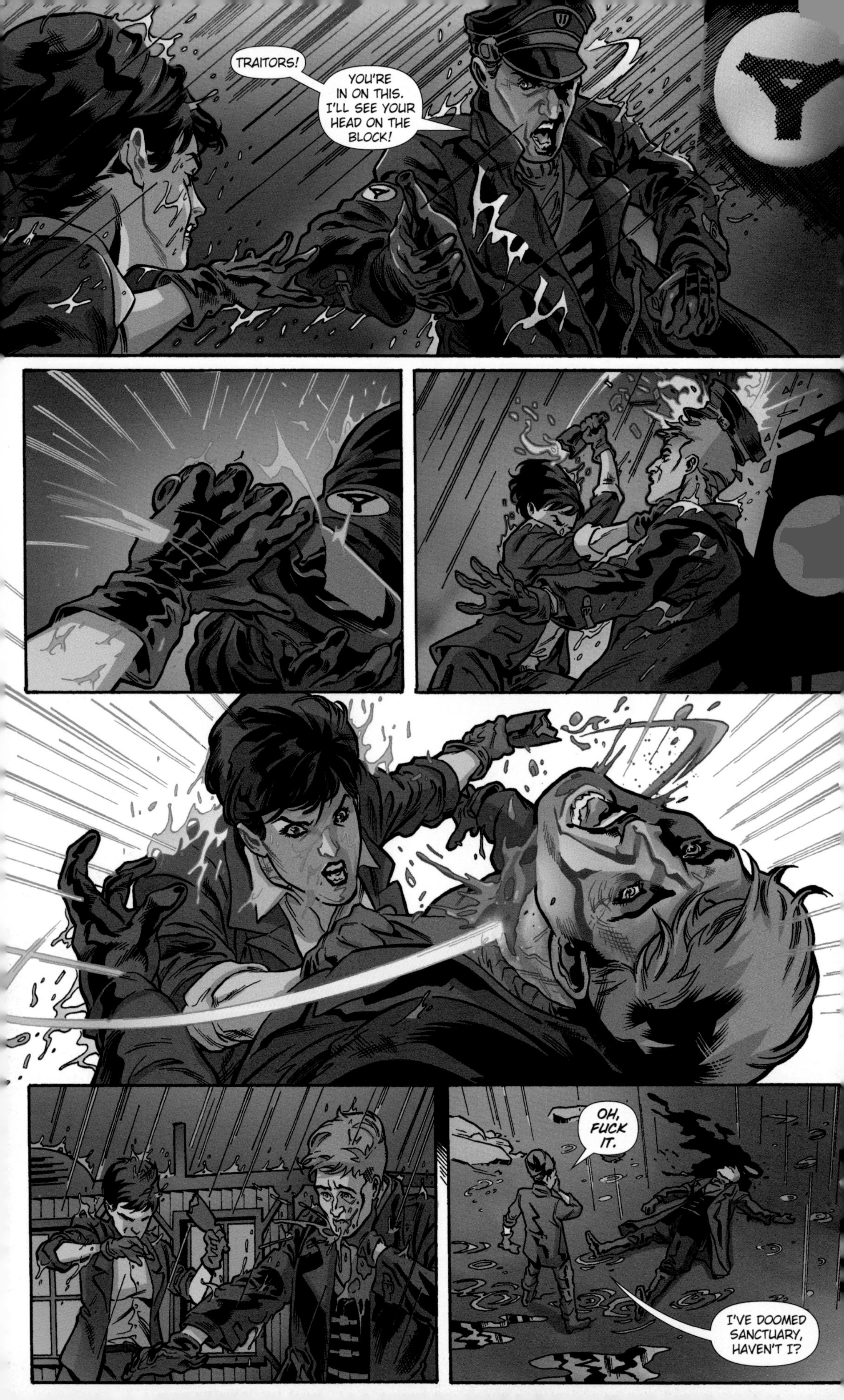
TRAITORS!
YOU'RE IN ON THIS. I'LL SEE YOUR HEAD ON THE BLOCK!
OH, FUCK IT.
I'VE DOOMED SANCTUARY, HAVEN'T I?

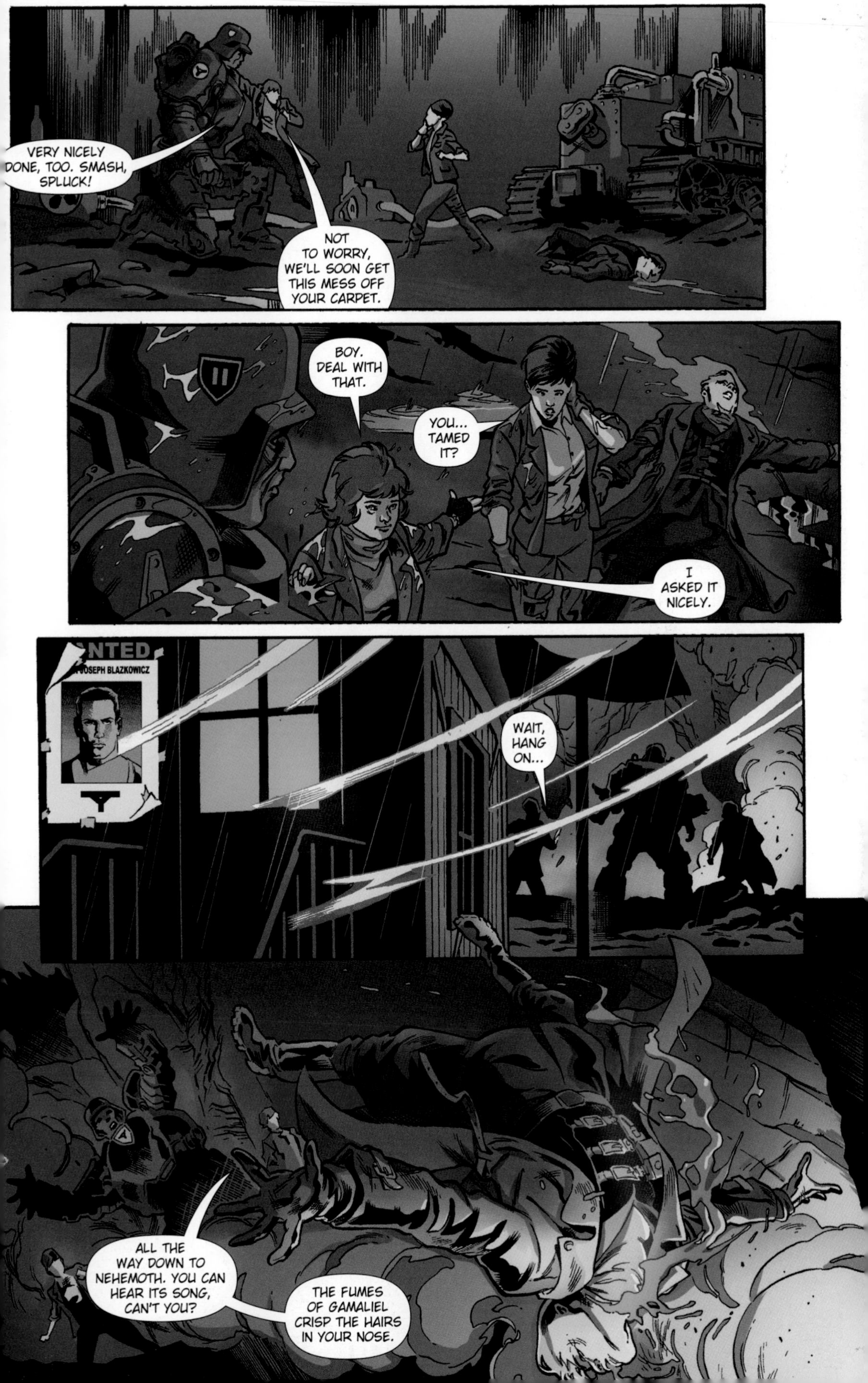
VERY NICELY DONE, TOO. SMASH, SPLUCK!
NOT TO WORRY, WE'LL SOON GET THIS MESS OFF YOUR CARPET.
BOY. DEAL WITH THAT.
YOU... TAMED IT?
I ASKED IT NICELY.
NTED
JOSEPH BLAZKOWICZ
WAIT, HANG ON...
ALL THE WAY DOWN TO NEHEMOTH. YOU CAN HEAR ITS SONG, CAN'T YOU?
THE FUMES OF GAMALIEL CRISP THE HAIRS IN YOUR NOSE.

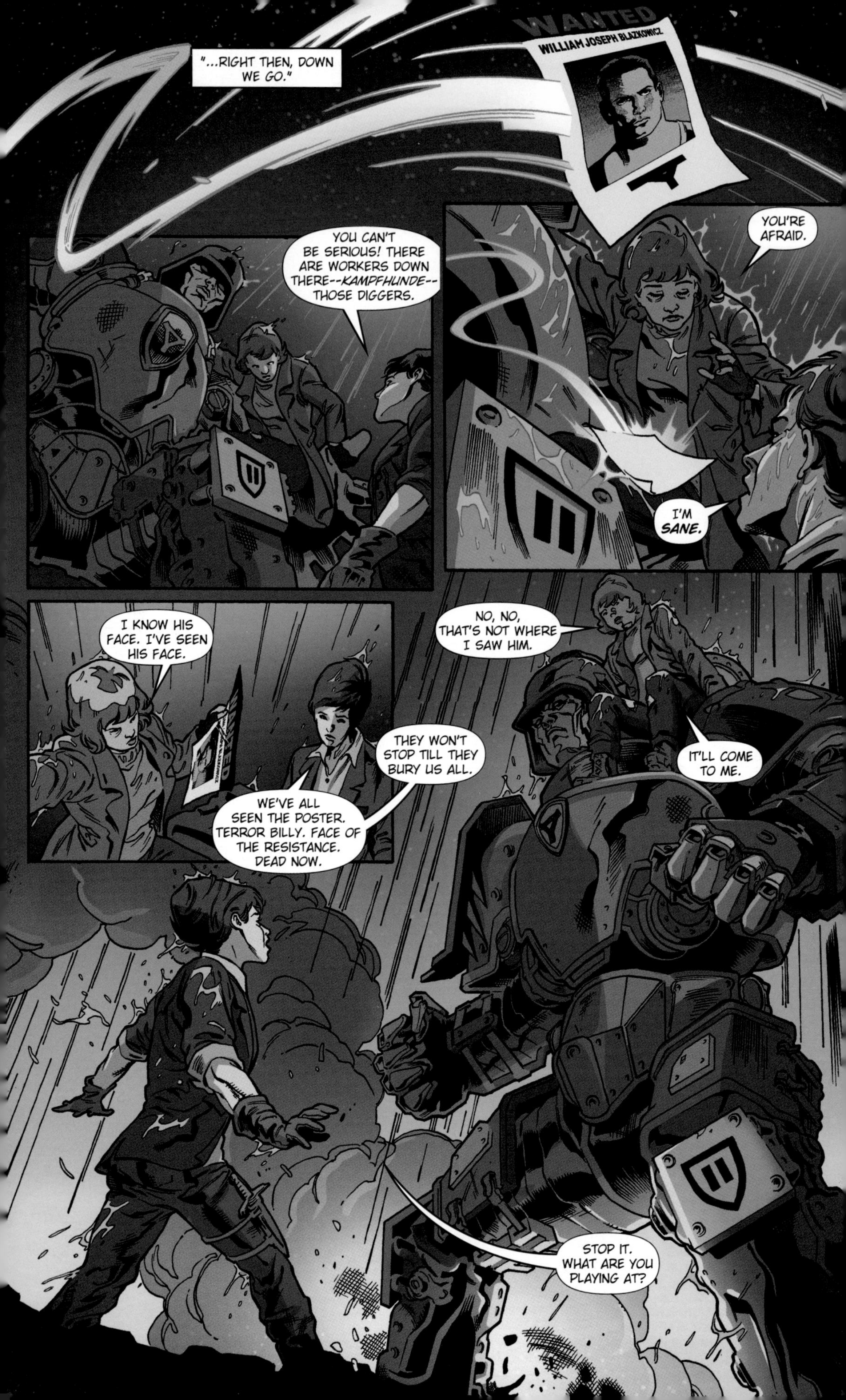
"...RIGHT THEN, DOWN WE GO."
WANTED
WILLIAM JOSEPH BLAZKOWICZ
YOU CAN'T BE SERIOUS! THERE ARE WORKERS DOWN THERE--*KAMPFHUNDE*--THOSE DIGGERS.
YOU'RE AFRAID.
I'M **SANE.**
I KNOW HIS FACE. I'VE SEEN HIS FACE.
WE'VE ALL SEEN THE POSTER. TERROR BILLY. FACE OF THE RESISTANCE. DEAD NOW.
THEY WON'T STOP TILL THEY BURY US ALL.
NO, NO, THAT'S NOT WHERE I SAW HIM.
IT'LL COME TO ME.
STOP IT. WHAT ARE YOU PLAYING AT?

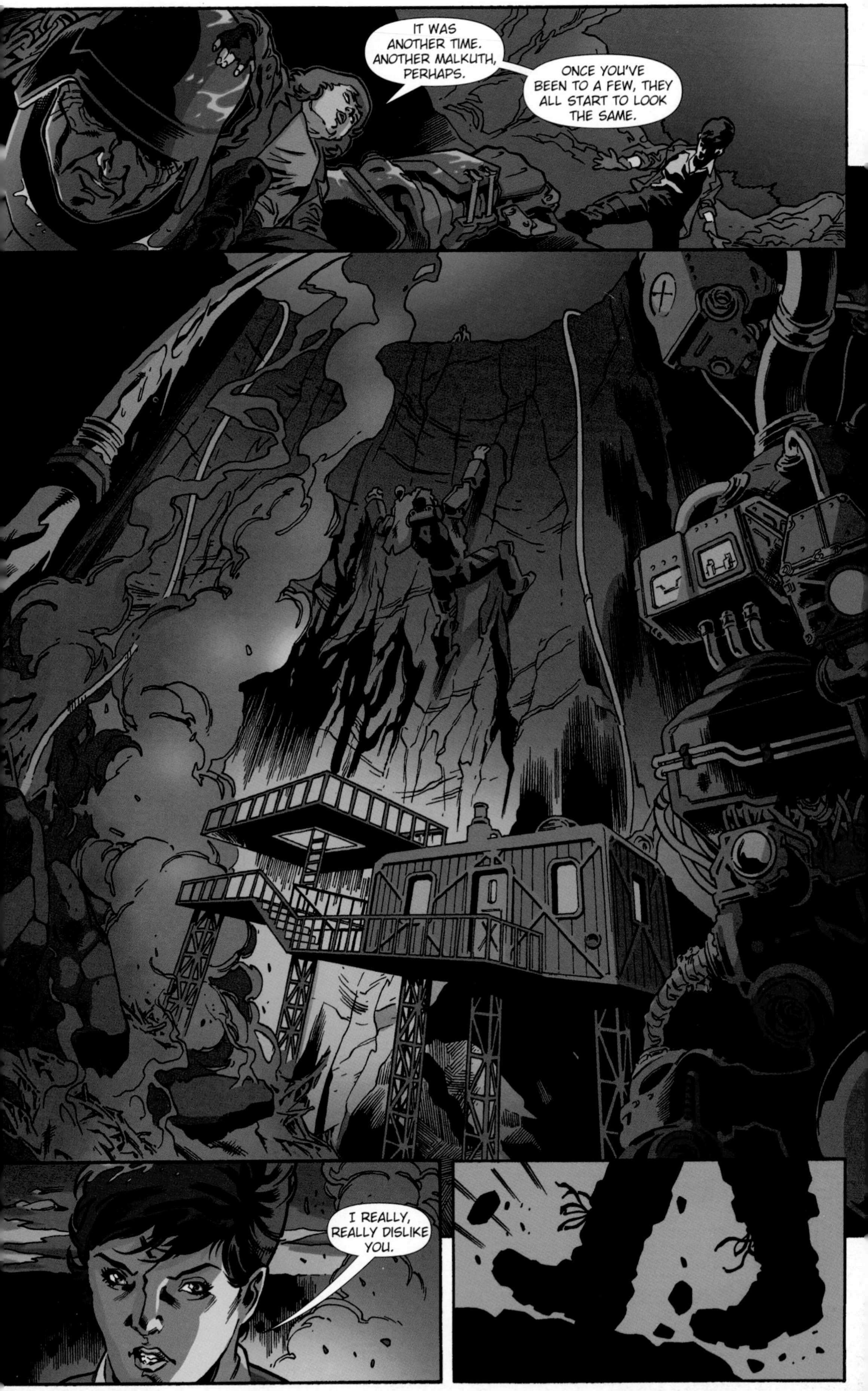
IT WAS ANOTHER TIME. ANOTHER MALKUTH, PERHAPS.
ONCE YOU'VE BEEN TO A FEW, THEY ALL START TO LOOK THE SAME.
I REALLY, REALLY DISLIKE YOU.

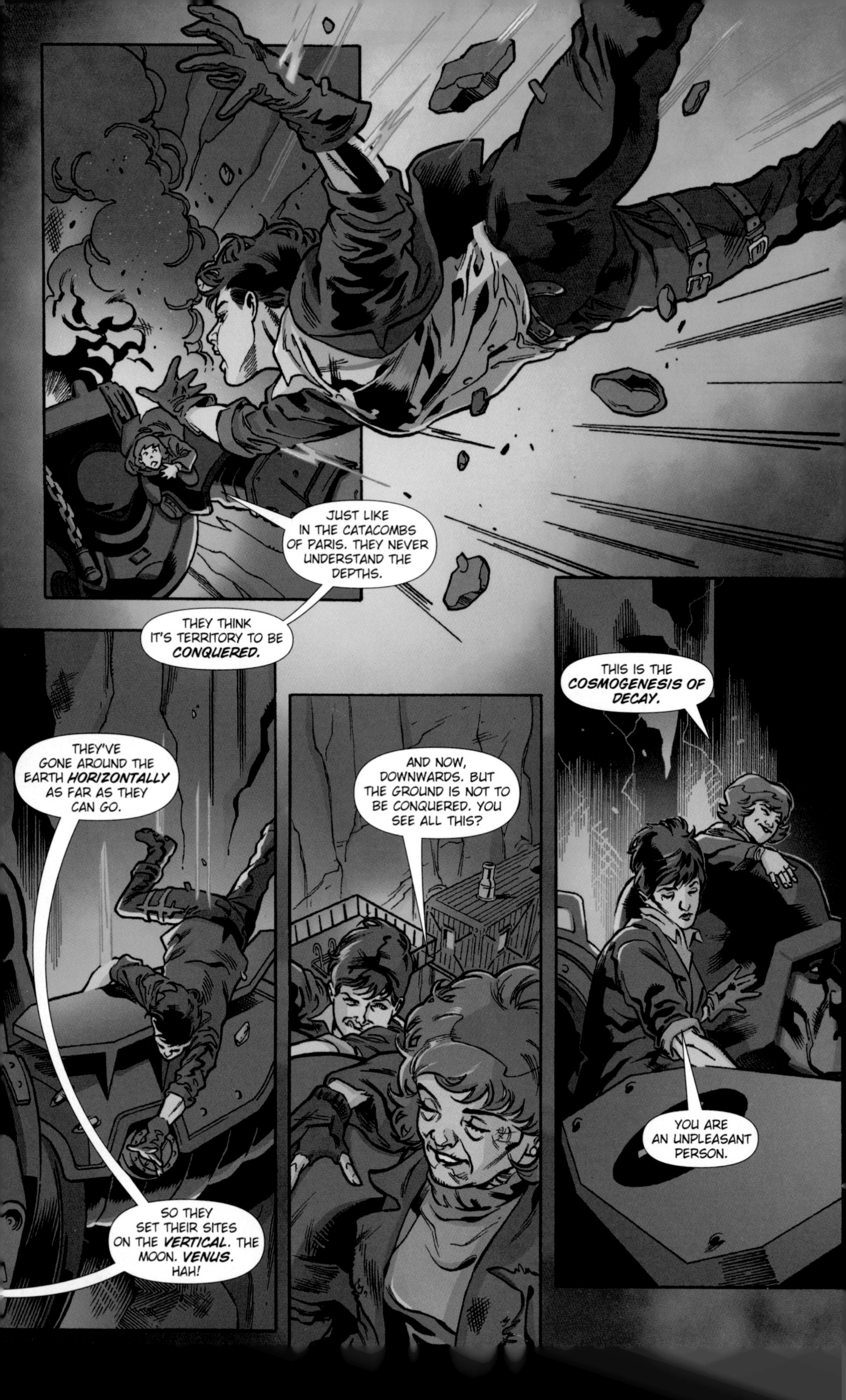
JUST LIKE IN THE CATACOMBS OF PARIS. THEY NEVER UNDERSTAND THE DEPTHS.
THEY THINK IT'S TERRITORY TO BE **CONQUERED.**
THEY'VE GONE AROUND THE EARTH ***HORIZONTALLY*** AS FAR AS THEY CAN GO.
SO THEY SET THEIR SITES ON THE ***VERTICAL***. THE MOON. ***VENUS***. HAH!
AND NOW, DOWNWARDS. BUT THE GROUND IS NOT TO BE CONQUERED. YOU SEE ALL THIS?
THIS IS THE ***COSMOGENESIS OF DECAY.***
YOU ARE AN UNPLEASANT PERSON.

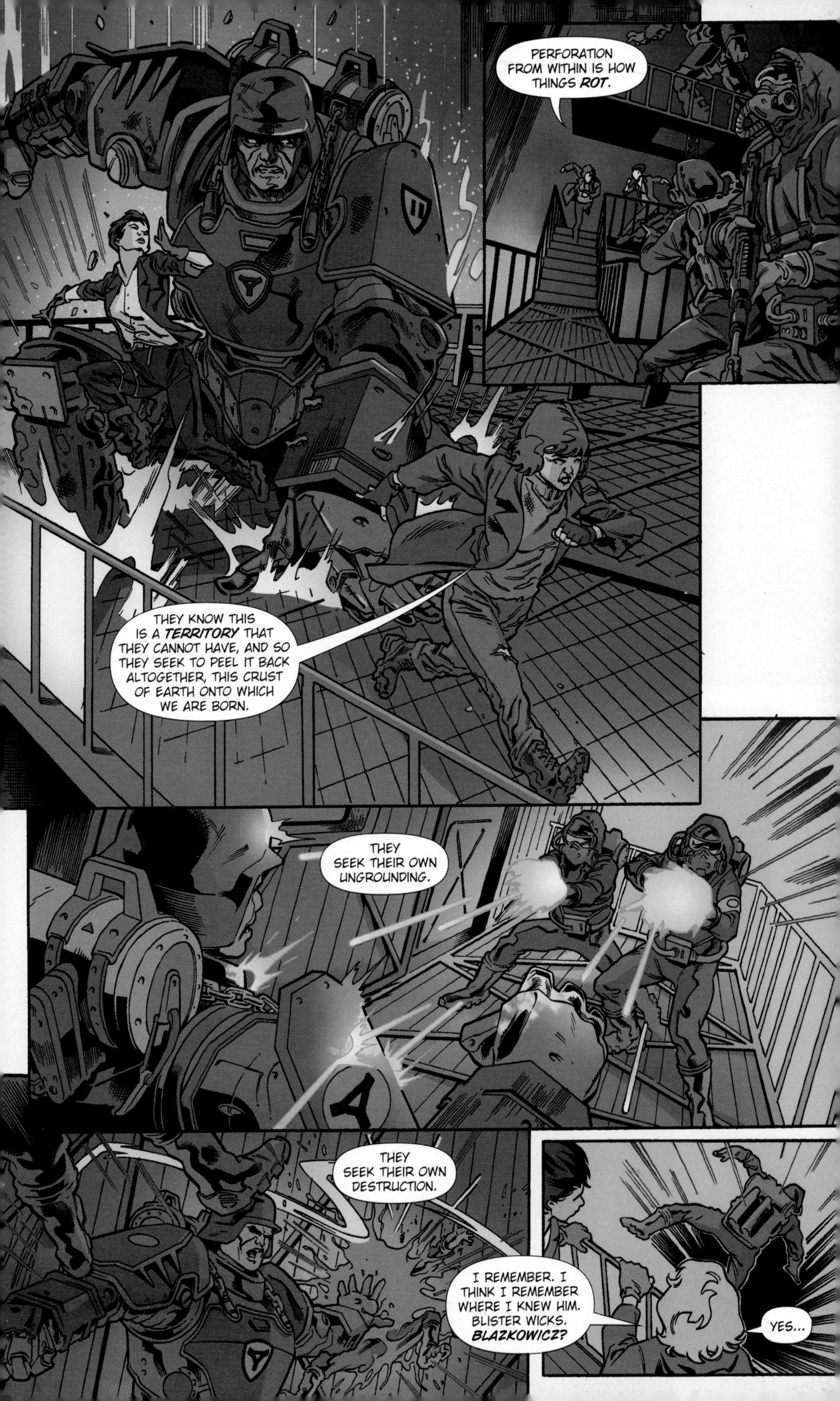
PERFORATION FROM WITHIN IS HOW THINGS ROT.
THEY KNOW THIS IS A TERRITORY THAT THEY CANNOT HAVE, AND SO THEY SEEK TO PEEL IT BACK ALTOGETHER, THIS CRUST OF EARTH ONTO WHICH WE ARE BORN.
THEY SEEK THEIR OWN UNGROUNDING.
THEY SEEK THEIR OWN DESTRUCTION.
I REMEMBER. I THINK I REMEMBER WHERE I KNEW HIM. BLISTER WICKS. BLAZKOWICZ?
YES...

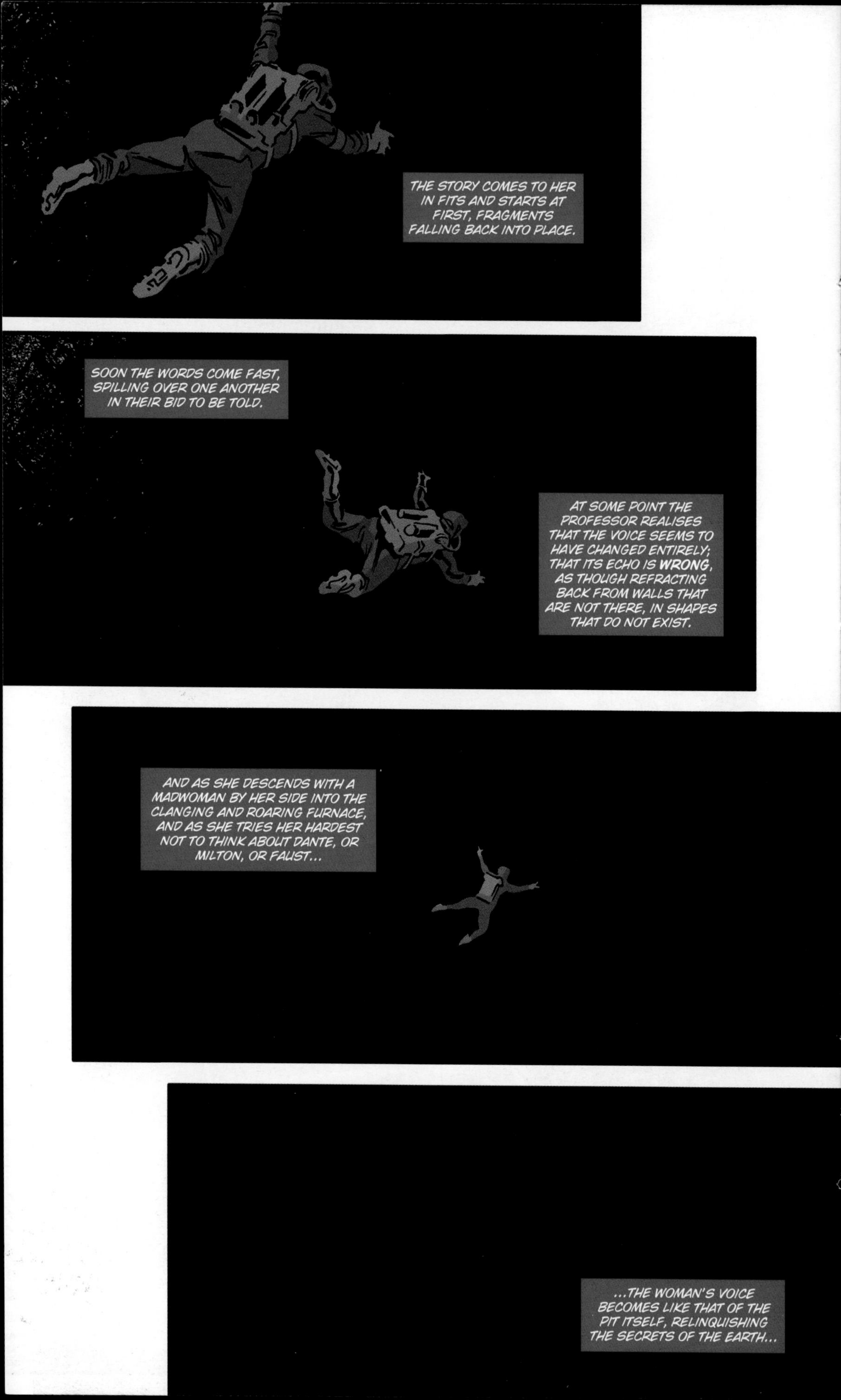
THE STORY COMES TO HER IN FITS AND STARTS AT FIRST, FRAGMENTS FALLING BACK INTO PLACE.
SOON THE WORDS COME FAST, SPILLING OVER ONE ANOTHER IN THEIR BID TO BE TOLD.
AT SOME POINT THE PROFESSOR REALISES THAT THE VOICE SEEMS TO HAVE CHANGED ENTIRELY; THAT ITS ECHO IS **WRONG**, AS THOUGH REFRACTING BACK FROM WALLS THAT ARE NOT THERE, IN SHAPES THAT DO NOT EXIST.
AND AS SHE DESCENDS WITH A MADWOMAN BY HER SIDE INTO THE CLANGING AND ROARING FURNACE, AND AS SHE TRIES HER HARDEST NOT TO THINK ABOUT DANTE, OR MILTON, OR FAUST...
...THE WOMAN'S VOICE BECOMES LIKE THAT OF THE PIT ITSELF, RELINQUISHING THE SECRETS OF THE EARTH...

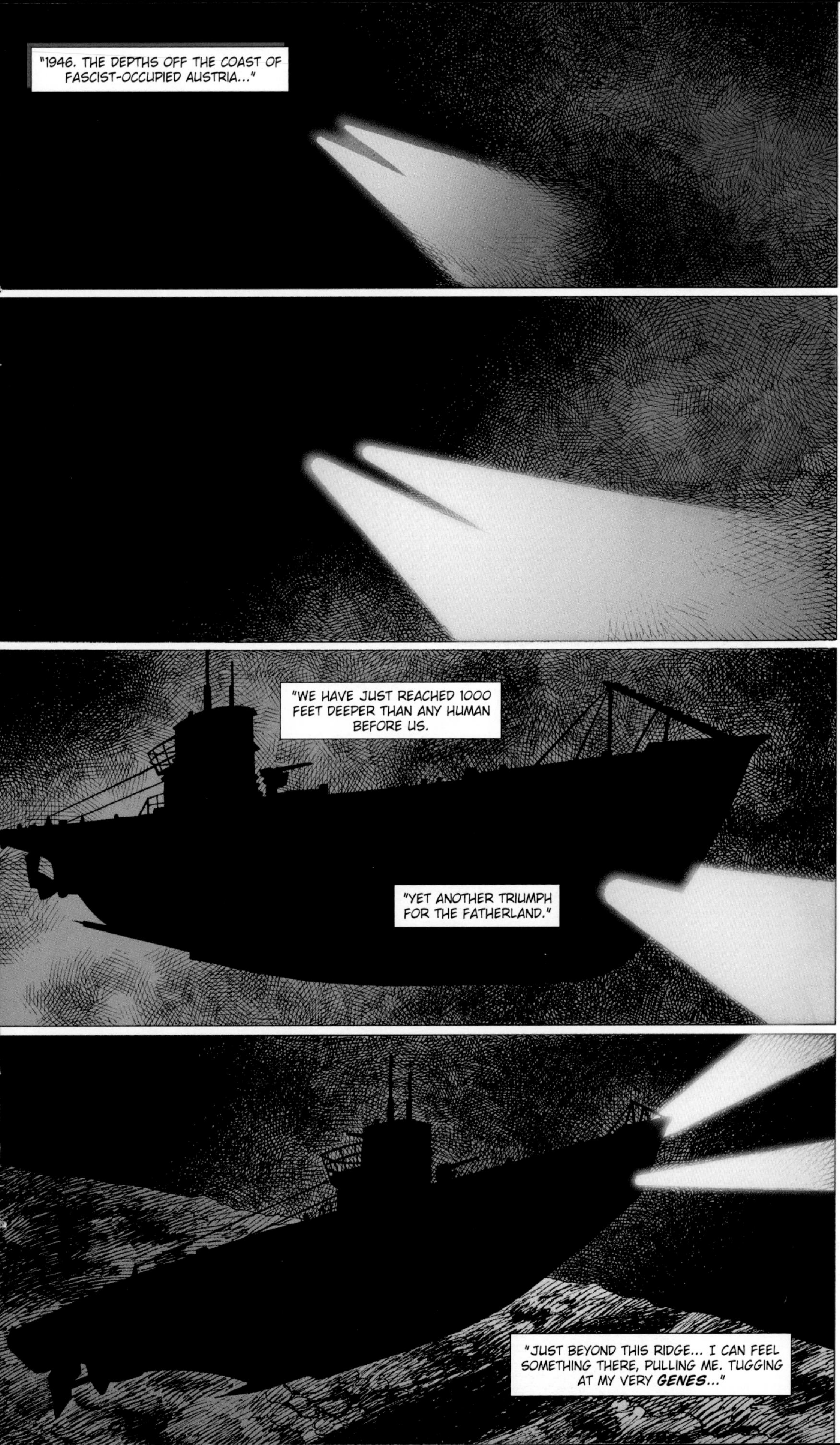
"1946. THE DEPTHS OFF THE COAST OF FASCIST-OCCUPIED AUSTRIA..."
"WE HAVE JUST REACHED 1000 FEET DEEPER THAN ANY HUMAN BEFORE US.
"YET ANOTHER TRIUMPH FOR THE FATHERLAND."
"JUST BEYOND THIS RIDGE... I CAN FEEL SOMETHING THERE, PULLING ME. TUGGING AT MY VERY GENES..."

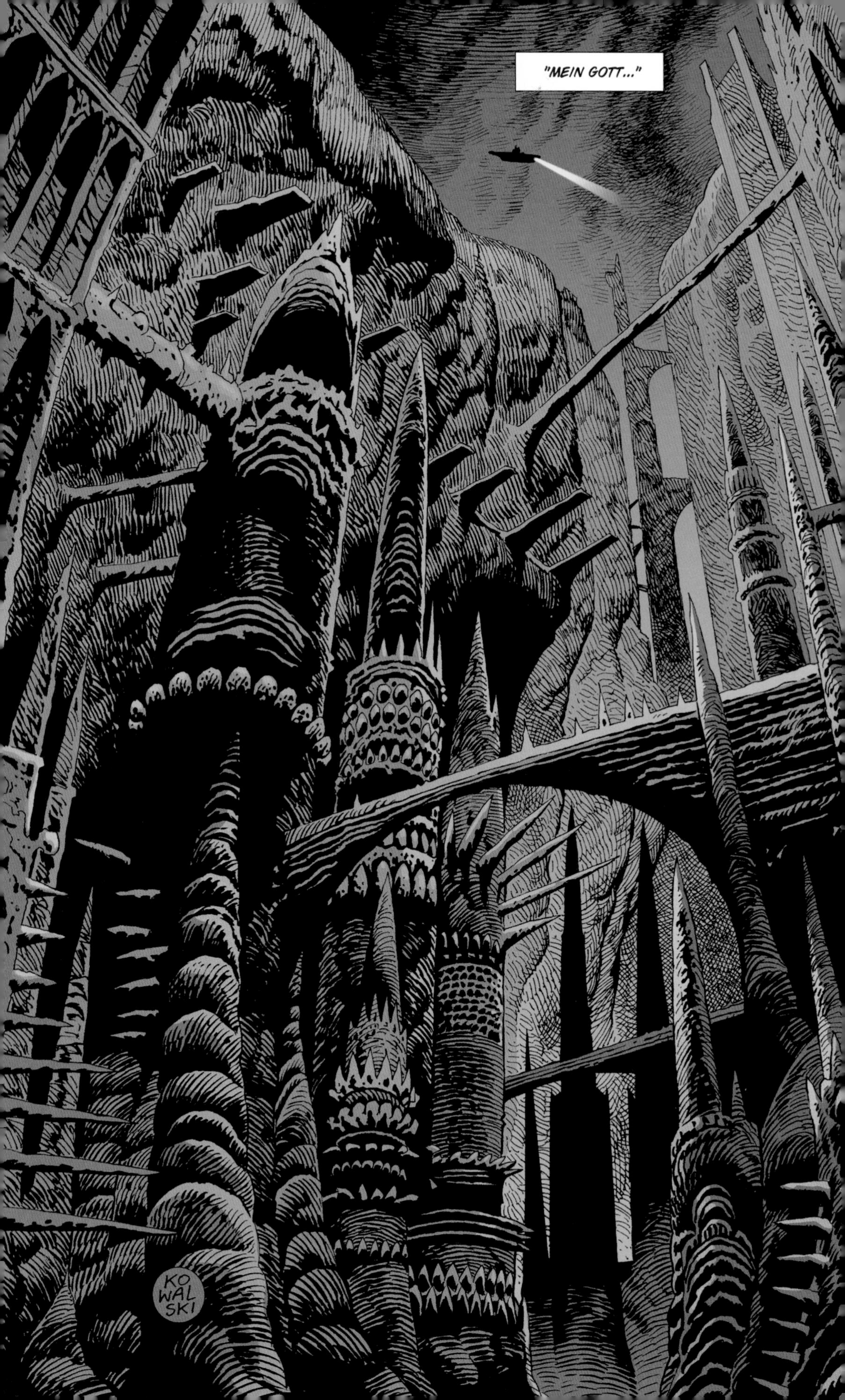
"MEIN GOTT..."
KOWALSKI

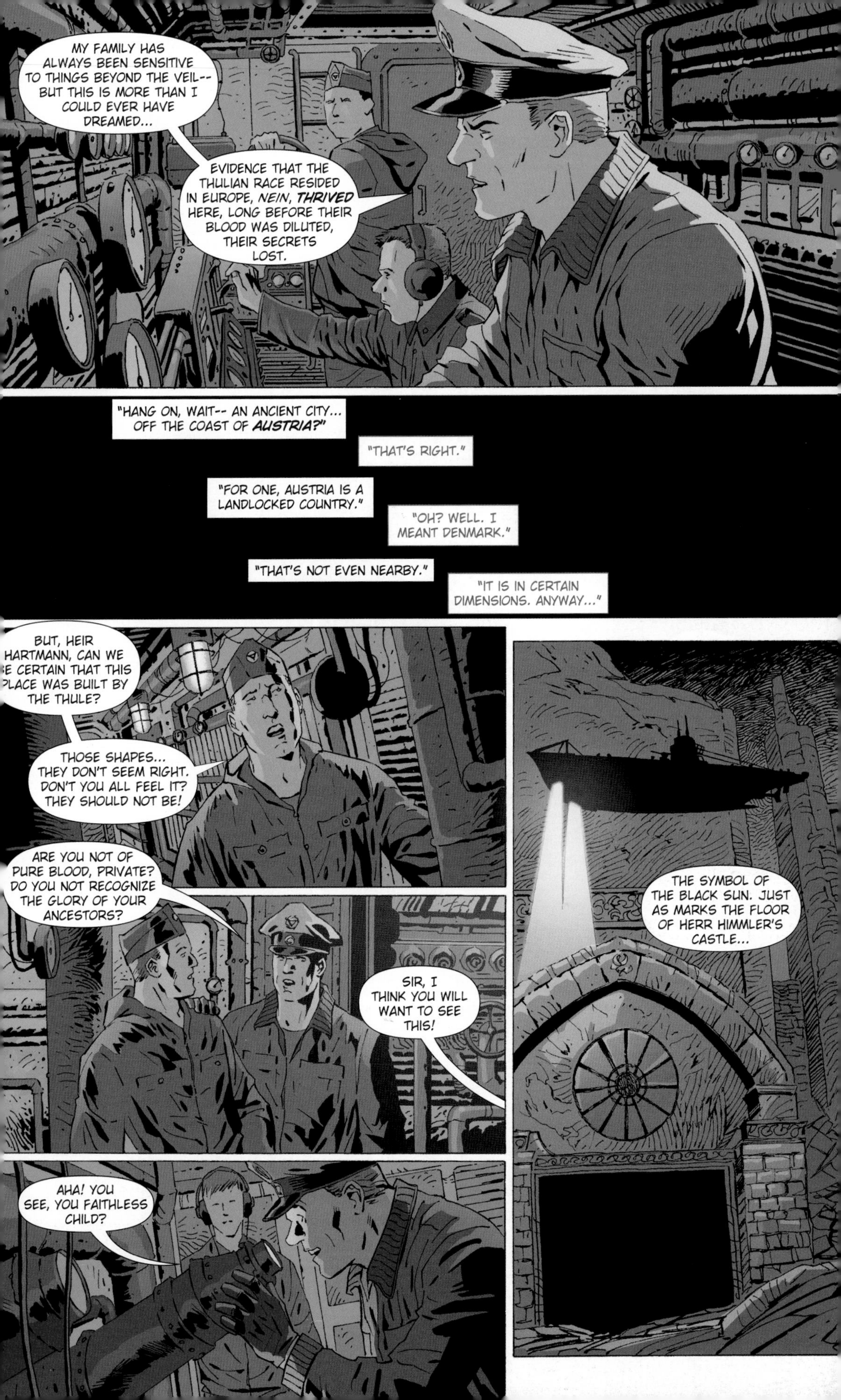
MY FAMILY HAS ALWAYS BEEN SENSITIVE TO THINGS BEYOND THE VEIL-- BUT THIS IS MORE THAN I COULD EVER HAVE DREAMED...
EVIDENCE THAT THE THULIAN RACE RESIDED IN EUROPE, NEIN, THRIVED HERE, LONG BEFORE THEIR BLOOD WAS DILUTED, THEIR SECRETS LOST.
"HANG ON, WAIT-- AN ANCIENT CITY... OFF THE COAST OF AUSTRIA?"
"THAT'S RIGHT."
"FOR ONE, AUSTRIA IS A LANDLOCKED COUNTRY."
"OH? WELL. I MEANT DENMARK."
"THAT'S NOT EVEN NEARBY."
"IT IS IN CERTAIN DIMENSIONS. ANYWAY..."
BUT, HEIR HARTMANN, CAN WE BE CERTAIN THAT THIS PLACE WAS BUILT BY THE THULE?
THOSE SHAPES... THEY DON'T SEEM RIGHT. DON'T YOU ALL FEEL IT? THEY SHOULD NOT BE!
ARE YOU NOT OF PURE BLOOD, PRIVATE? DO YOU NOT RECOGNIZE THE GLORY OF YOUR ANCESTORS?
SIR, I THINK YOU WILL WANT TO SEE THIS!
AHA! YOU SEE, YOU FAITHLESS CHILD?
THE SYMBOL OF THE BLACK SUN. JUST AS MARKS THE FLOOR OF HERR HIMMLER'S CASTLE...

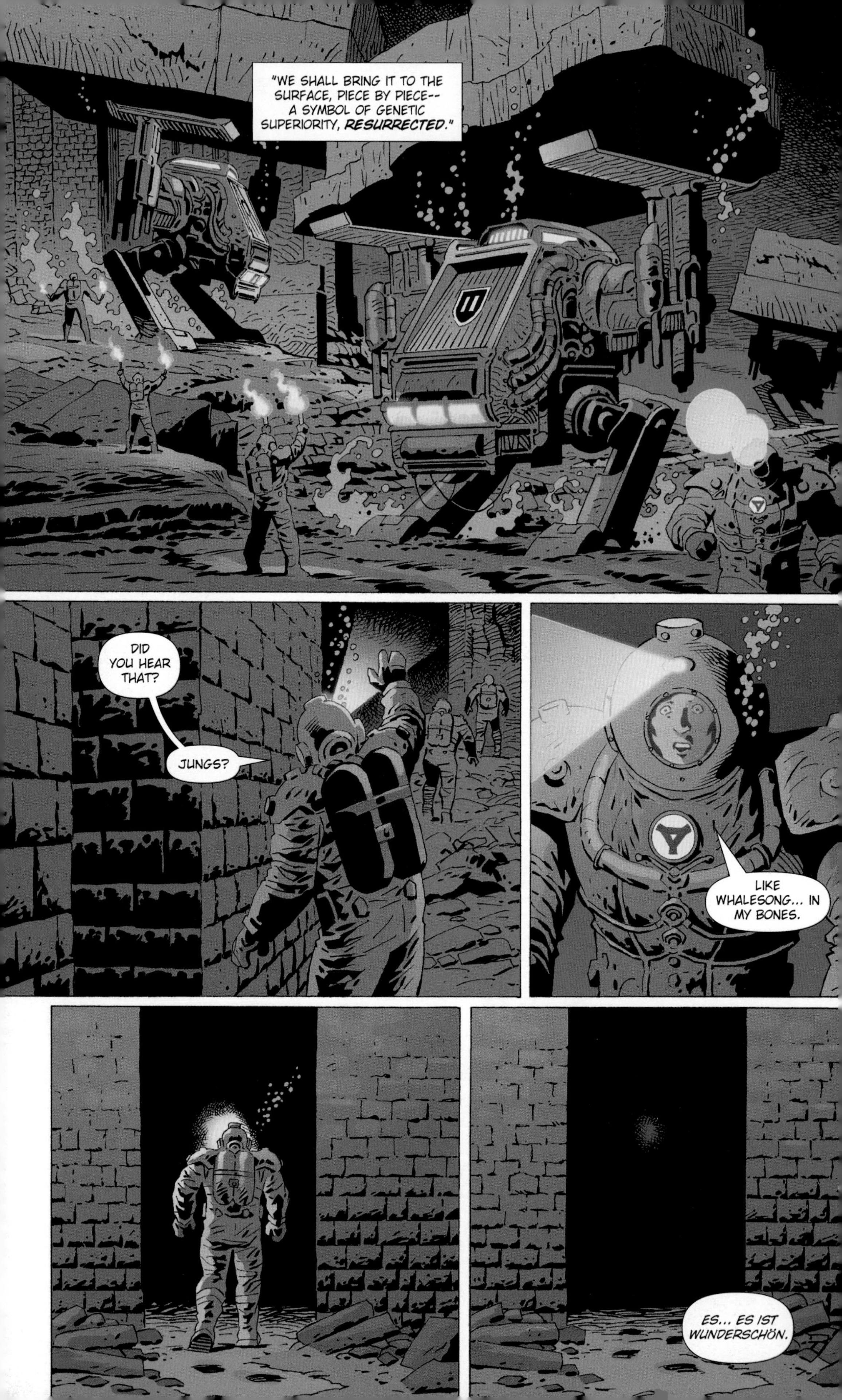

"WE SHALL BRING IT TO THE SURFACE, PIECE BY PIECE-- A SYMBOL OF GENETIC SUPERIORITY, ***RESURRECTED.***"
DID YOU HEAR THAT?
JUNGS?
LIKE WHALESONG... IN MY BONES.
ES... ES IST WUNDERSCHÖN.

I FOR ONE CAN'T WAIT. AN ANCIENT THULIAN CITY, LOST TO TIME AND SHORE EROSION, RECOVERED AND RIPE FOR EXPLORATION?

THINK OF ALL WE CAN LEARN. OF ALL TO BE *UNCOVERED*.

WE SHALL SEE IF YOUR ENTHUSIASM REMAINS WHEN YOU BEGIN TO HAVE THE NIGHTMARES, WISSENSCHAFTLER.

NO MAN SLEEPS WELL IN HERR HARTMANN'S NEW CASTLE **WOLFENSTEIN**

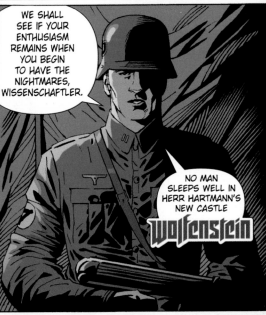

FASCINATING. PERHAPS SOMETHING TO DO WITH REVERBERATION? LOW FREQUENCY SOUNDS CAN CAUSE PAIN, NAUSEA, AND SO FORTH.

THEY'RE STARING AT US...

THE VILLAGERS? DON'T WORRY. WEAK, PEASANT STOCK. DIDN'T EVEN GRUMBLE WHEN WE DEMOLISHED THEIR CHURCH TO MAKE WAY FOR THE CASTLE.

WE HAULED A PREHISTORIC PALACE FROM THE DEPTHS AND THEY JUST LOOKED AT IT AS IF THEY'D SEEN IT A THOUSAND TIMES BEFORE.

FEEBLE MINDED, YOU SEE.

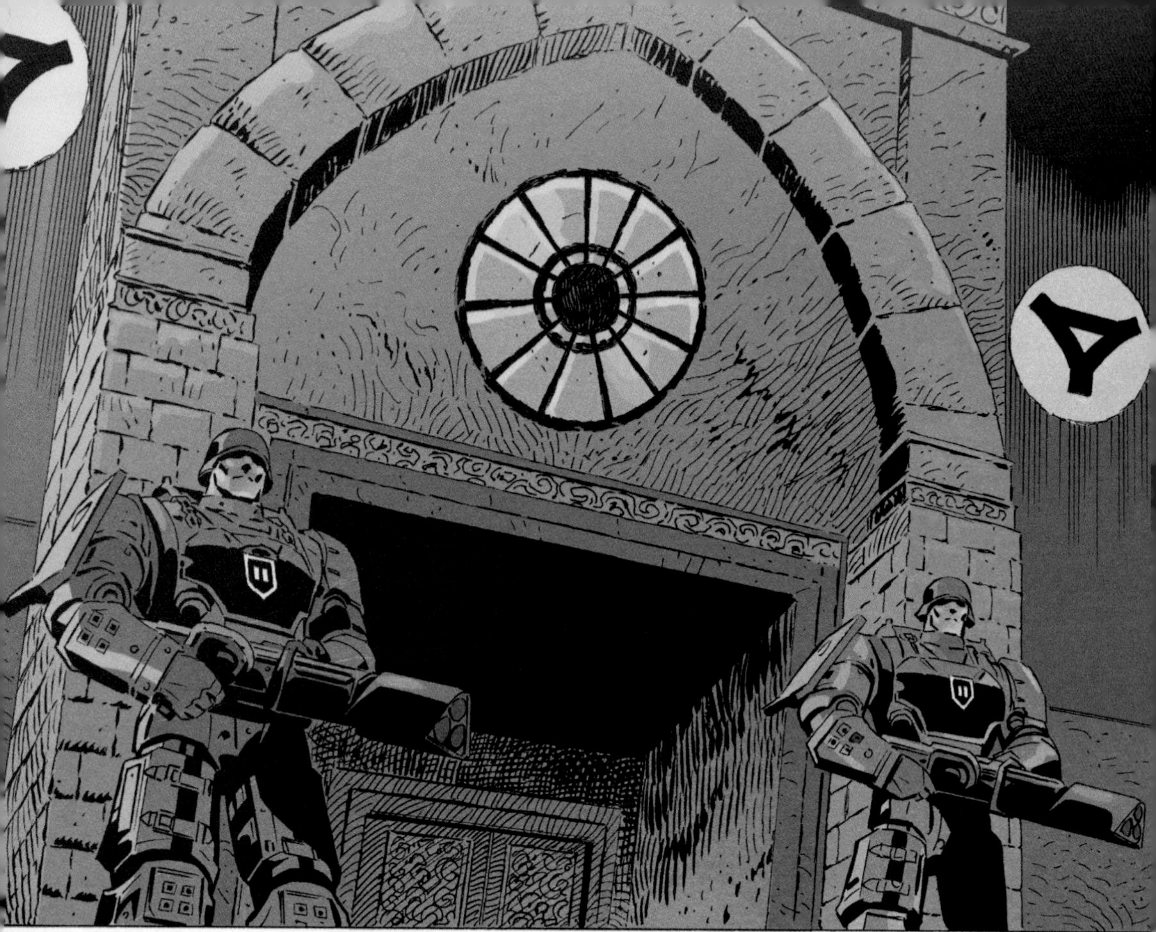

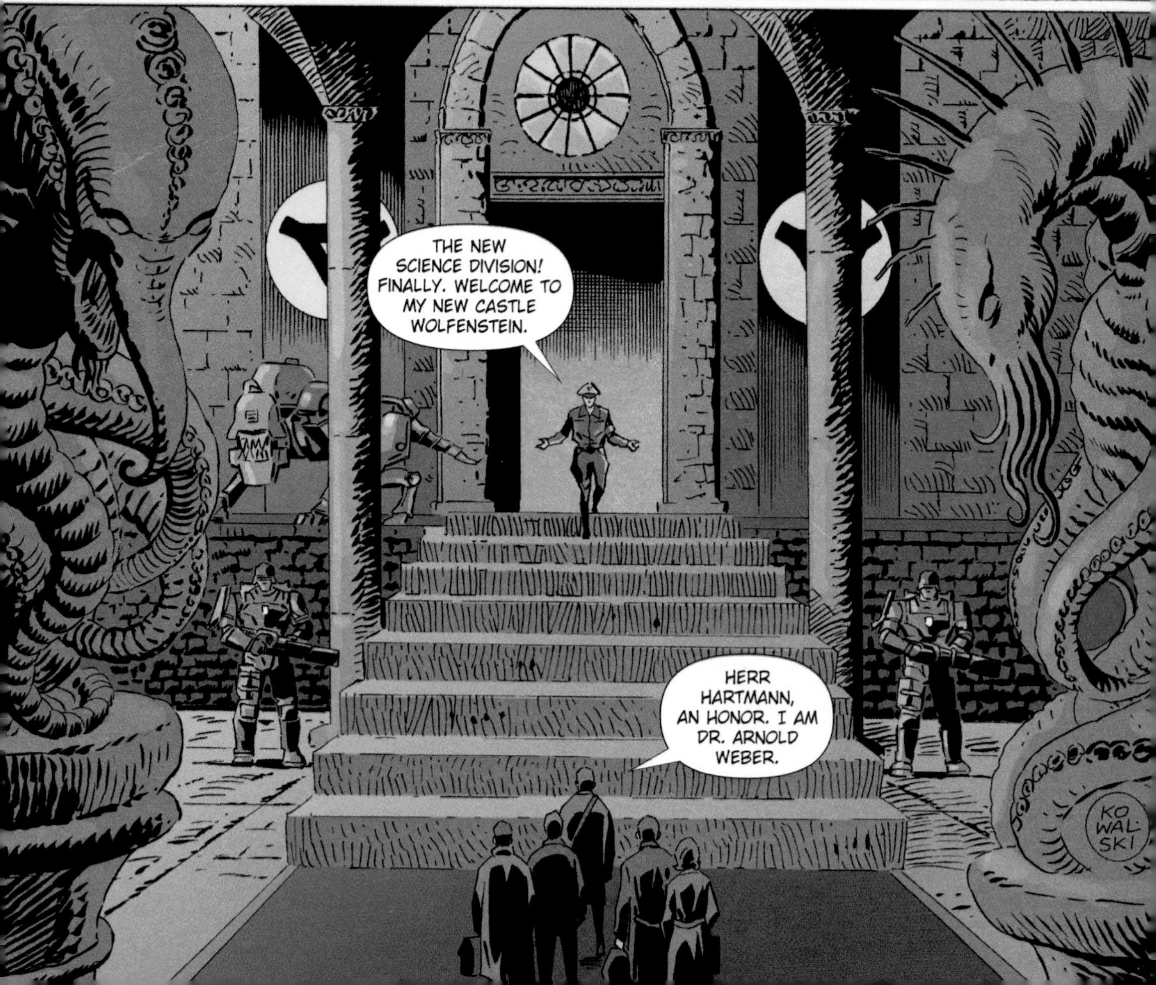
THE NEW SCIENCE DIVISION! FINALLY. WELCOME TO MY NEW CASTLE WOLFENSTEIN.
HERR HARTMANN, AN HONOR. I AM DR. ARNOLD WEBER.
KOWALSKI

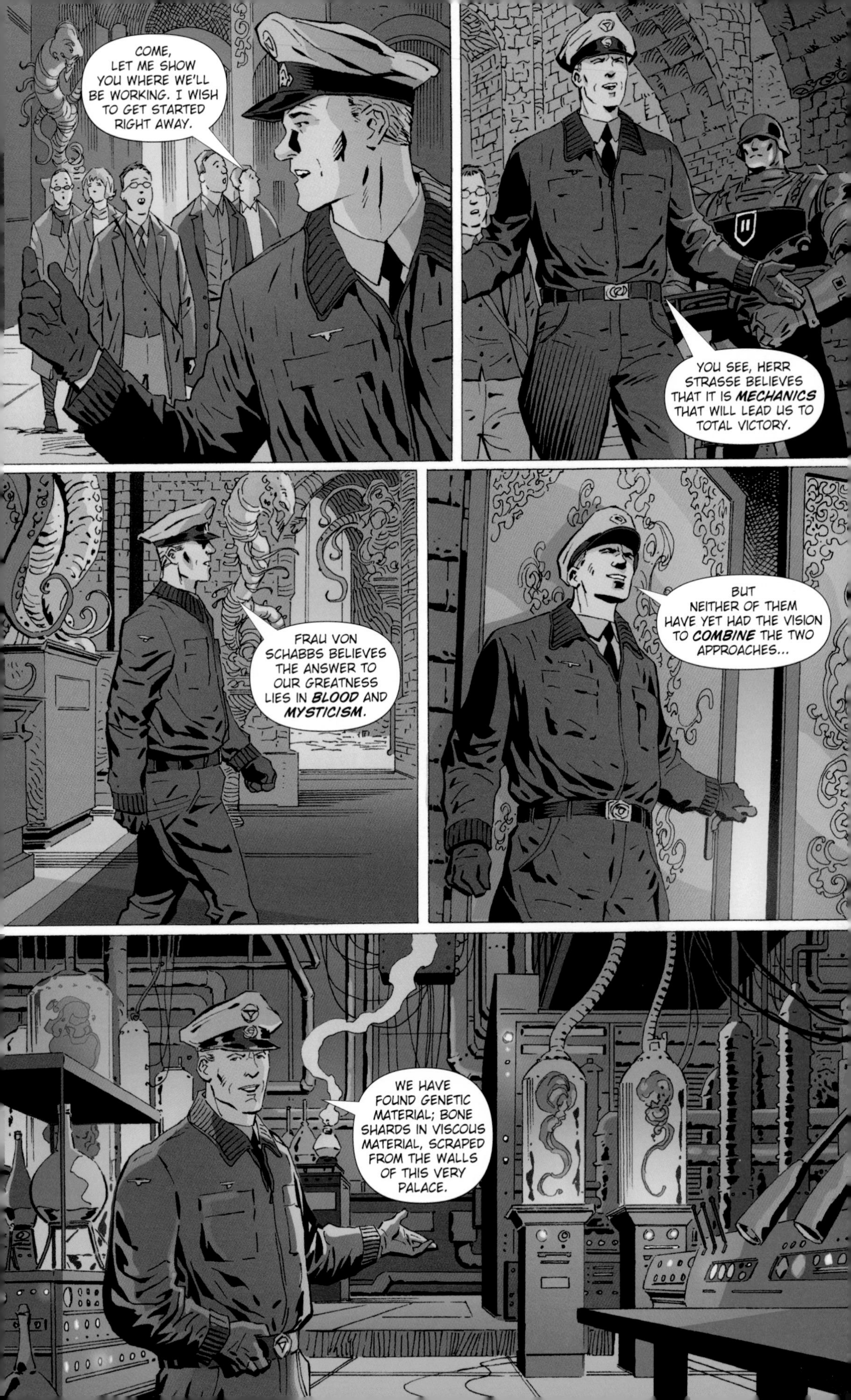
COME, LET ME SHOW YOU WHERE WE'LL BE WORKING. I WISH TO GET STARTED RIGHT AWAY.
YOU SEE, HERR STRASSE BELIEVES THAT IT IS MECHANICS THAT WILL LEAD US TO TOTAL VICTORY.
FRAU VON SCHABBS BELIEVES THE ANSWER TO OUR GREATNESS LIES IN BLOOD AND MYSTICISM.
BUT NEITHER OF THEM HAVE YET HAD THE VISION TO COMBINE THE TWO APPROACHES...
WE HAVE FOUND GENETIC MATERIAL; BONE SHARDS IN VISCOUS MATERIAL, SCRAPED FROM THE WALLS OF THIS VERY PALACE.

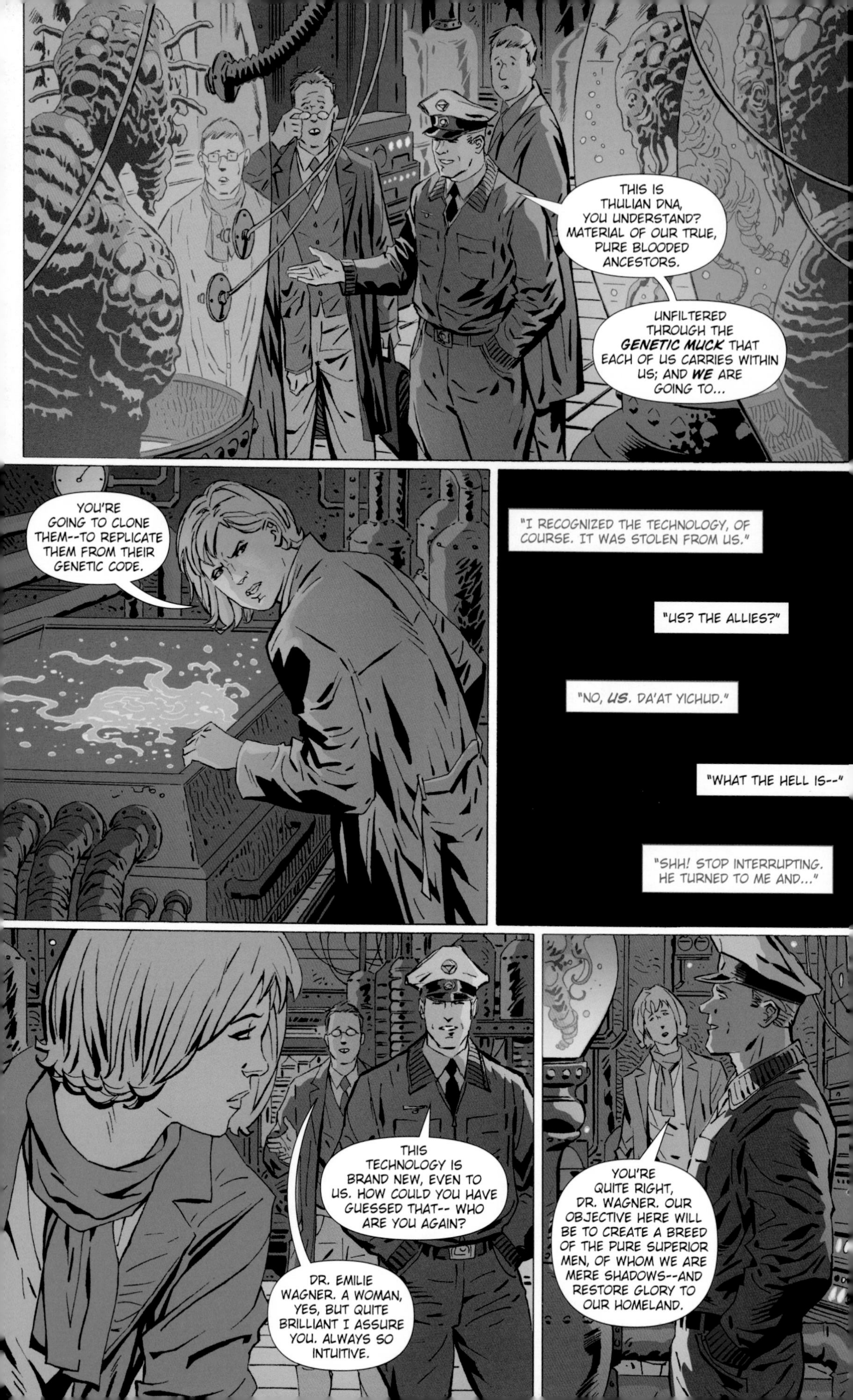
THIS IS THULIAN DNA, YOU UNDERSTAND? MATERIAL OF OUR TRUE, PURE BLOODED ANCESTORS.
UNFILTERED THROUGH THE GENETIC MUCK THAT EACH OF US CARRIES WITHIN US; AND WE ARE GOING TO...
YOU'RE GOING TO CLONE THEM--TO REPLICATE THEM FROM THEIR GENETIC CODE.
"I RECOGNIZED THE TECHNOLOGY, OF COURSE. IT WAS STOLEN FROM US."
"US? THE ALLIES?"
"NO, US. DA'AT YICHUD."
"WHAT THE HELL IS--"
"SHH! STOP INTERRUPTING. HE TURNED TO ME AND..."
THIS TECHNOLOGY IS BRAND NEW, EVEN TO US. HOW COULD YOU HAVE GUESSED THAT-- WHO ARE YOU AGAIN?
DR. EMILIE WAGNER. A WOMAN, YES, BUT QUITE BRILLIANT I ASSURE YOU. ALWAYS SO INTUITIVE.
YOU'RE QUITE RIGHT, DR. WAGNER. OUR OBJECTIVE HERE WILL BE TO CREATE A BREED OF THE PURE SUPERIOR MEN, OF WHOM WE ARE MERE SHADOWS--AND RESTORE GLORY TO OUR HOMELAND.

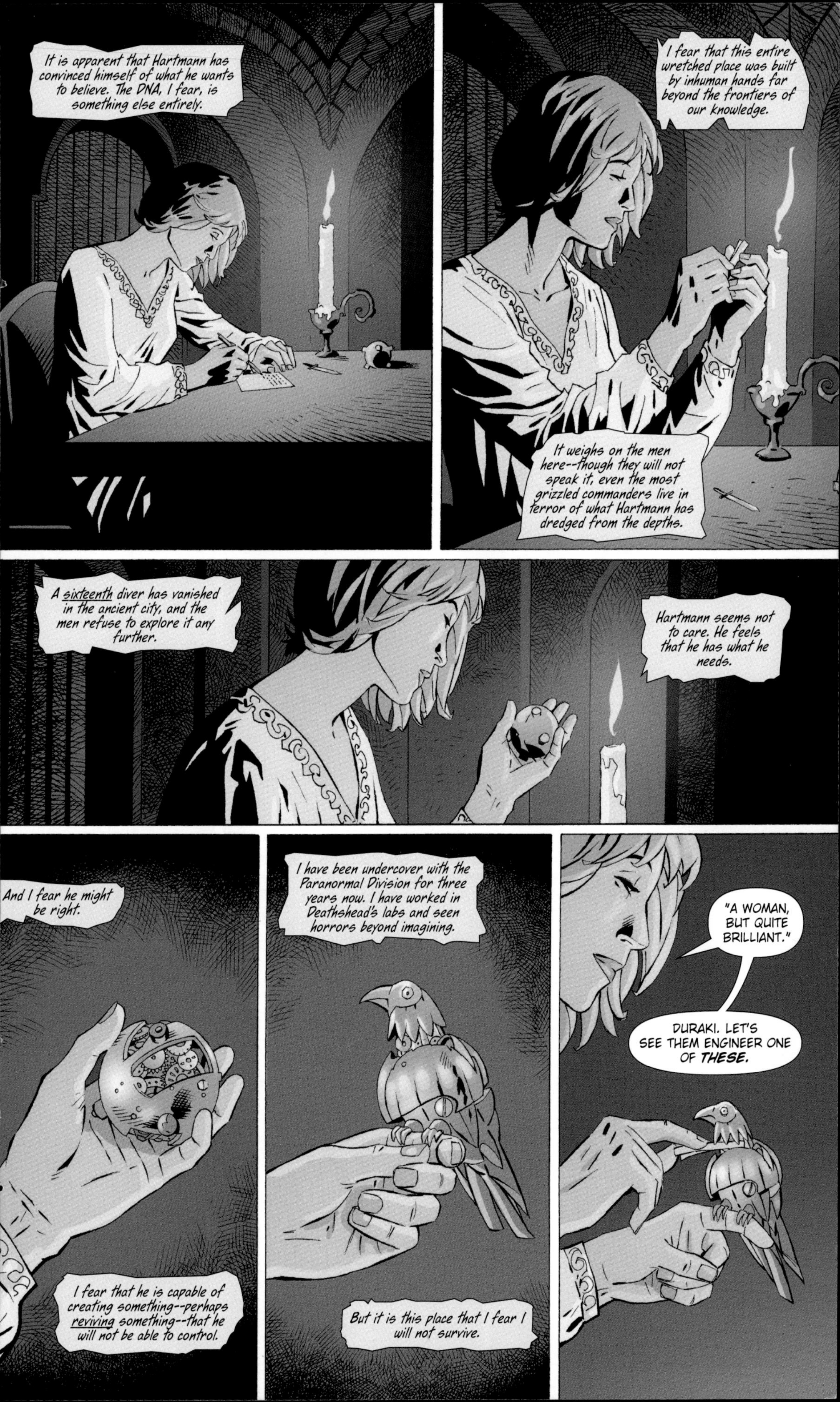
It is apparent that Hartmann has convinced himself of what he wants to believe. The DNA, I fear, is something else entirely.
I fear that this entire wretched place was built by inhuman hands far beyond the frontiers of our knowledge.
It weighs on the men here--though they will not speak it, even the most grizzled commanders live in terror of what Hartmann has dredged from the depths.
A sixteenth diver has vanished in the ancient city, and the men refuse to explore it any further.
Hartmann seems not to care. He feels that he has what he needs.
And I fear he might be right.
I fear that he is capable of creating something--perhaps reviving something--that he will not be able to control.
I have been undercover with the Paranormal Division for three years now. I have worked in Deathshead's labs and seen horrors beyond imagining.
But it is this place that I fear I will not survive.
"A WOMAN, BUT QUITE BRILLIANT."
DURAKI. LET'S SEE THEM ENGINEER ONE OF THESE.

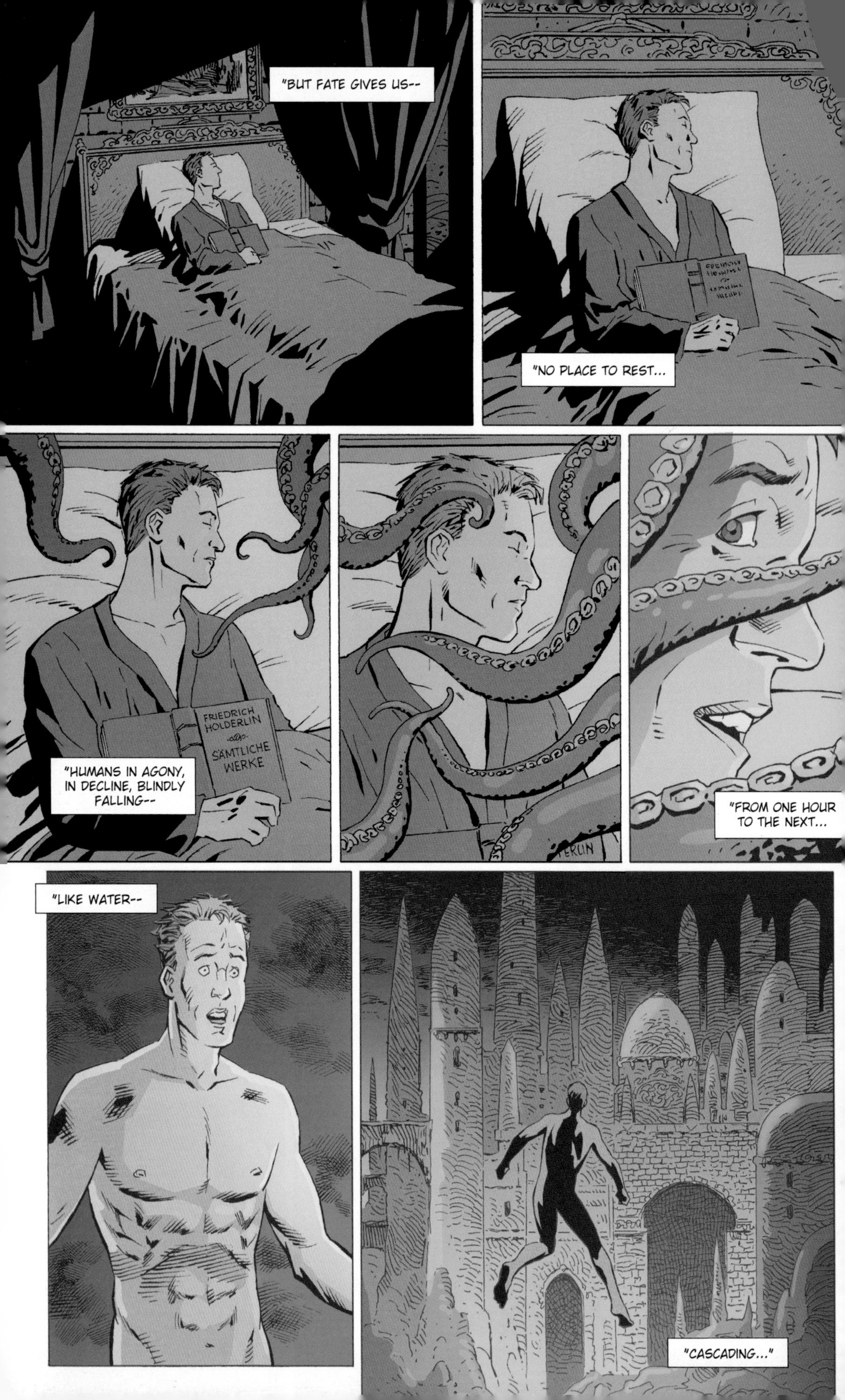
"BUT FATE GIVES US--
"NO PLACE TO REST...
FRIEDRICH HOLDERLIN SÄMTLICHE WERKE
"HUMANS IN AGONY, IN DECLINE, BLINDLY FALLING--
"FROM ONE HOUR TO THE NEXT...
"LIKE WATER--
"CASCADING..."

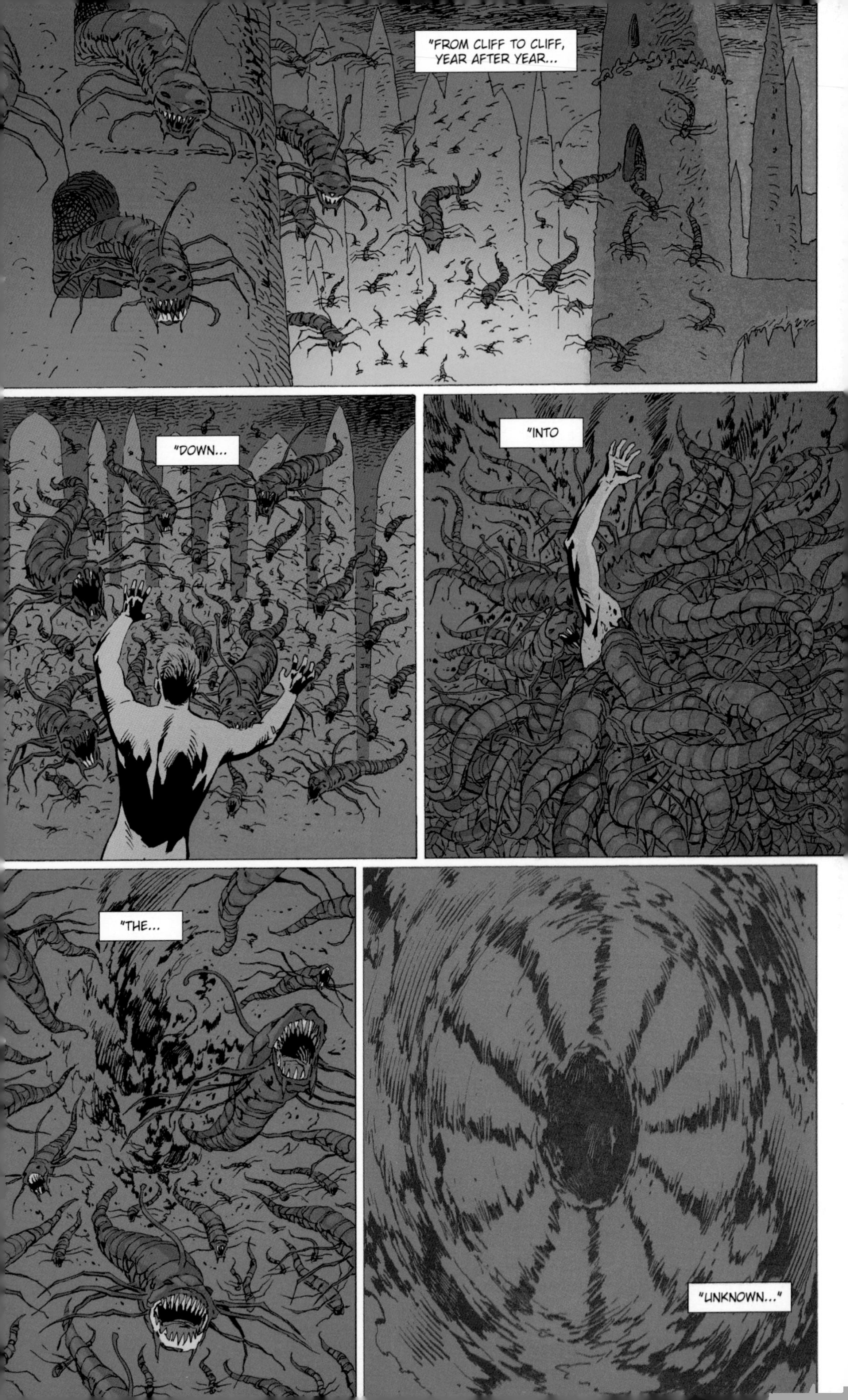
"FROM CLIFF TO CLIFF, YEAR AFTER YEAR...
"DOWN...
"INTO
"THE...
"UNKNOWN..."

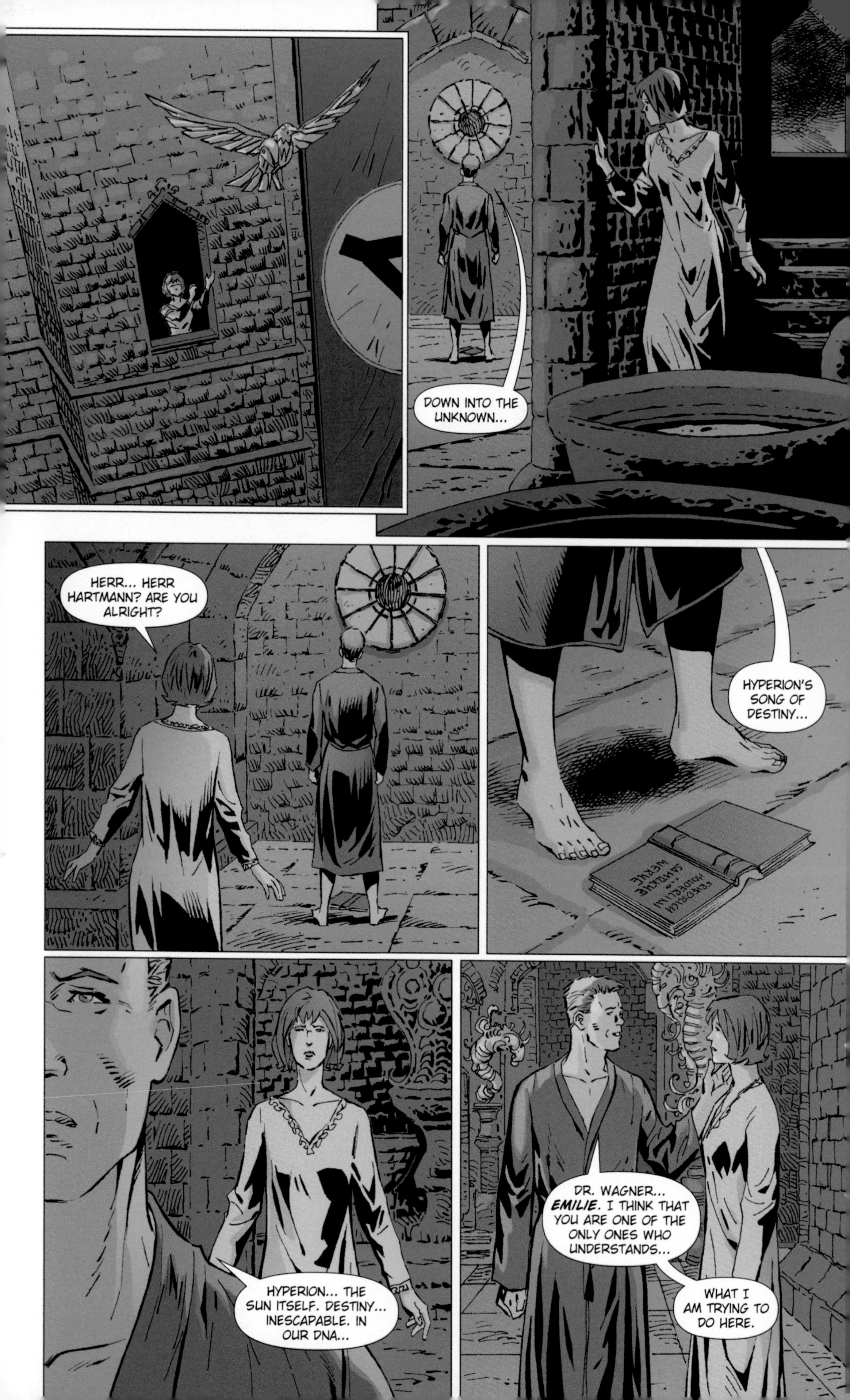
DOWN INTO THE UNKNOWN...
HERR... HERR HARTMANN? ARE YOU ALRIGHT?
HYPERION'S SONG OF DESTINY...
HYPERION... THE SUN ITSELF. DESTINY... INESCAPABLE. IN OUR DNA...
DR. WAGNER... **EMILIE**. I THINK THAT YOU ARE ONE OF THE ONLY ONES WHO UNDERSTANDS...
WHAT I AM TRYING TO DO HERE.

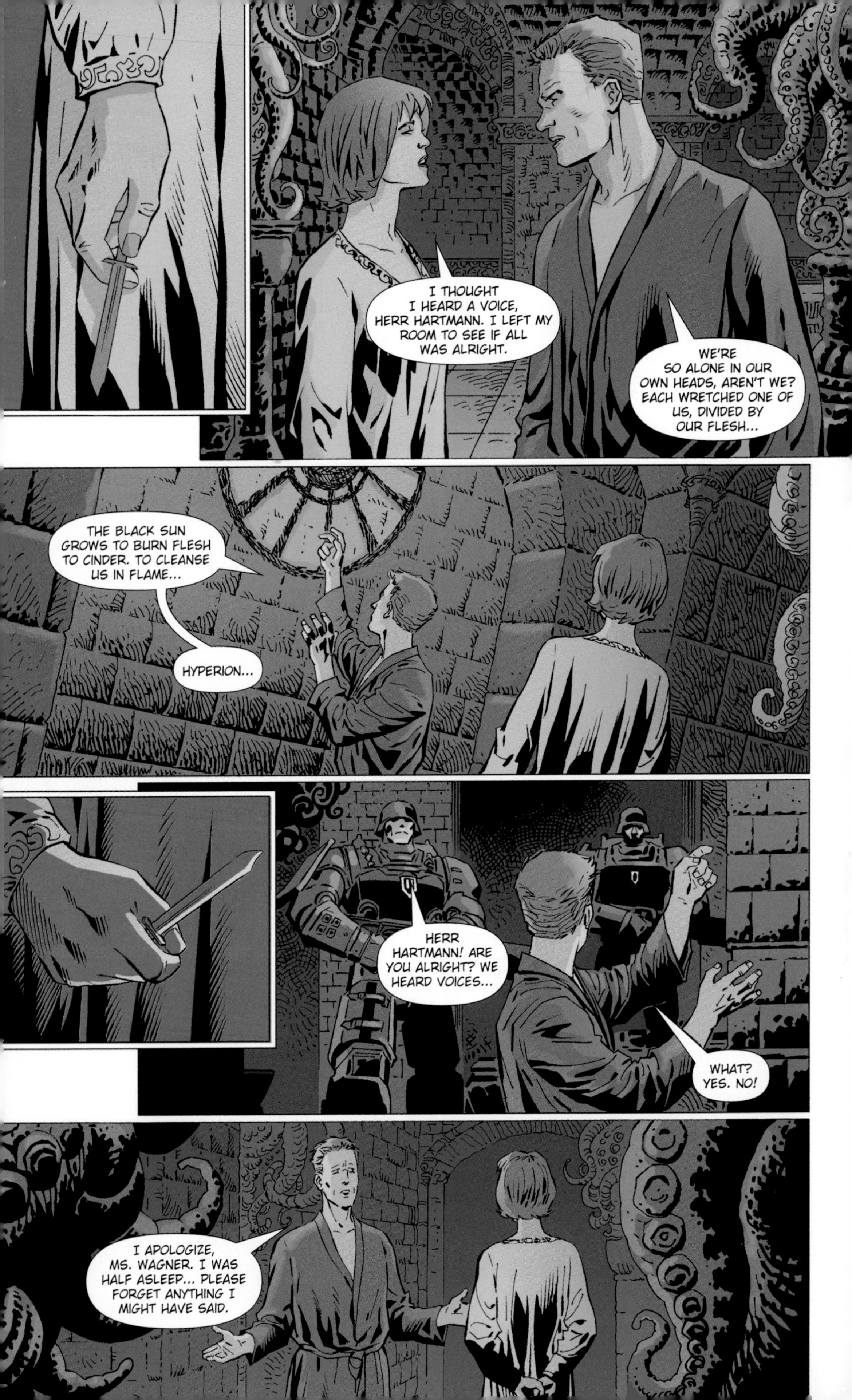
I THOUGHT I HEARD A VOICE, HERR HARTMANN. I LEFT MY ROOM TO SEE IF ALL WAS ALRIGHT.
WE'RE SO ALONE IN OUR OWN HEADS, AREN'T WE? EACH WRETCHED ONE OF US, DIVIDED BY OUR FLESH...
THE BLACK SUN GROWS TO BURN FLESH TO CINDER. TO CLEANSE US IN FLAME...
HYPERION...
HERR HARTMANN! ARE YOU ALRIGHT? WE HEARD VOICES...
WHAT? YES. NO!
I APOLOGIZE, MS. WAGNER. I WAS HALF ASLEEP... PLEASE FORGET ANYTHING I MIGHT HAVE SAID.

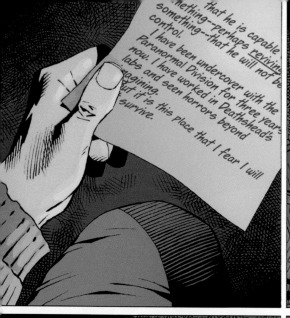

that he is capable of
something—perhaps reviving
something—that he will not be able to
control.
I have been undercover with the
Paranormal Division for three years
now. I have worked in Deathshead's
labs and seen horrors beyond
imagining.
But it is this place that I fear I will not
survive.

THE MESSAGE
WAS RECEIVED VIA
UNCONVENTIONAL NETWORKS,
BUT CERTAINLY SEEMS
LEGITIMATE.

WHAT DO YOU
WANT TO DO, CAPTAIN
BLAZKOWICZ?

I WANT TO
GO BLOW UP SOME
FASCISTS.

IT WON'T
BE EASY.

YEAH.

VERY GOOD.
THE MESSAGE
MENTIONS THAT
NEW WOLFENSTEIN
IS LOCATED ON A
CLIFFTOP.

A BIG ENOUGH
EXPLOSION AT THE RIGHT
PLACE SHOULD SEND THE
ENTIRE THING STRAIGHT
TO HELL.

YEAH.

"NOW ALL THEY NEEDED TO DO WAS GET TERROR
BILLY'S SQUAD INTO OCCUPIED SLOVENIA WITH A
FEW TONNES OF PLASTIC EXPLOSIVE."

"NOW IT'S SLOVENIA?
YOU SAID DENMARK."

"SLOVENIA. I *DEFINITELY*
SAID SLOVENIA."

SO YOU
DON'T SPEAK
THE LANGUAGE
AT ALL, MR.
BLAZKOWICZ?

NEIN.

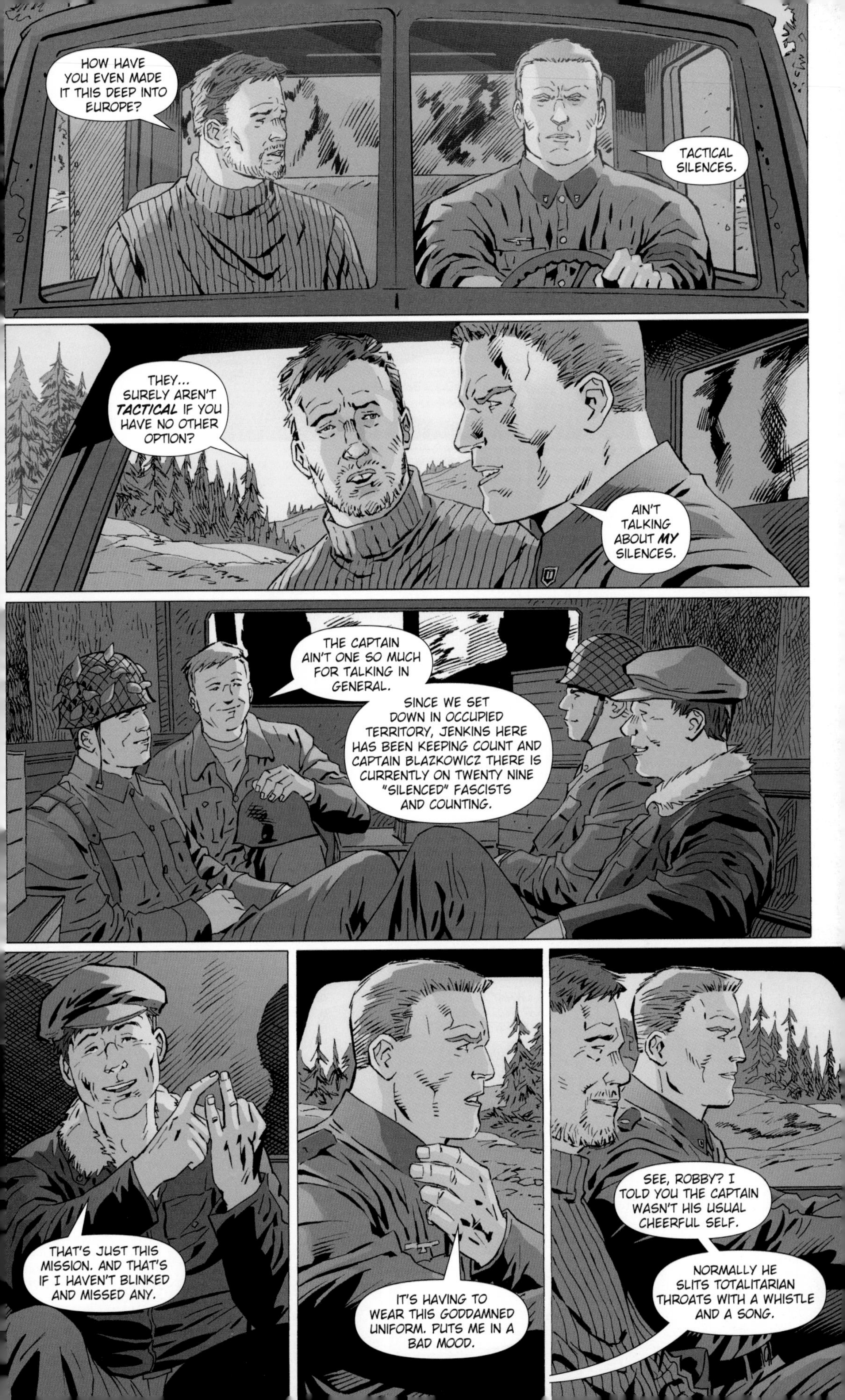
HOW HAVE YOU EVEN MADE IT THIS DEEP INTO EUROPE?
TACTICAL SILENCES.
THEY... SURELY AREN'T *TACTICAL* IF YOU HAVE NO OTHER OPTION?
AIN'T TALKING ABOUT *MY* SILENCES.
THE CAPTAIN AIN'T ONE SO MUCH FOR TALKING IN GENERAL.
SINCE WE SET DOWN IN OCCUPIED TERRITORY, JENKINS HERE HAS BEEN KEEPING COUNT AND CAPTAIN BLAZKOWICZ THERE IS CURRENTLY ON TWENTY NINE "SILENCED" FASCISTS AND COUNTING.
THAT'S JUST THIS MISSION. AND THAT'S IF I HAVEN'T BLINKED AND MISSED ANY.
IT'S HAVING TO WEAR THIS GODDAMNED UNIFORM. PUTS ME IN A BAD MOOD.
SEE, ROBBY? I TOLD YOU THE CAPTAIN WASN'T HIS USUAL CHEERFUL SELF.
NORMALLY HE SLITS TOTALITARIAN THROATS WITH A WHISTLE AND A SONG.

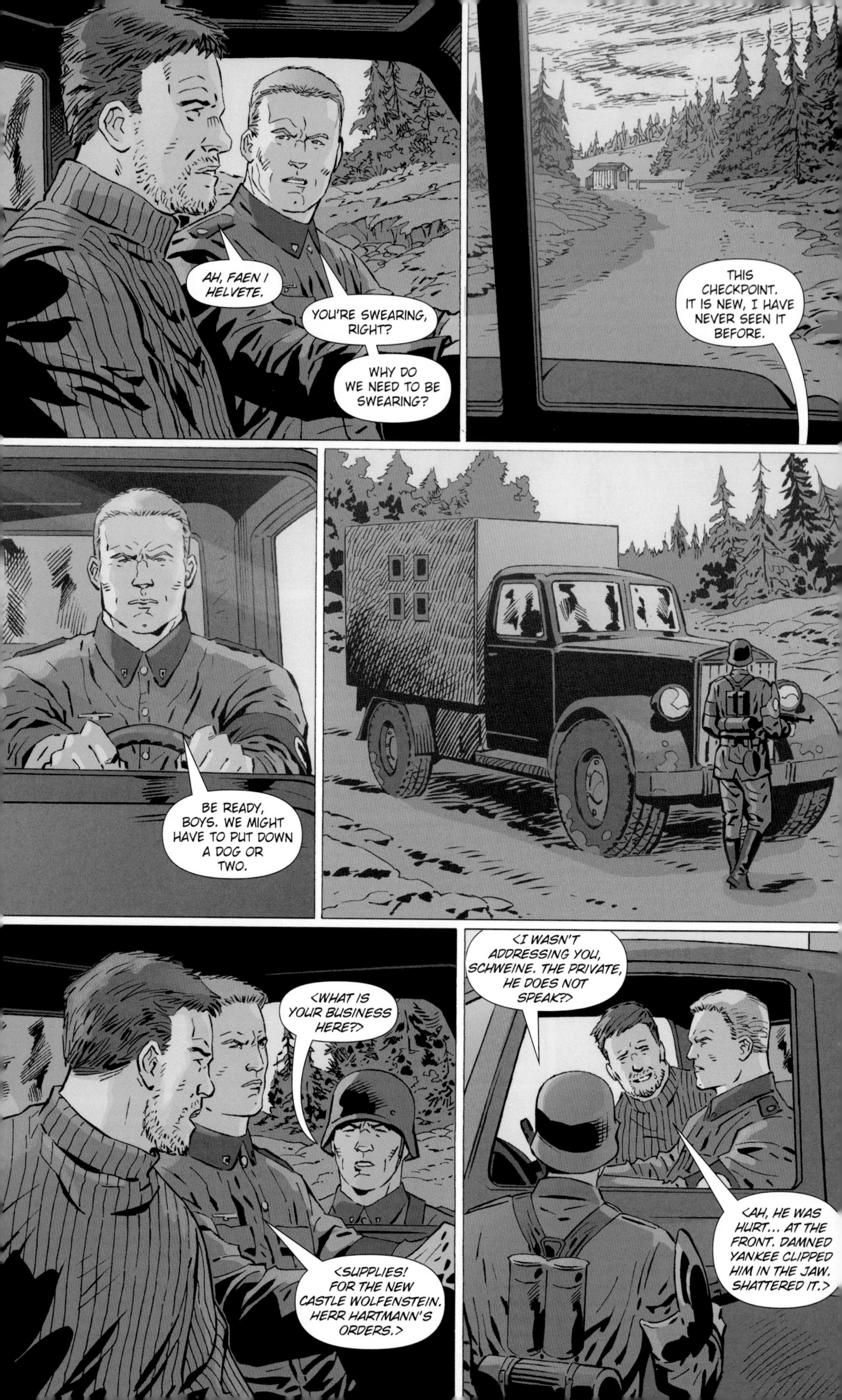
AH, FAEN I HELVETE.
YOU'RE SWEARING, RIGHT?
WHY DO WE NEED TO BE SWEARING?
THIS CHECKPOINT. IT IS NEW, I HAVE NEVER SEEN IT BEFORE.
BE READY, BOYS. WE MIGHT HAVE TO PUT DOWN A DOG OR TWO.
<WHAT IS YOUR BUSINESS HERE?>
<SUPPLIES! FOR THE NEW CASTLE WOLFENSTEIN. HERR HARTMANN'S ORDERS.>
<I WASN'T ADDRESSING YOU, SCHWEINE. THE PRIVATE, HE DOES NOT SPEAK?>
<AH, HE WAS HURT... AT THE FRONT. DAMNED YANKEE CLIPPED HIM IN THE JAW. SHATTERED IT.>

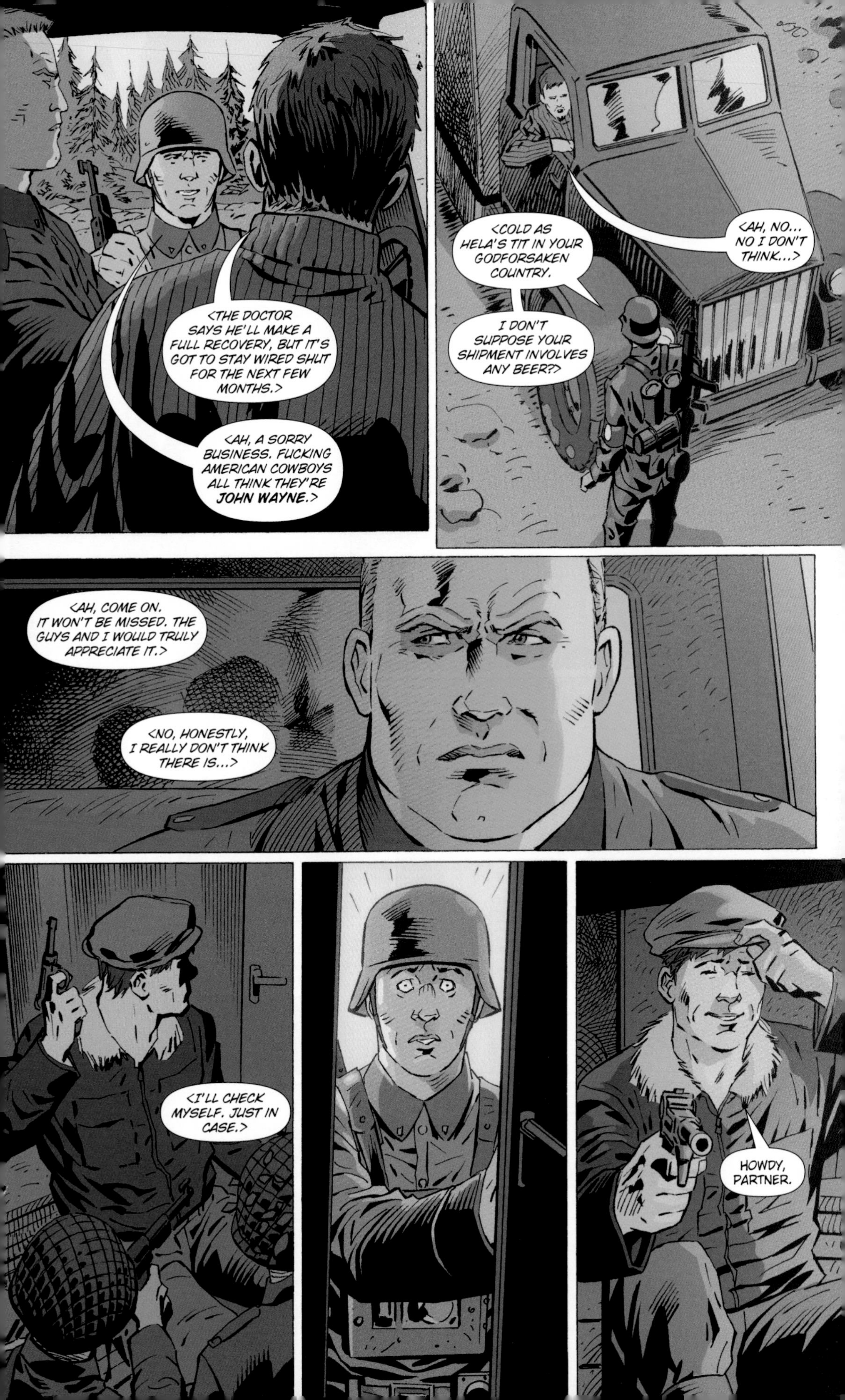

<THE DOCTOR SAYS HE'LL MAKE A FULL RECOVERY, BUT IT'S GOT TO STAY WIRED SHUT FOR THE NEXT FEW MONTHS.>
<AH, A SORRY BUSINESS. FUCKING AMERICAN COWBOYS ALL THINK THEY'RE JOHN WAYNE.>
<COLD AS HELA'S TIT IN YOUR GODFORSAKEN COUNTRY.
I DON'T SUPPOSE YOUR SHIPMENT INVOLVES ANY BEER?>
<AH, NO... NO I DON'T THINK...>
<AH, COME ON. IT WON'T BE MISSED. THE GUYS AND I WOULD TRULY APPRECIATE IT.>
<NO, HONESTLY, I REALLY DON'T THINK THERE IS...>
<I'LL CHECK MYSELF. JUST IN CASE.>
HOWDY, PARTNER.

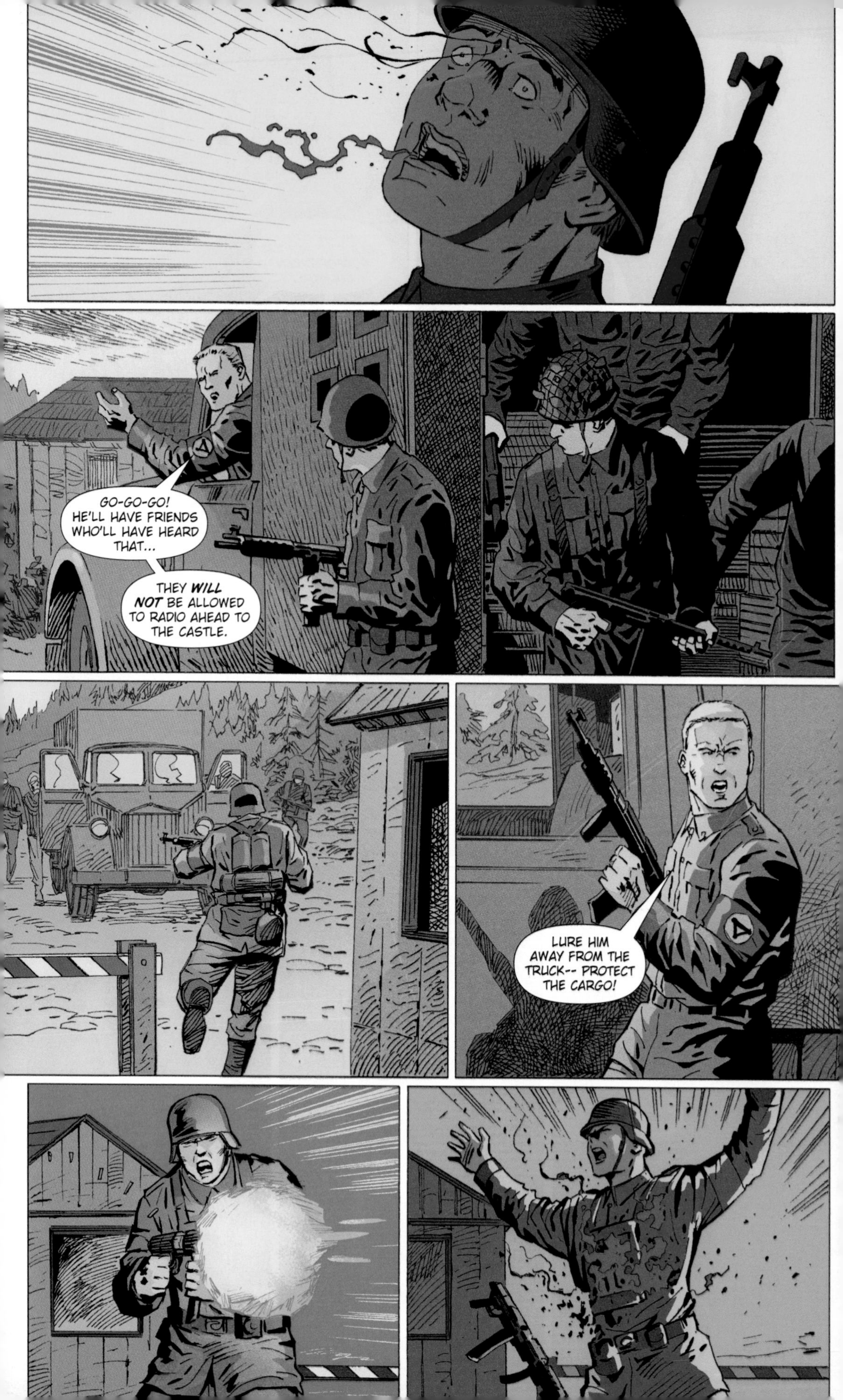
GO-GO-GO! HE'LL HAVE FRIENDS WHO'LL HAVE HEARD THAT...
THEY WILL NOT BE ALLOWED TO RADIO AHEAD TO THE CASTLE.
LURE HIM AWAY FROM THE TRUCK-- PROTECT THE CARGO!

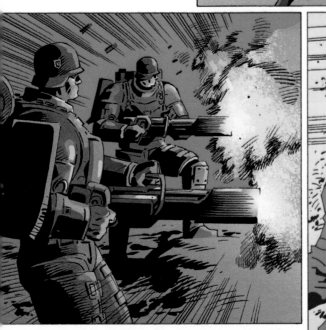

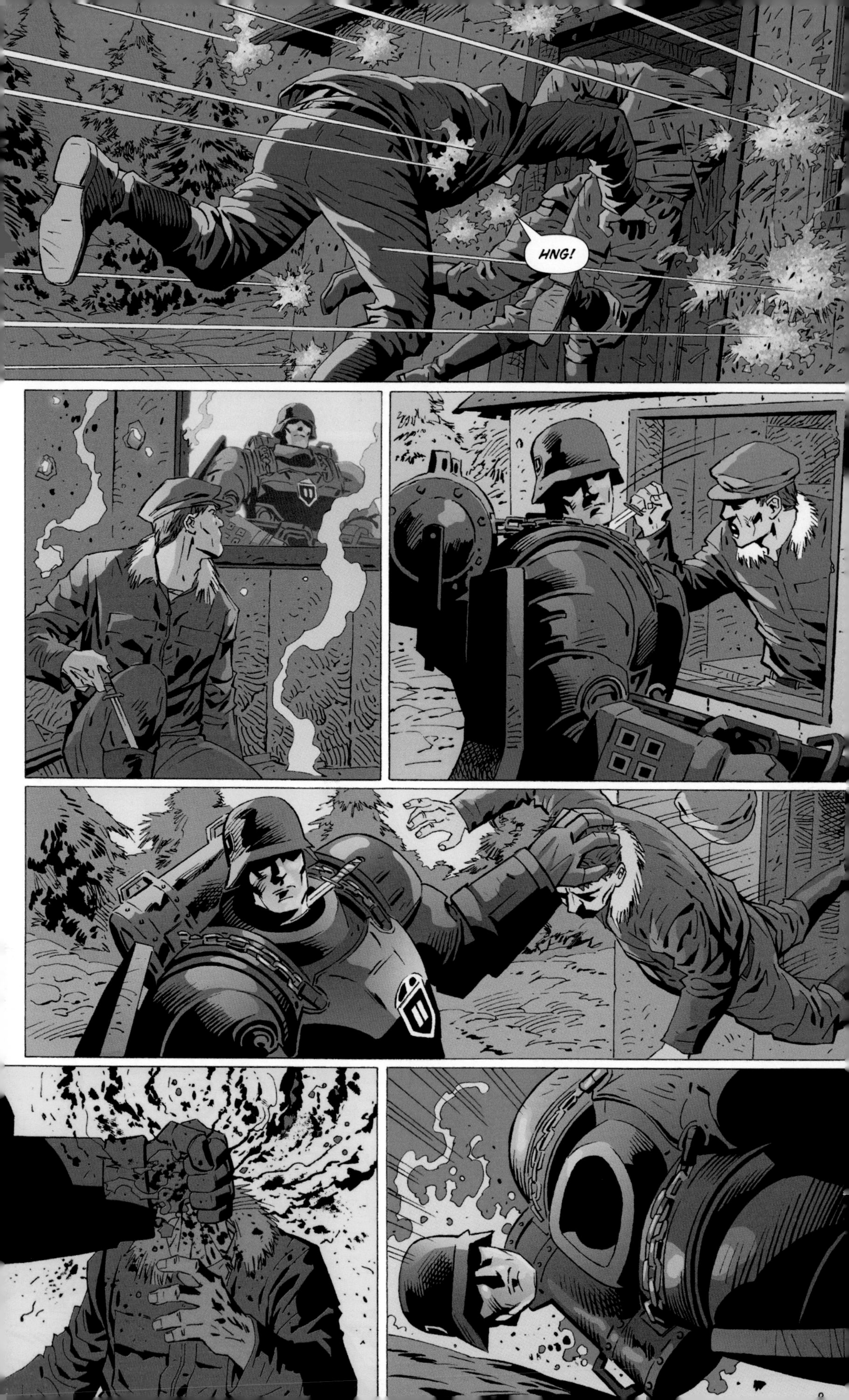
HNG!

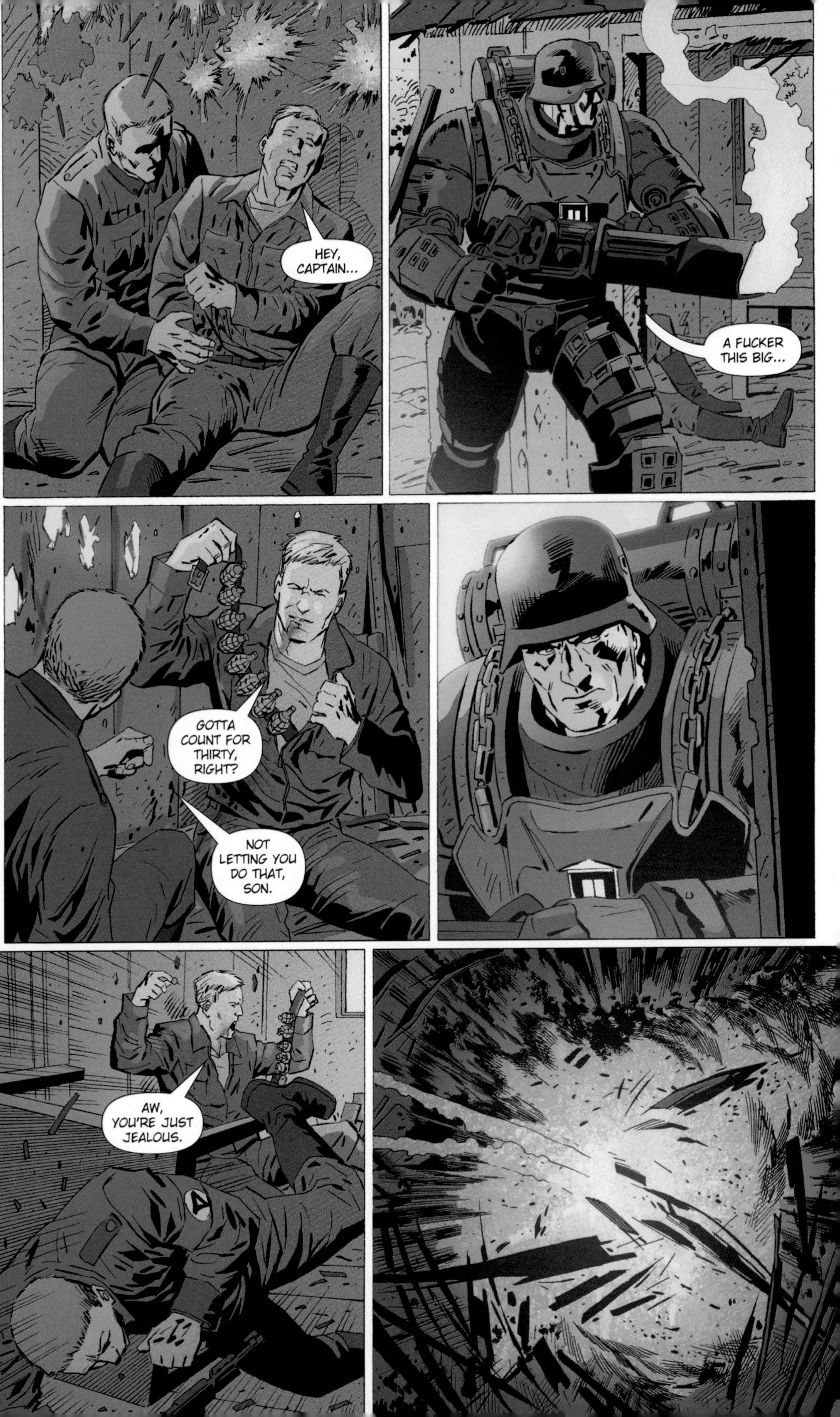
HEY, CAPTAIN...
A FUCKER THIS BIG...
GOTTA COUNT FOR THIRTY, RIGHT?
NOT LETTING YOU DO THAT, SON.
AW, YOU'RE JUST JEALOUS.

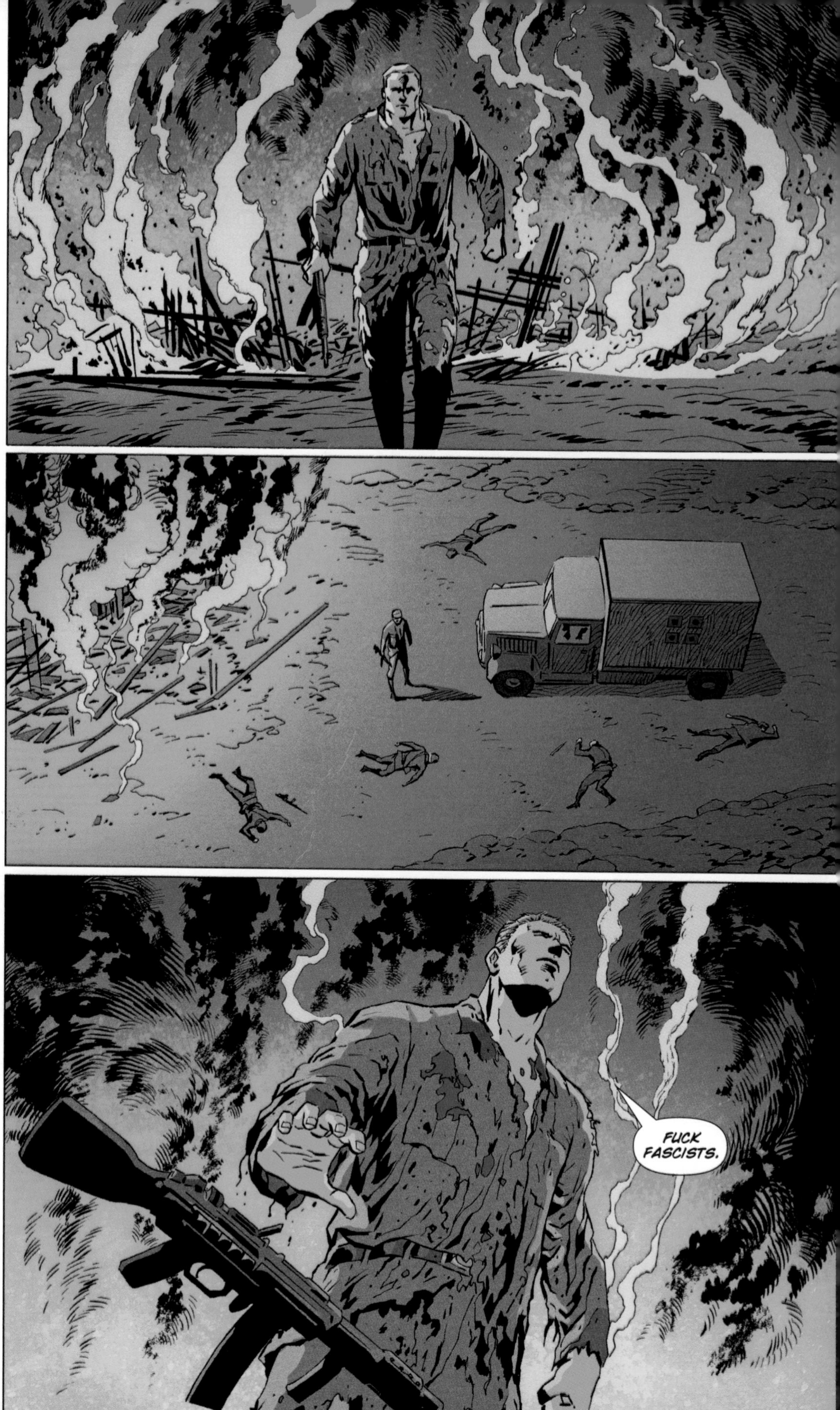
FUCK FASCISTS.

TM

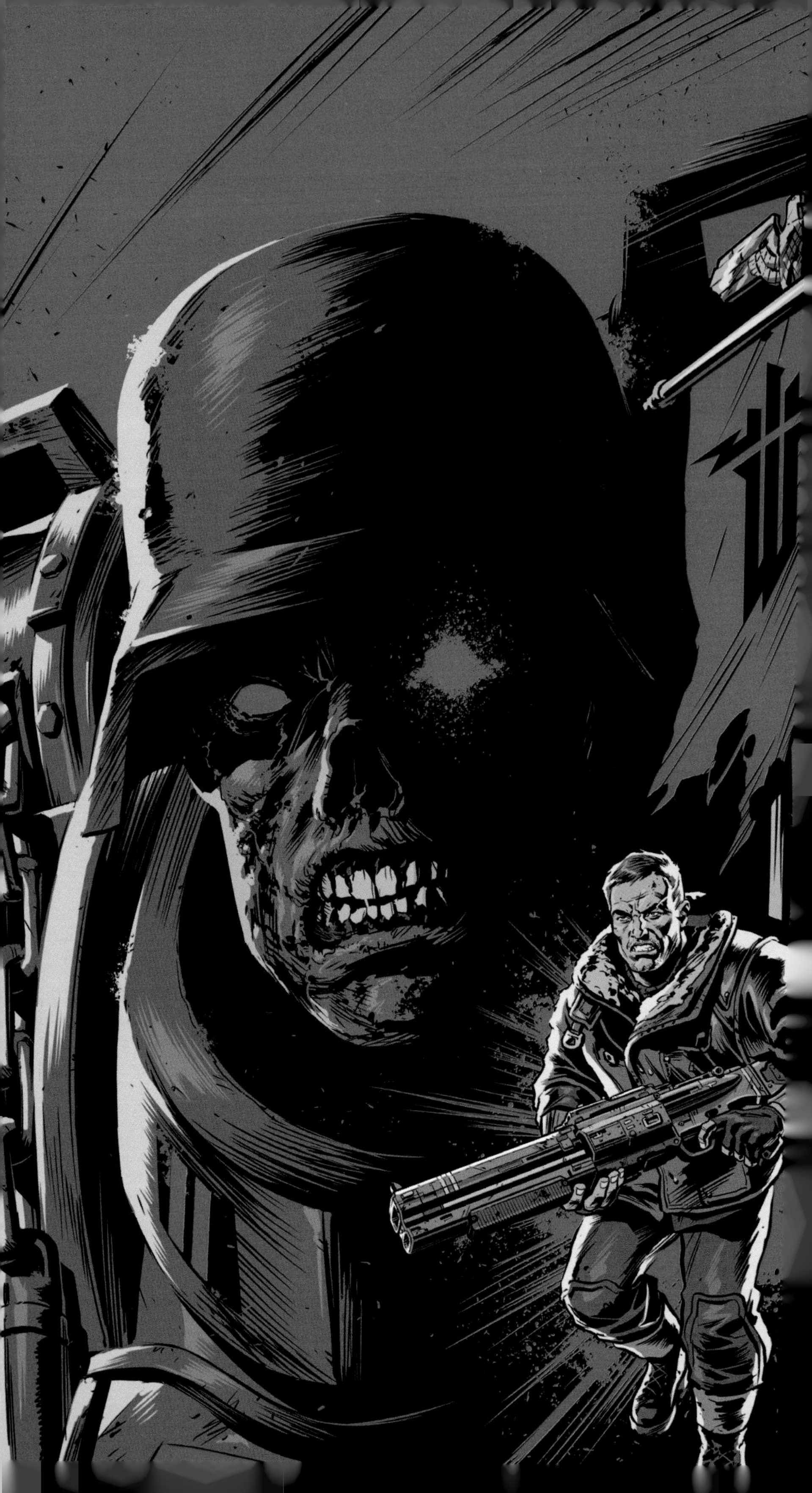

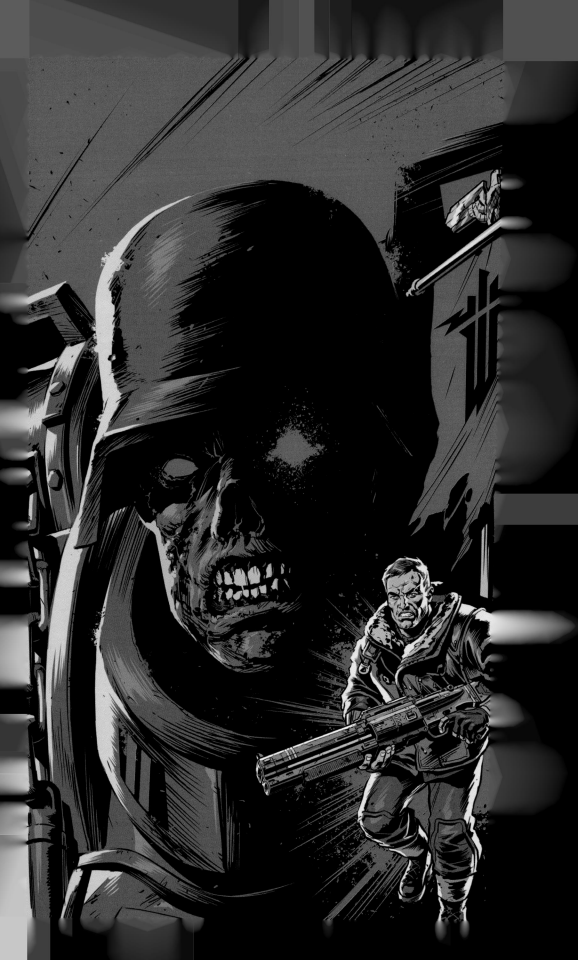

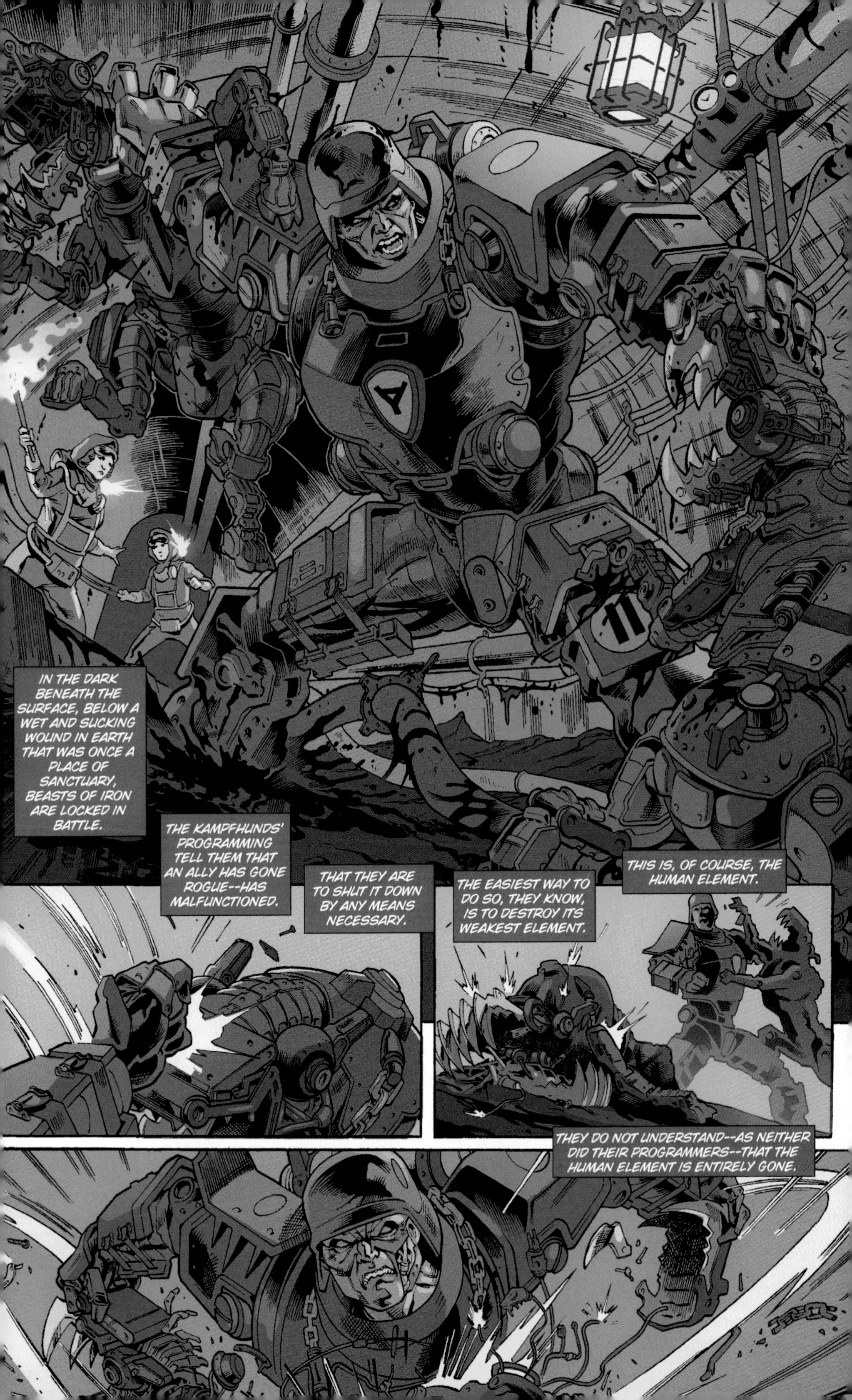
IN THE DARK BENEATH THE SURFACE, BELOW A WET AND SUCKING WOUND IN EARTH THAT WAS ONCE A PLACE OF SANCTUARY, BEASTS OF IRON ARE LOCKED IN BATTLE.
THE KAMPFHUNDS' PROGRAMMING TELL THEM THAT AN ALLY HAS GONE ROGUE--HAS MALFUNCTIONED.
THAT THEY ARE TO SHUT IT DOWN BY ANY MEANS NECESSARY.
THE EASIEST WAY TO DO SO, THEY KNOW, IS TO DESTROY ITS WEAKEST ELEMENT.
THIS IS, OF COURSE, THE HUMAN ELEMENT.
THEY DO NOT UNDERSTAND--AS NEITHER DID THEIR PROGRAMMERS--THAT THE HUMAN ELEMENT IS ENTIRELY GONE.

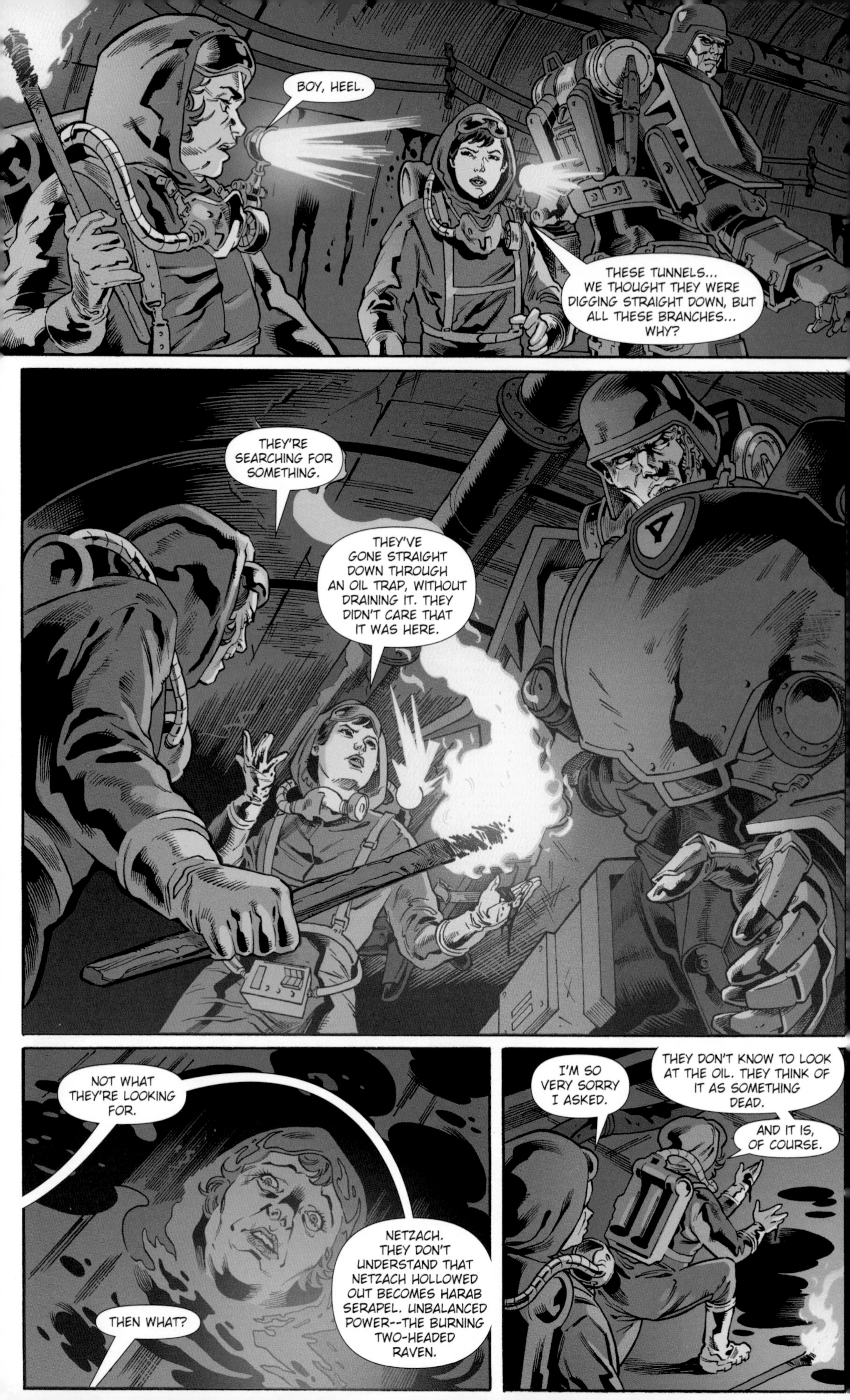
BOY, HEEL.
THESE TUNNELS... WE THOUGHT THEY WERE DIGGING STRAIGHT DOWN, BUT ALL THESE BRANCHES... WHY?
THEY'RE SEARCHING FOR SOMETHING.
THEY'VE GONE STRAIGHT DOWN THROUGH AN OIL TRAP, WITHOUT DRAINING IT. THEY DIDN'T CARE THAT IT WAS HERE.
NOT WHAT THEY'RE LOOKING FOR.
THEN WHAT?
NETZACH. THEY DON'T UNDERSTAND THAT NETZACH HOLLOWED OUT BECOMES HARAB SERAPEL. UNBALANCED POWER--THE BURNING TWO-HEADED RAVEN.
I'M SO VERY SORRY I ASKED.
THEY DON'T KNOW TO LOOK AT THE OIL. THEY THINK OF IT AS SOMETHING DEAD.
AND IT IS, OF COURSE.

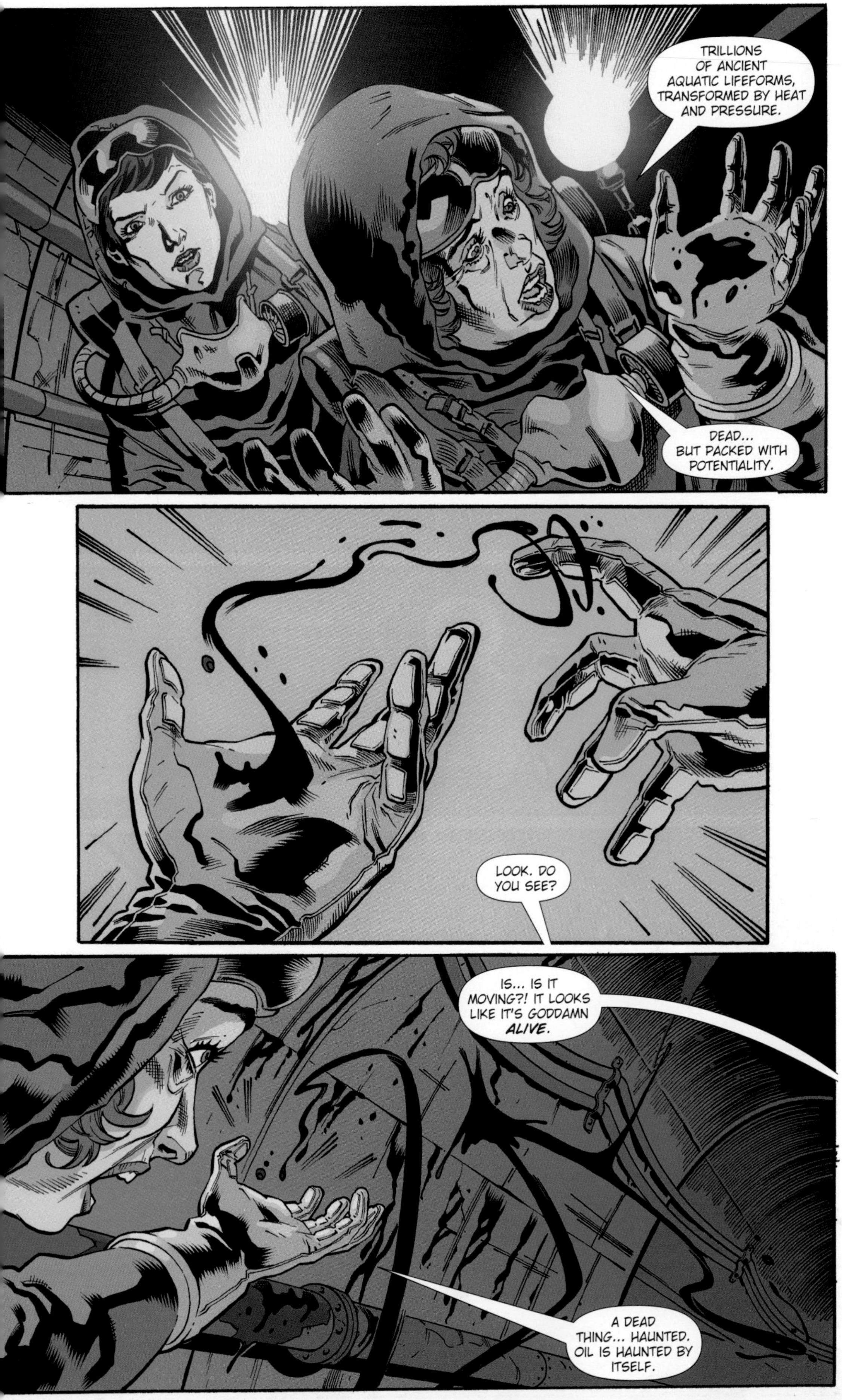
TRILLIONS OF ANCIENT AQUATIC LIFEFORMS, TRANSFORMED BY HEAT AND PRESSURE.
DEAD... BUT PACKED WITH POTENTIALITY.
LOOK. DO YOU SEE?
IS... IS IT MOVING?! IT LOOKS LIKE IT'S GODDAMN *ALIVE*.
A DEAD THING... HAUNTED. OIL IS HAUNTED BY ITSELF.

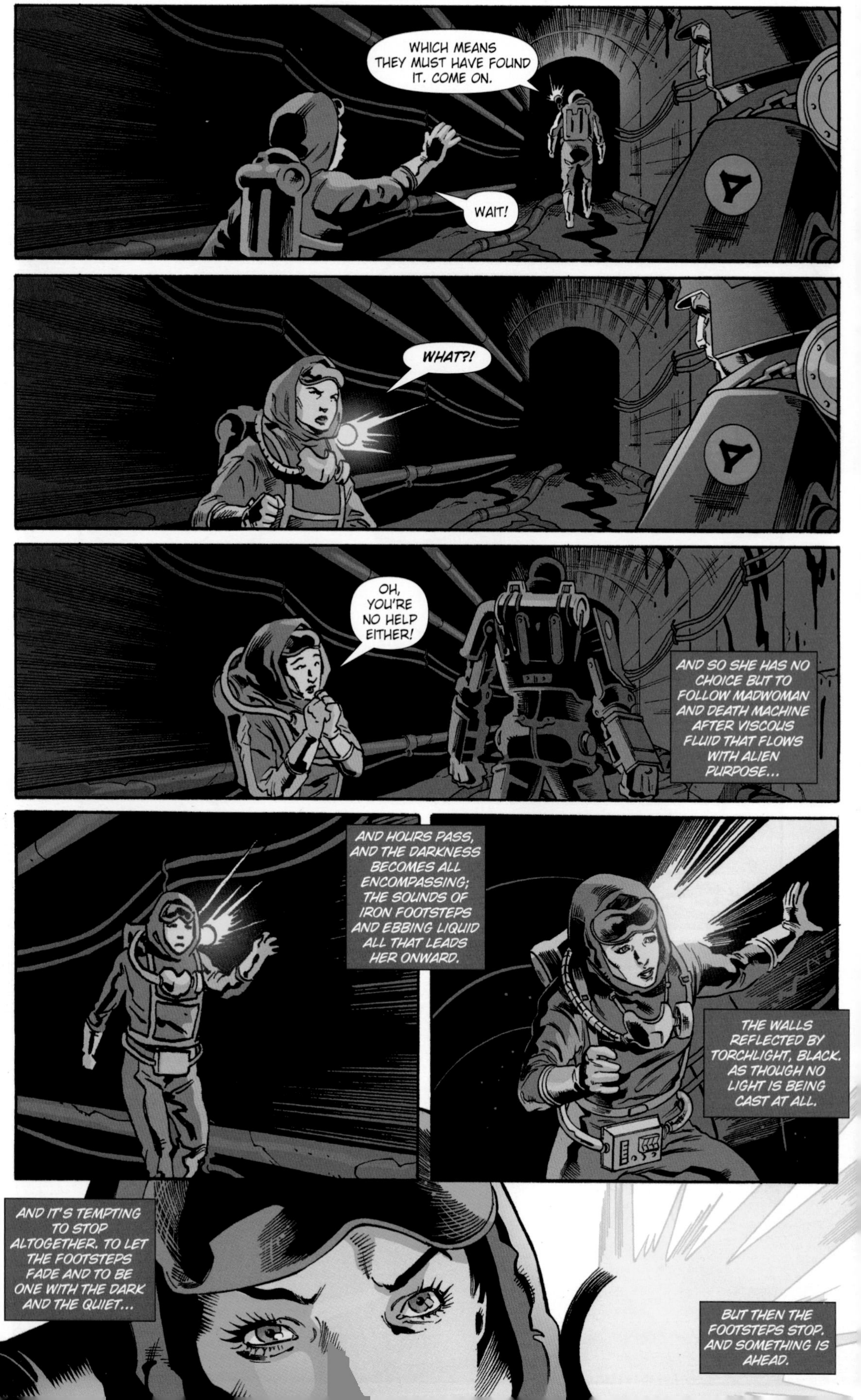

WHICH MEANS THEY MUST HAVE FOUND IT. COME ON.
WAIT!
WHAT?!
OH, YOU'RE NO HELP EITHER!
AND SO SHE HAS NO CHOICE BUT TO FOLLOW MADWOMAN AND DEATH MACHINE AFTER VISCOUS FLUID THAT FLOWS WITH ALIEN PURPOSE...
AND HOURS PASS, AND THE DARKNESS BECOMES ALL ENCOMPASSING; THE SOUNDS OF IRON FOOTSTEPS AND EBBING LIQUID ALL THAT LEADS HER ONWARD.
THE WALLS REFLECTED BY TORCHLIGHT, BLACK. AS THOUGH NO LIGHT IS BEING CAST AT ALL.
AND IT'S TEMPTING TO STOP ALTOGETHER. TO LET THE FOOTSTEPS FADE AND TO BE ONE WITH THE DARK AND THE QUIET...
BUT THEN THE FOOTSTEPS STOP. AND SOMETHING IS AHEAD.

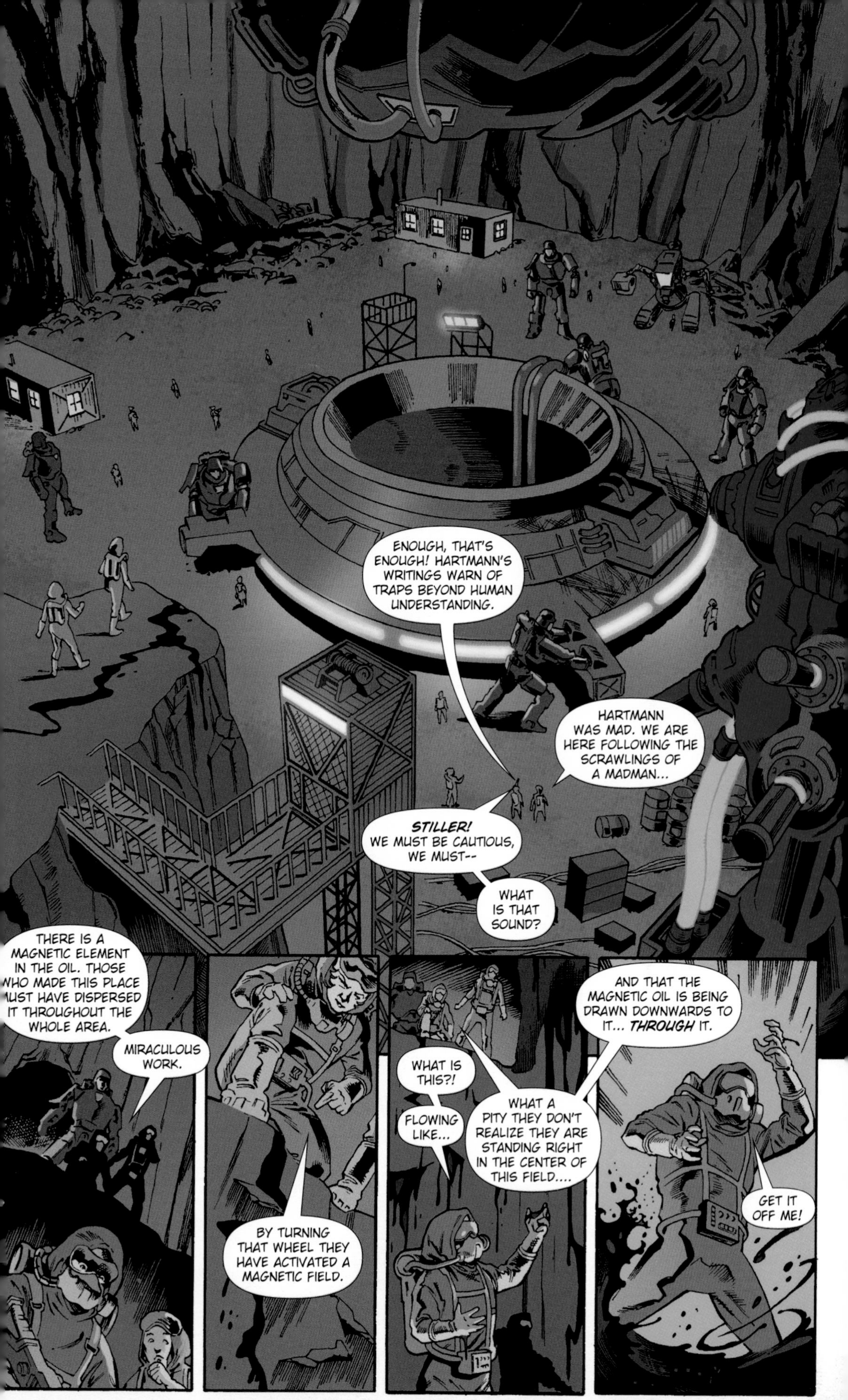

ENOUGH, THAT'S ENOUGH! HARTMANN'S WRITINGS WARN OF TRAPS BEYOND HUMAN UNDERSTANDING.
HARTMANN WAS MAD. WE ARE HERE FOLLOWING THE SCRAWLINGS OF A MADMAN...
STILLER! WE MUST BE CAUTIOUS, WE MUST--
WHAT IS THAT SOUND?
THERE IS A MAGNETIC ELEMENT IN THE OIL. THOSE WHO MADE THIS PLACE MUST HAVE DISPERSED IT THROUGHOUT THE WHOLE AREA.
MIRACULOUS WORK.
BY TURNING THAT WHEEL THEY HAVE ACTIVATED A MAGNETIC FIELD.
WHAT IS THIS?!
FLOWING LIKE...
WHAT A PITY THEY DON'T REALIZE THEY ARE STANDING RIGHT IN THE CENTER OF THIS FIELD....
AND THAT THE MAGNETIC OIL IS BEING DRAWN DOWNWARDS TO IT... THROUGH IT.
GET IT OFF ME!

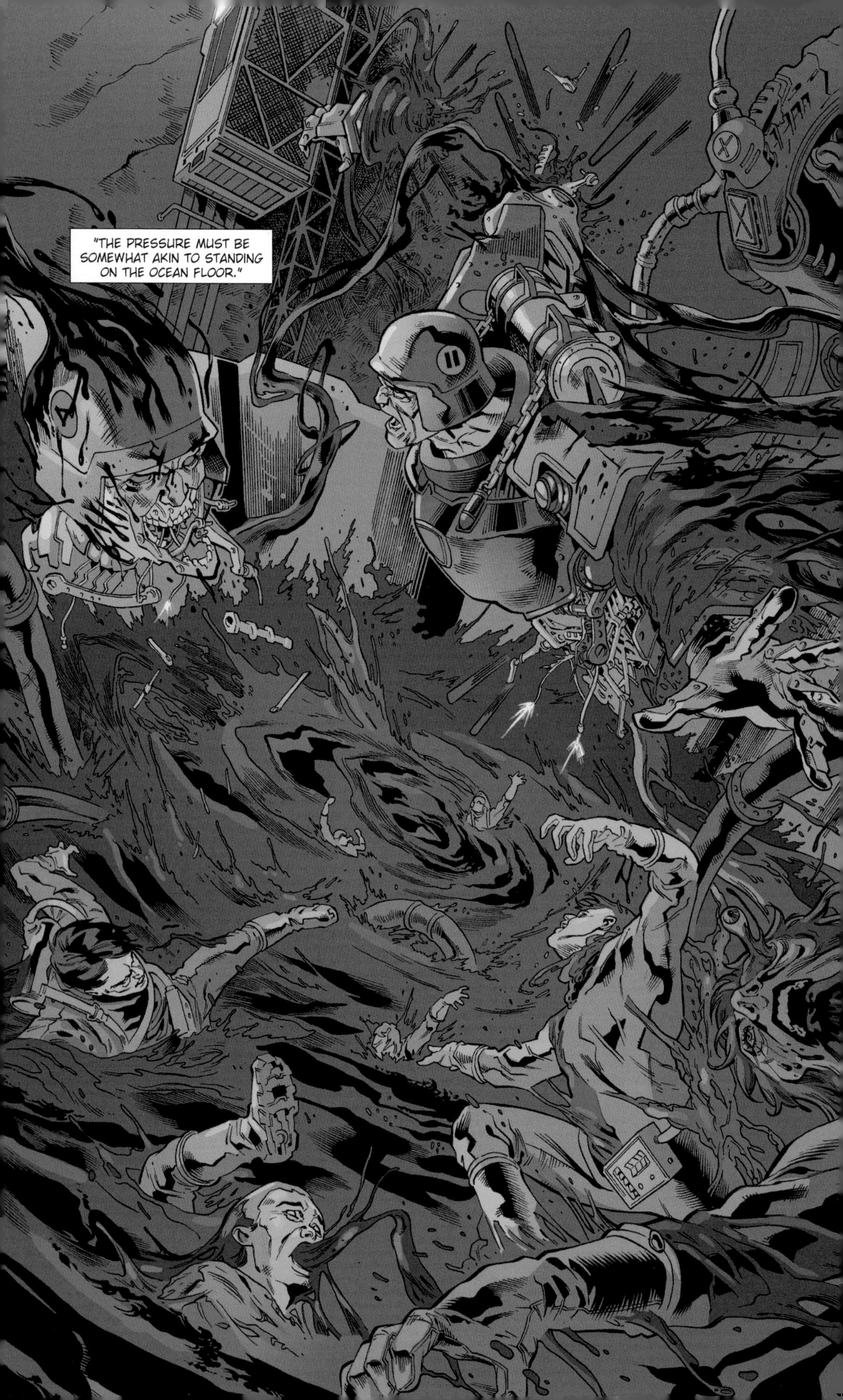
"THE PRESSURE MUST BE SOMEWHAT AKIN TO STANDING ON THE OCEAN FLOOR."

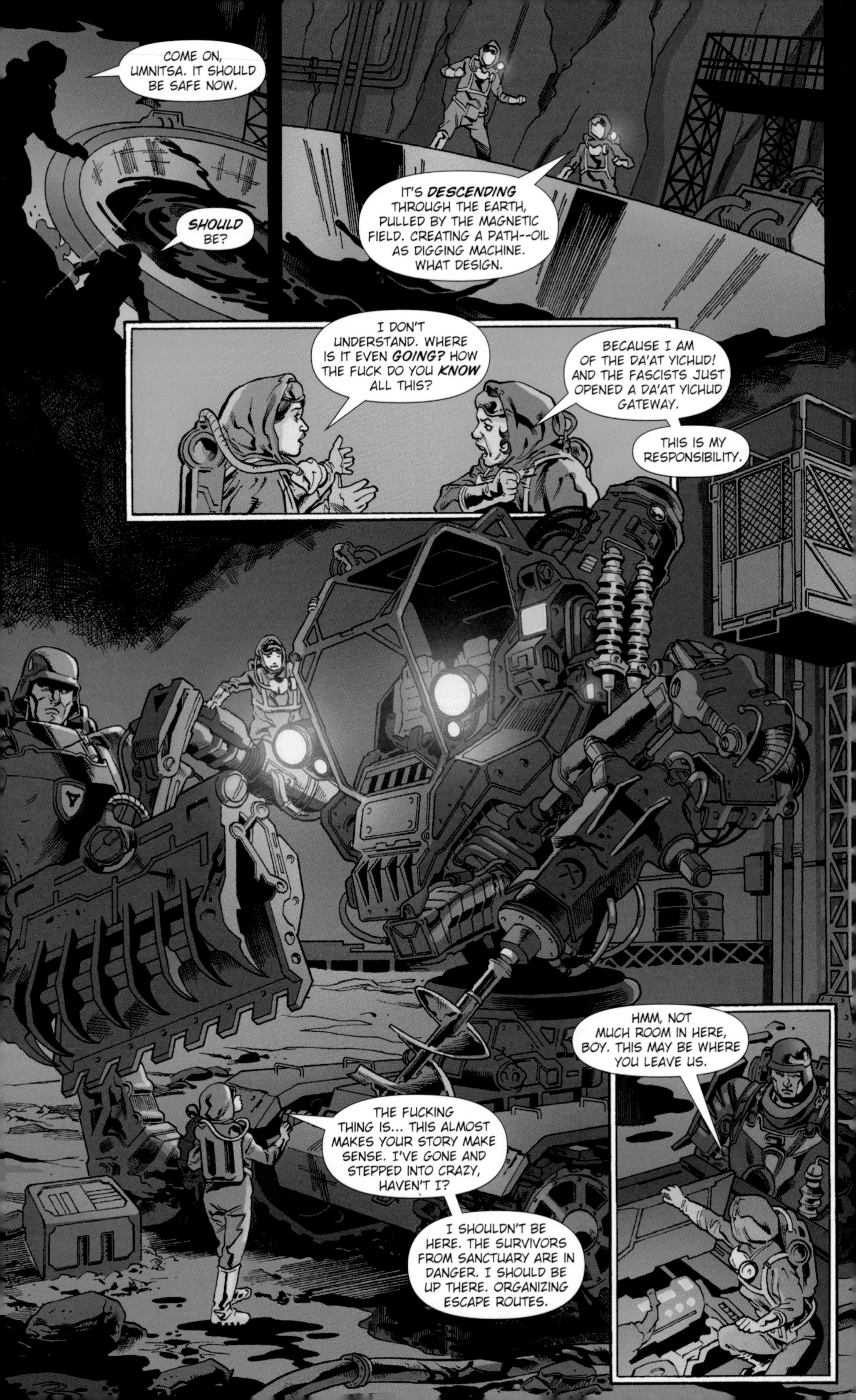
COME ON, UMNITSA. IT SHOULD BE SAFE NOW.
SHOULD BE?
IT'S DESCENDING THROUGH THE EARTH, PULLED BY THE MAGNETIC FIELD. CREATING A PATH--OIL AS DIGGING MACHINE. WHAT DESIGN.
I DON'T UNDERSTAND. WHERE IS IT EVEN GOING? HOW THE FUCK DO YOU KNOW ALL THIS?
BECAUSE I AM OF THE DA'AT YICHUD! AND THE FASCISTS JUST OPENED A DA'AT YICHUD GATEWAY.
THIS IS MY RESPONSIBILITY.
THE FUCKING THING IS... THIS ALMOST MAKES YOUR STORY MAKE SENSE. I'VE GONE AND STEPPED INTO CRAZY, HAVEN'T I?
I SHOULDN'T BE HERE. THE SURVIVORS FROM SANCTUARY ARE IN DANGER. I SHOULD BE UP THERE. ORGANIZING ESCAPE ROUTES.
HMM, NOT MUCH ROOM IN HERE, BOY. THIS MAY BE WHERE YOU LEAVE US.

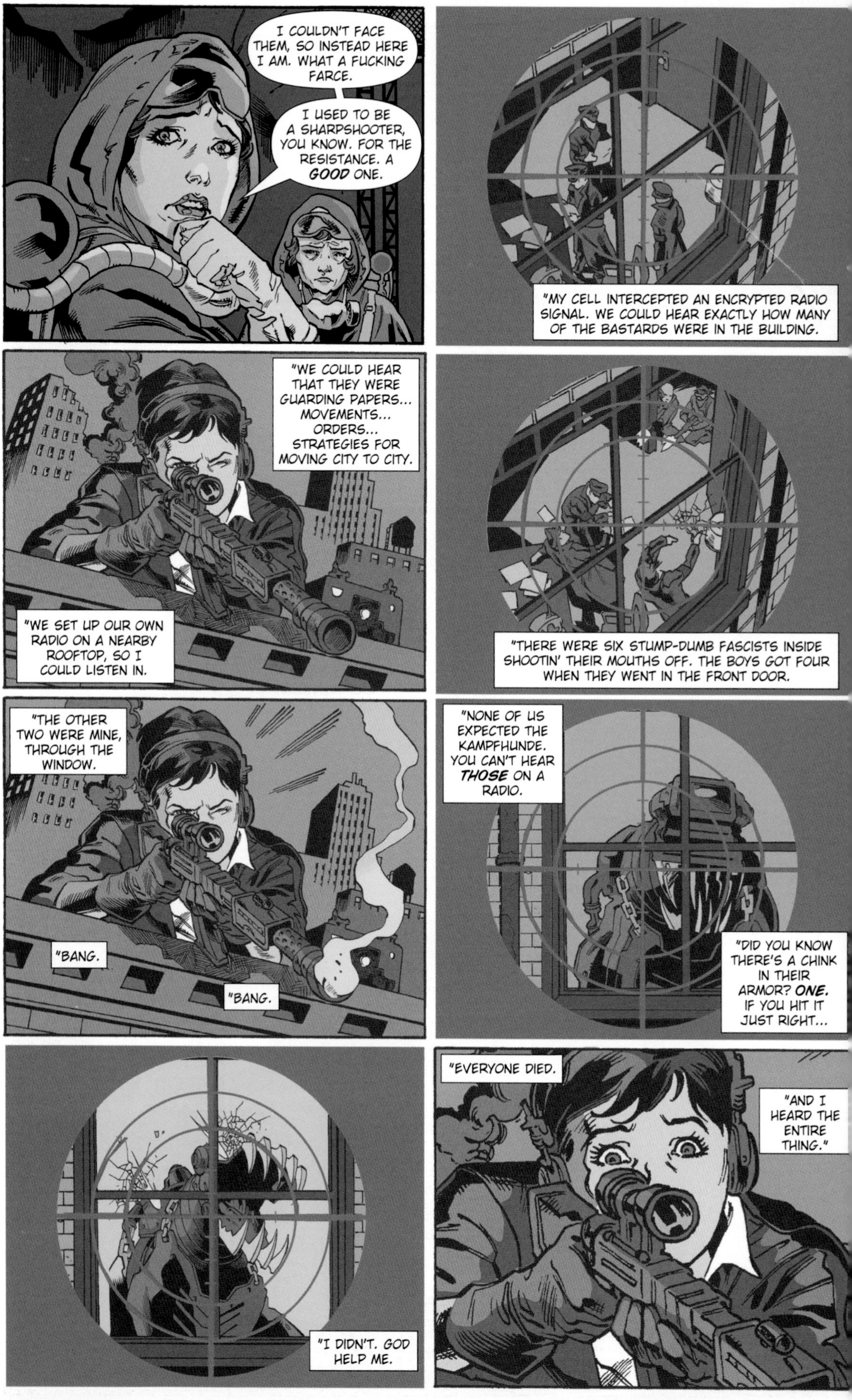
I COULDN'T FACE THEM, SO INSTEAD HERE I AM. WHAT A FUCKING FARCE.
I USED TO BE A SHARPSHOOTER, YOU KNOW. FOR THE RESISTANCE. A GOOD ONE.
"MY CELL INTERCEPTED AN ENCRYPTED RADIO SIGNAL. WE COULD HEAR EXACTLY HOW MANY OF THE BASTARDS WERE IN THE BUILDING.
"WE COULD HEAR THAT THEY WERE GUARDING PAPERS... MOVEMENTS... ORDERS... STRATEGIES FOR MOVING CITY TO CITY.
"WE SET UP OUR OWN RADIO ON A NEARBY ROOFTOP, SO I COULD LISTEN IN.
"THERE WERE SIX STUMP-DUMB FASCISTS INSIDE SHOOTIN' THEIR MOUTHS OFF. THE BOYS GOT FOUR WHEN THEY WENT IN THE FRONT DOOR.
"THE OTHER TWO WERE MINE, THROUGH THE WINDOW.
"BANG.
"BANG.
"NONE OF US EXPECTED THE KAMPFHUNDE. YOU CAN'T HEAR THOSE ON A RADIO.
"DID YOU KNOW THERE'S A CHINK IN THEIR ARMOR? ONE. IF YOU HIT IT JUST RIGHT...
"I DIDN'T. GOD HELP ME.
"EVERYONE DIED.
"AND I HEARD THE ENTIRE THING."

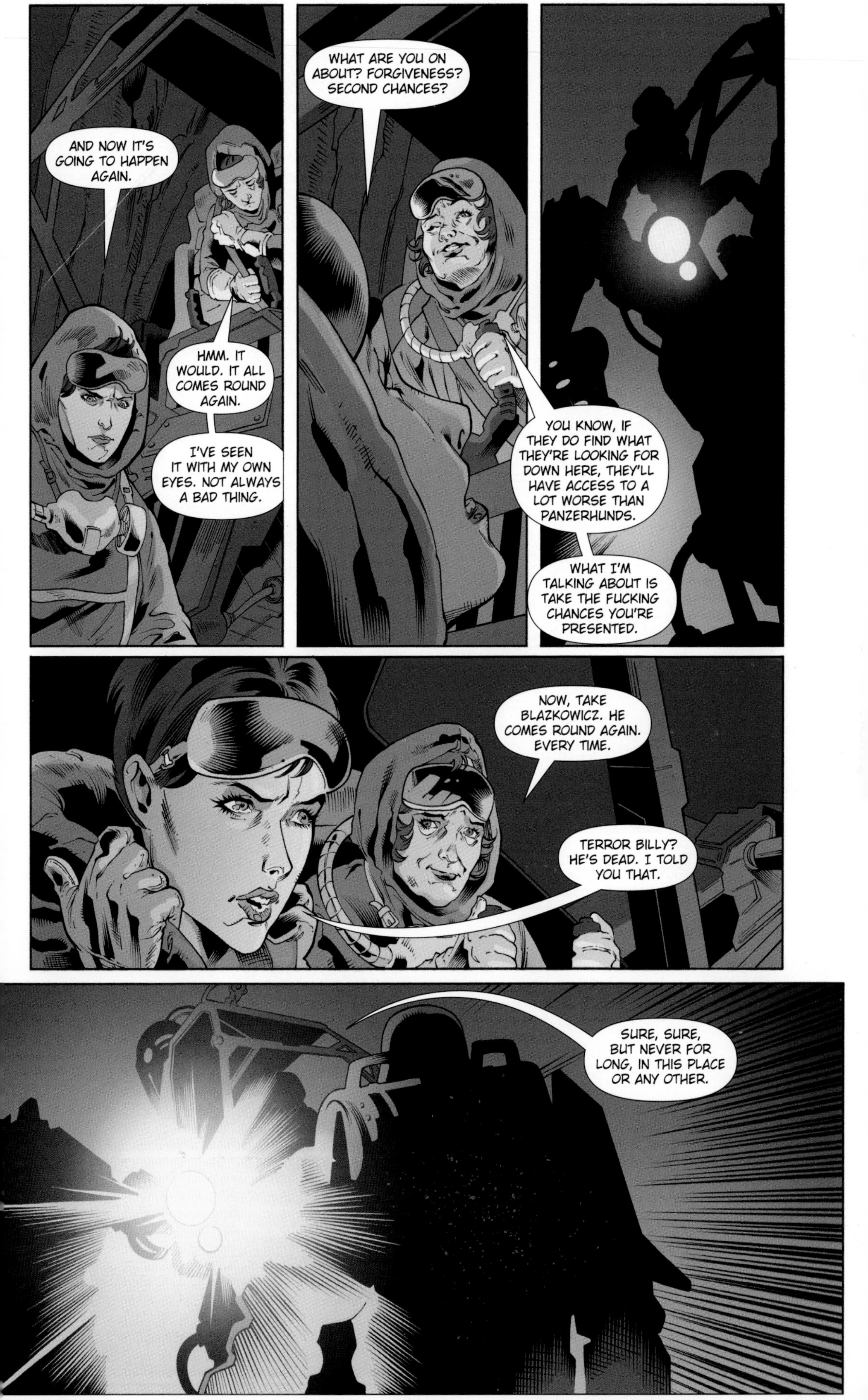
AND NOW IT'S GOING TO HAPPEN AGAIN.
HMM. IT WOULD. IT ALL COMES ROUND AGAIN.
I'VE SEEN IT WITH MY OWN EYES. NOT ALWAYS A BAD THING.
WHAT ARE YOU ON ABOUT? FORGIVENESS? SECOND CHANCES?
YOU KNOW, IF THEY DO FIND WHAT THEY'RE LOOKING FOR DOWN HERE, THEY'LL HAVE ACCESS TO A LOT WORSE THAN PANZERHUNDS.
WHAT I'M TALKING ABOUT IS TAKE THE FUCKING CHANCES YOU'RE PRESENTED.
NOW, TAKE BLAZKOWICZ. HE COMES ROUND AGAIN. EVERY TIME.
TERROR BILLY? HE'S DEAD. I TOLD YOU THAT.
SURE, SURE, BUT NEVER FOR LONG, IN THIS PLACE OR ANY OTHER.

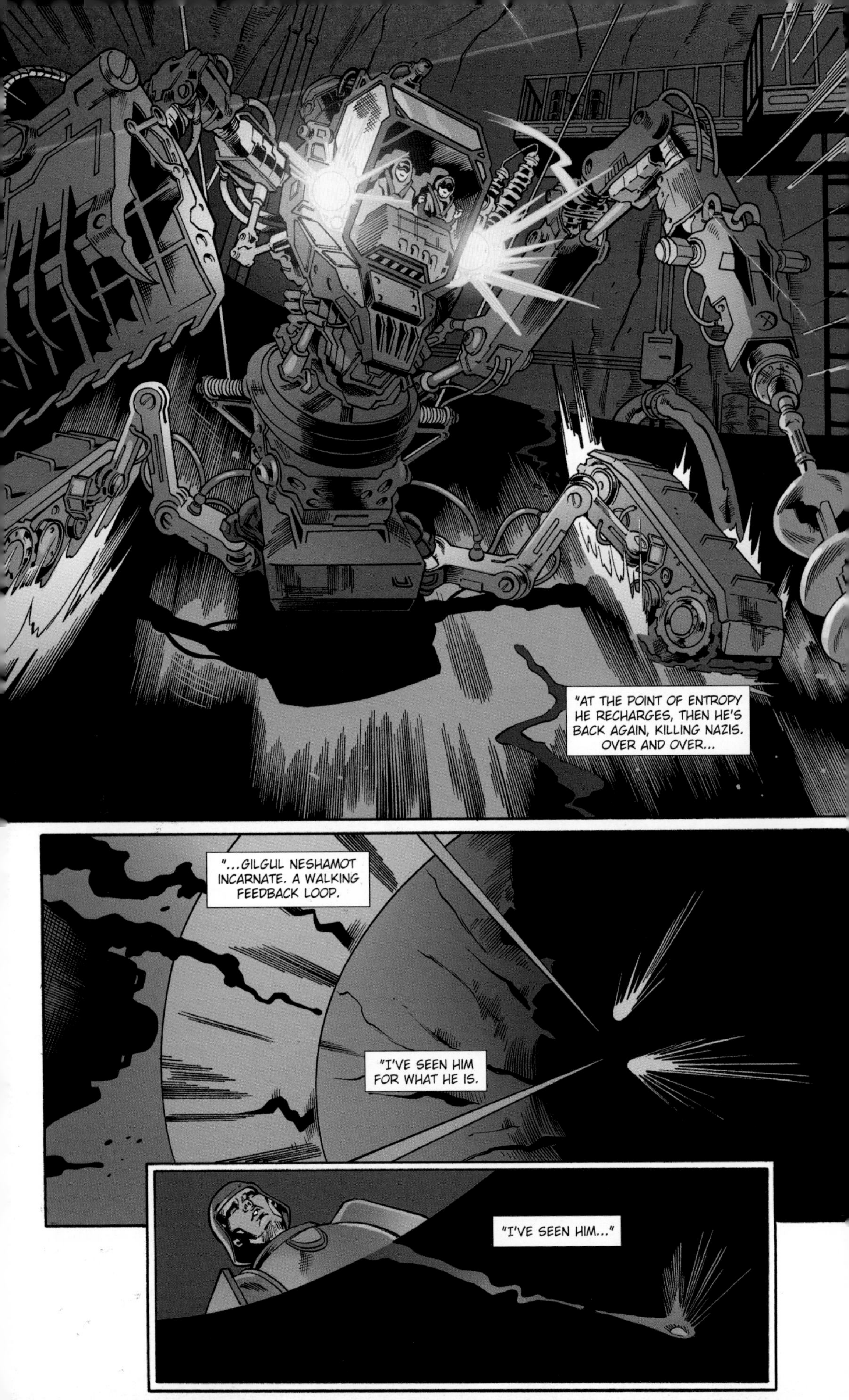
"AT THE POINT OF ENTROPY HE RECHARGES, THEN HE'S BACK AGAIN, KILLING NAZIS. OVER AND OVER...
"...GILGUL NESHAMOT INCARNATE. A WALKING FEEDBACK LOOP.
"I'VE SEEN HIM FOR WHAT HE IS.
"I'VE SEEN HIM..."

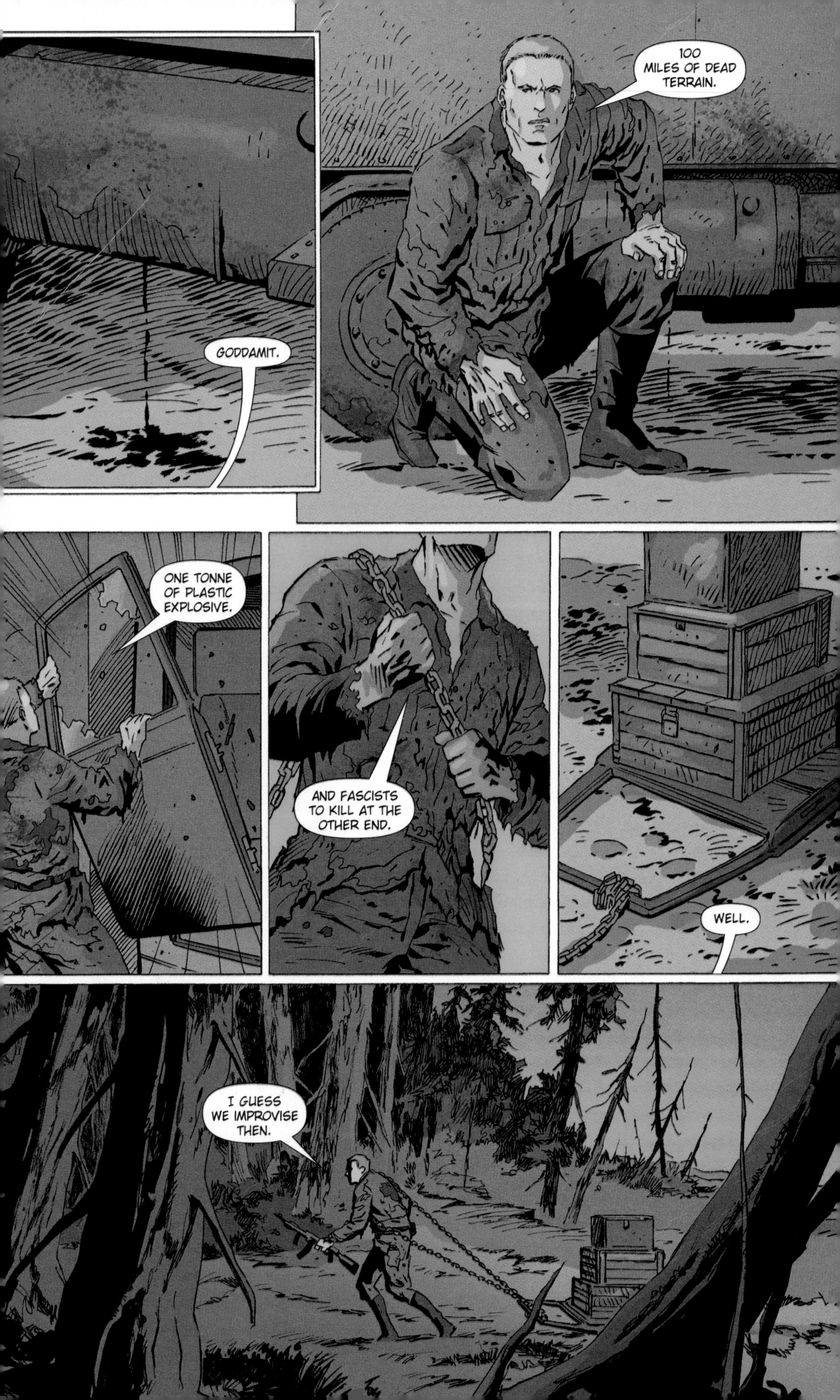
100
MILES OF DEAD
TERRAIN.
GODDAMIT.
ONE TONNE
OF PLASTIC
EXPLOSIVE.
AND FASCISTS
TO KILL AT THE
OTHER END.
WELL.
I GUESS
WE IMPROVISE
THEN.

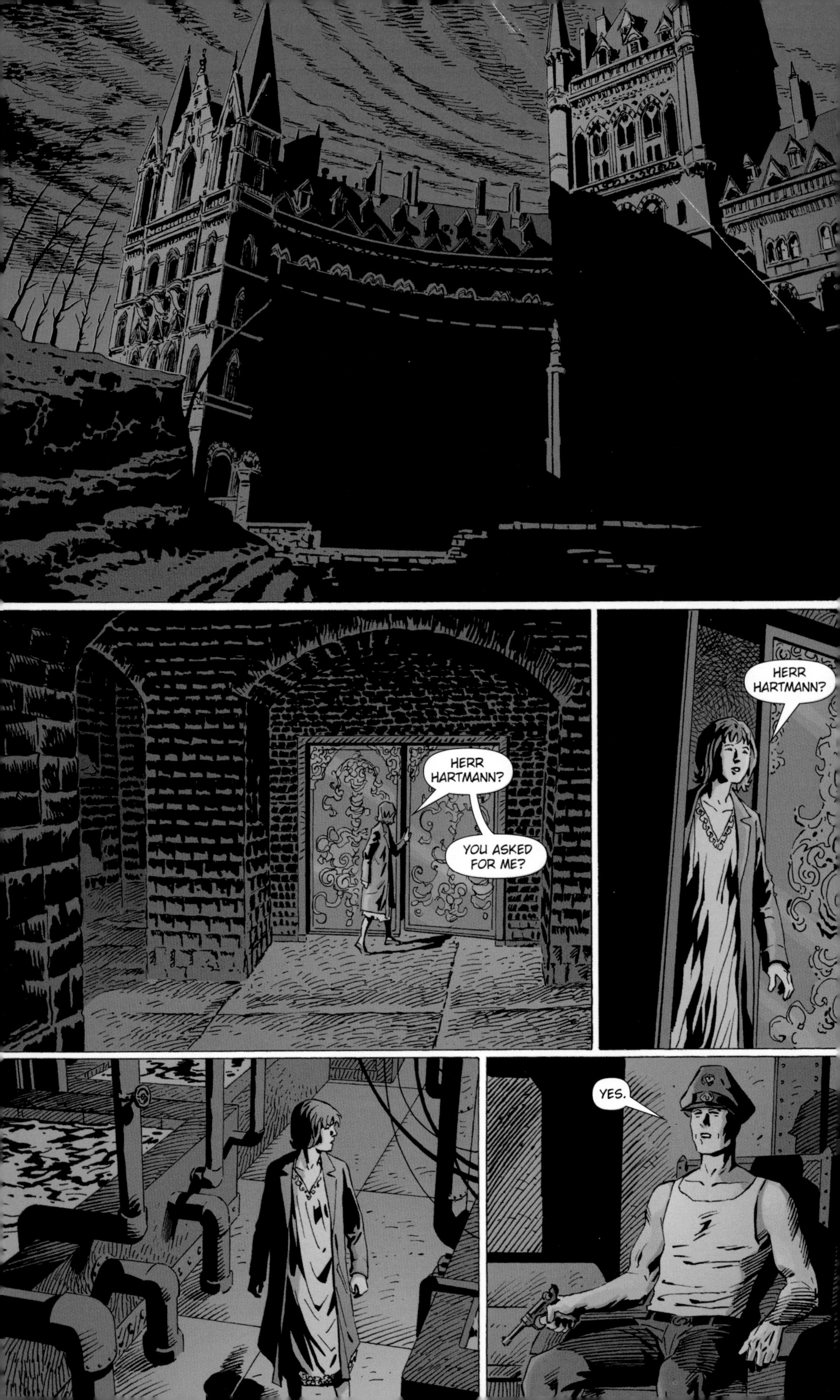
HERR HARTMANN?
YOU ASKED FOR ME?
HERR HARTMANN?
YES.

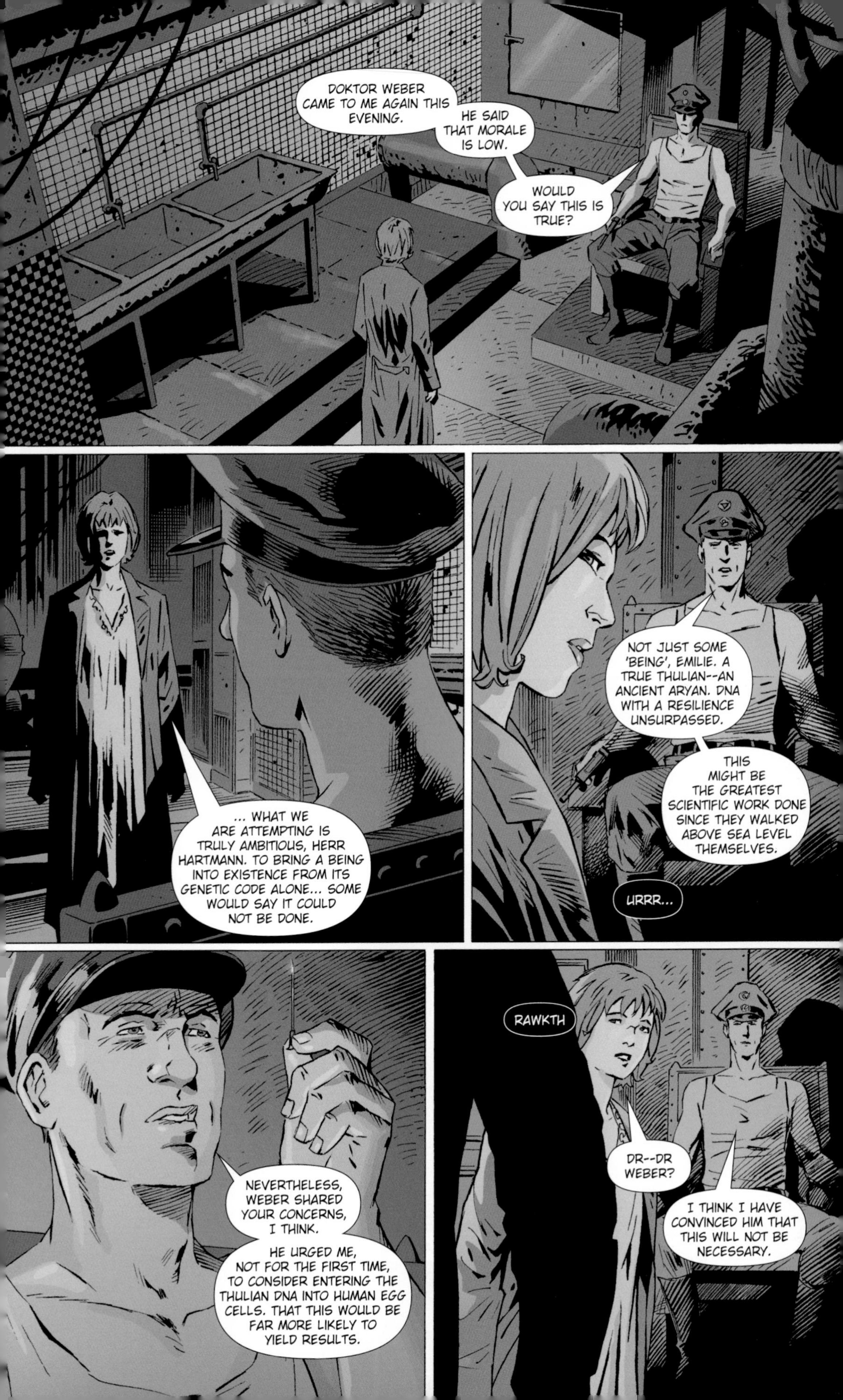

DOKTOR WEBER CAME TO ME AGAIN THIS EVENING.
HE SAID THAT MORALE IS LOW.
WOULD YOU SAY THIS IS TRUE?
... WHAT WE ARE ATTEMPTING IS TRULY AMBITIOUS, HERR HARTMANN. TO BRING A BEING INTO EXISTENCE FROM ITS GENETIC CODE ALONE... SOME WOULD SAY IT COULD NOT BE DONE.
NOT JUST SOME 'BEING', EMILIE. A TRUE THULIAN--AN ANCIENT ARYAN. DNA WITH A RESILIENCE UNSURPASSED.
THIS MIGHT BE THE GREATEST SCIENTIFIC WORK DONE SINCE THEY WALKED ABOVE SEA LEVEL THEMSELVES.
URRR...
NEVERTHELESS, WEBER SHARED YOUR CONCERNS, I THINK.
HE URGED ME, NOT FOR THE FIRST TIME, TO CONSIDER ENTERING THE THULIAN DNA INTO HUMAN EGG CELLS. THAT THIS WOULD BE FAR MORE LIKELY TO YIELD RESULTS.
RAWKTH
DR--DR WEBER?
I THINK I HAVE CONVINCED HIM THAT THIS WILL NOT BE NECESSARY.

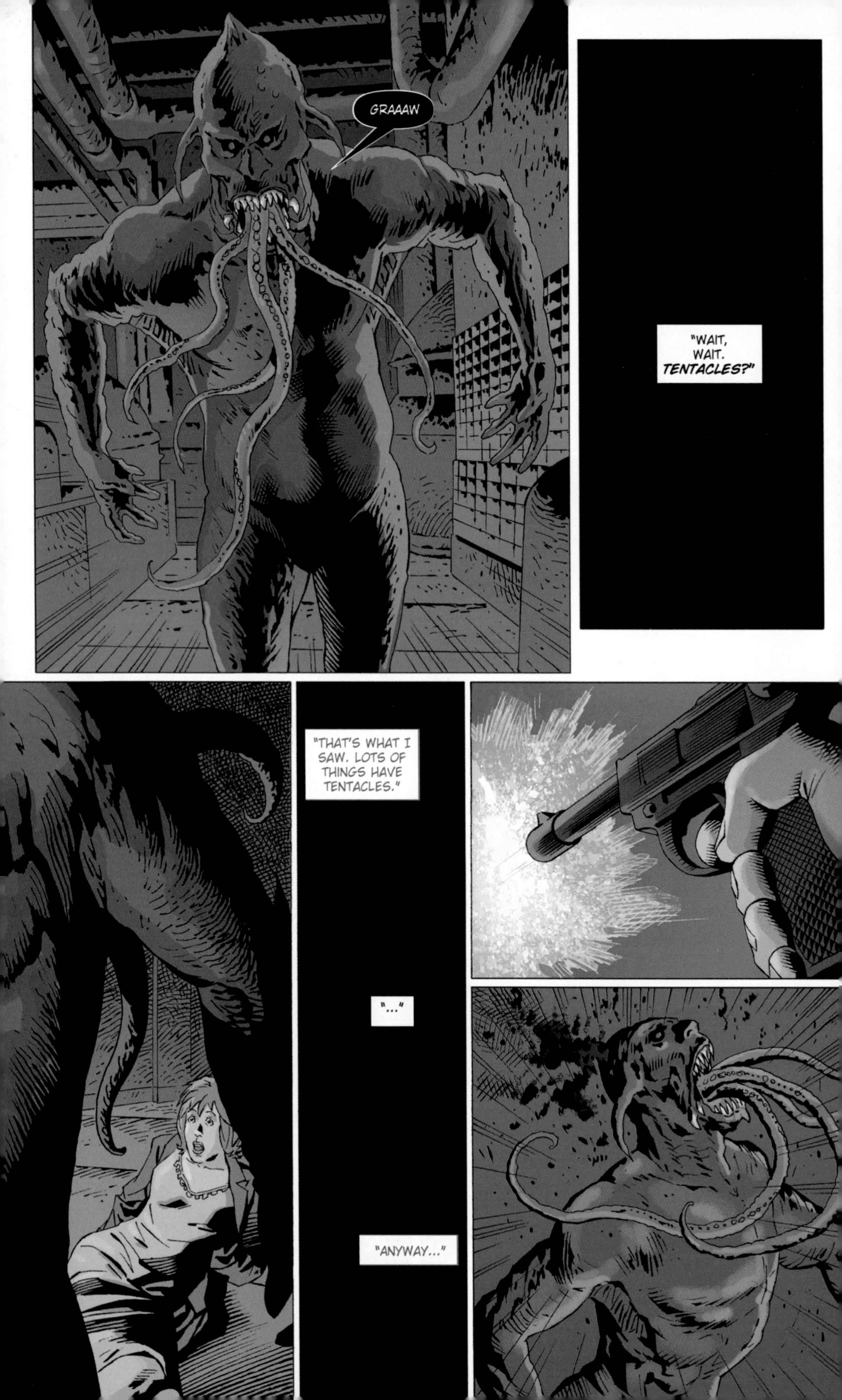
GRAAAW
"WAIT, WAIT. *TENTACLES?*"
"THAT'S WHAT I SAW. LOTS OF THINGS HAVE TENTACLES."
"..."
"ANYWAY..."

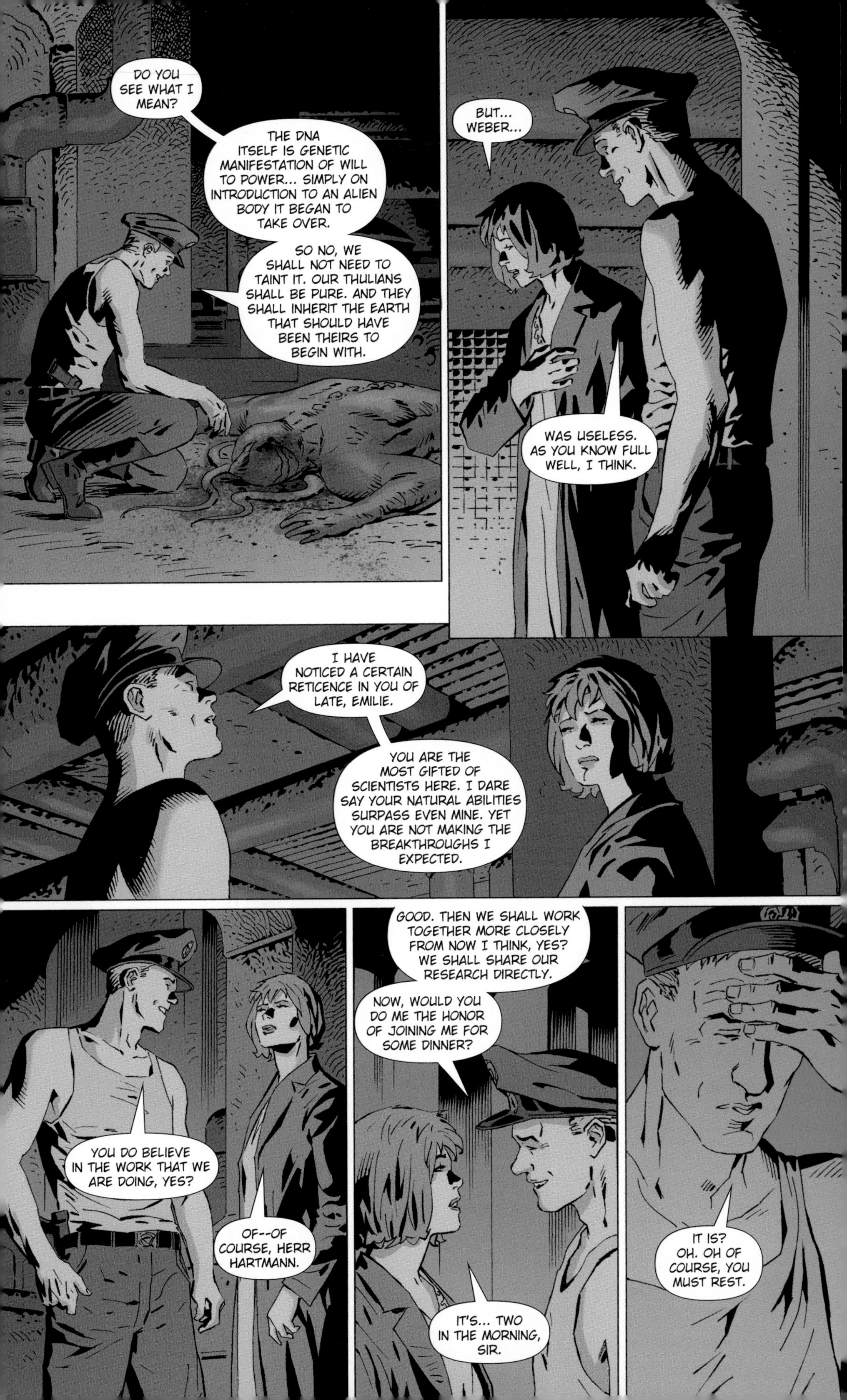
DO YOU SEE WHAT I MEAN?
THE DNA ITSELF IS GENETIC MANIFESTATION OF WILL TO POWER... SIMPLY ON INTRODUCTION TO AN ALIEN BODY IT BEGAN TO TAKE OVER.
SO NO, WE SHALL NOT NEED TO TAINT IT. OUR THULIANS SHALL BE PURE. AND THEY SHALL INHERIT THE EARTH THAT SHOULD HAVE BEEN THEIRS TO BEGIN WITH.
BUT... WEBER...
WAS USELESS. AS YOU KNOW FULL WELL, I THINK.
I HAVE NOTICED A CERTAIN RETICENCE IN YOU OF LATE, EMILIE.
YOU ARE THE MOST GIFTED OF SCIENTISTS HERE. I DARE SAY YOUR NATURAL ABILITIES SURPASS EVEN MINE. YET YOU ARE NOT MAKING THE BREAKTHROUGHS I EXPECTED.
YOU DO BELIEVE IN THE WORK THAT WE ARE DOING, YES?
OF--OF COURSE, HERR HARTMANN.
GOOD. THEN WE SHALL WORK TOGETHER MORE CLOSELY FROM NOW I THINK, YES? WE SHALL SHARE OUR RESEARCH DIRECTLY.
NOW, WOULD YOU DO ME THE HONOR OF JOINING ME FOR SOME DINNER?
IT'S... TWO IN THE MORNING, SIR.
IT IS? OH. OH OF COURSE, YOU MUST REST.

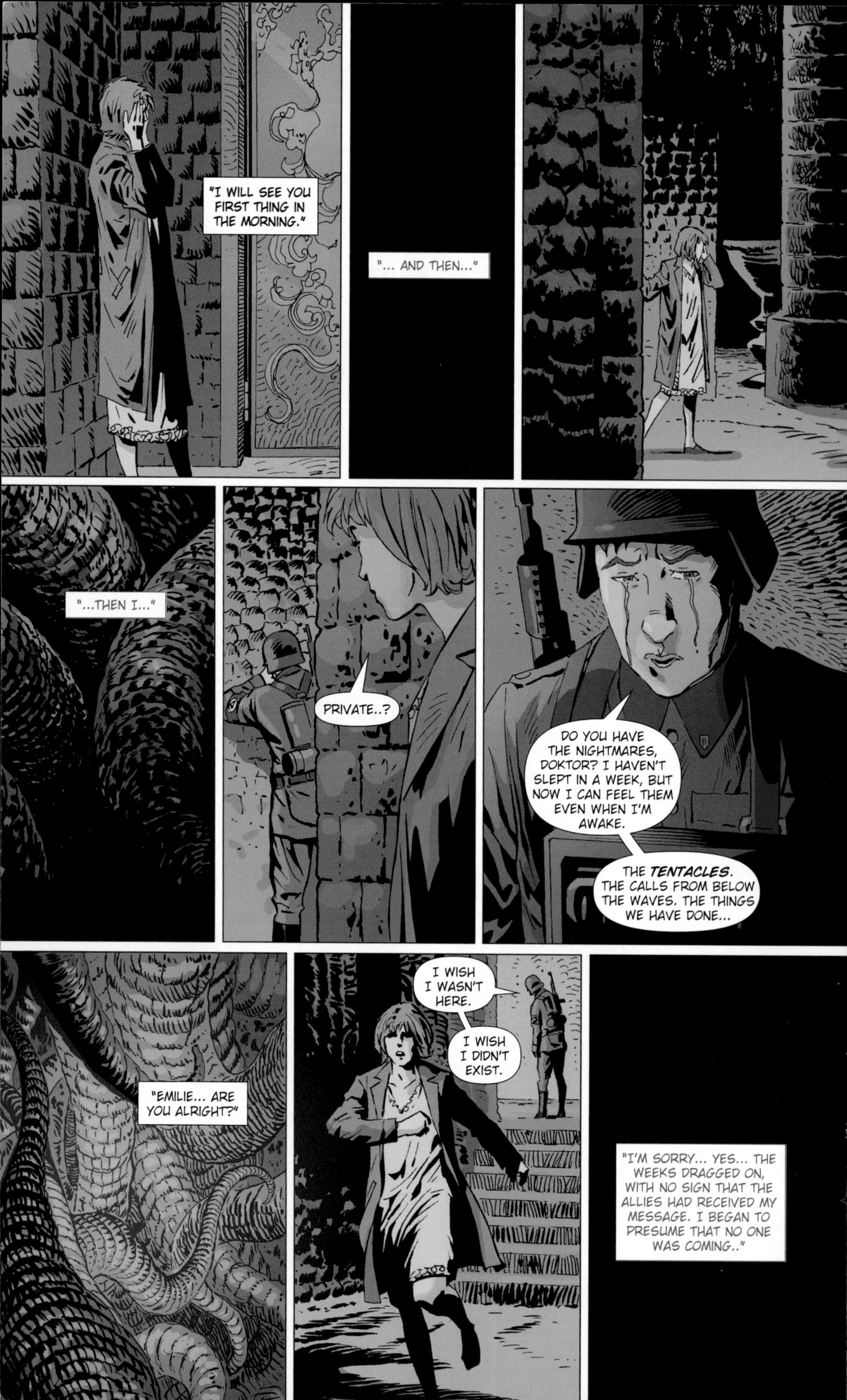
"I WILL SEE YOU FIRST THING IN THE MORNING."
"... AND THEN..."
"...THEN I..."
PRIVATE..?
DO YOU HAVE THE NIGHTMARES, DOKTOR? I HAVEN'T SLEPT IN A WEEK, BUT NOW I CAN FEEL THEM EVEN WHEN I'M AWAKE.
THE TENTACLES. THE CALLS FROM BELOW THE WAVES. THE THINGS WE HAVE DONE...
"EMILIE... ARE YOU ALRIGHT?"
I WISH I WASN'T HERE.
I WISH I DIDN'T EXIST.
"I'M SORRY... YES... THE WEEKS DRAGGED ON, WITH NO SIGN THAT THE ALLIES HAD RECEIVED MY MESSAGE. I BEGAN TO PRESUME THAT NO ONE WAS COMING.."

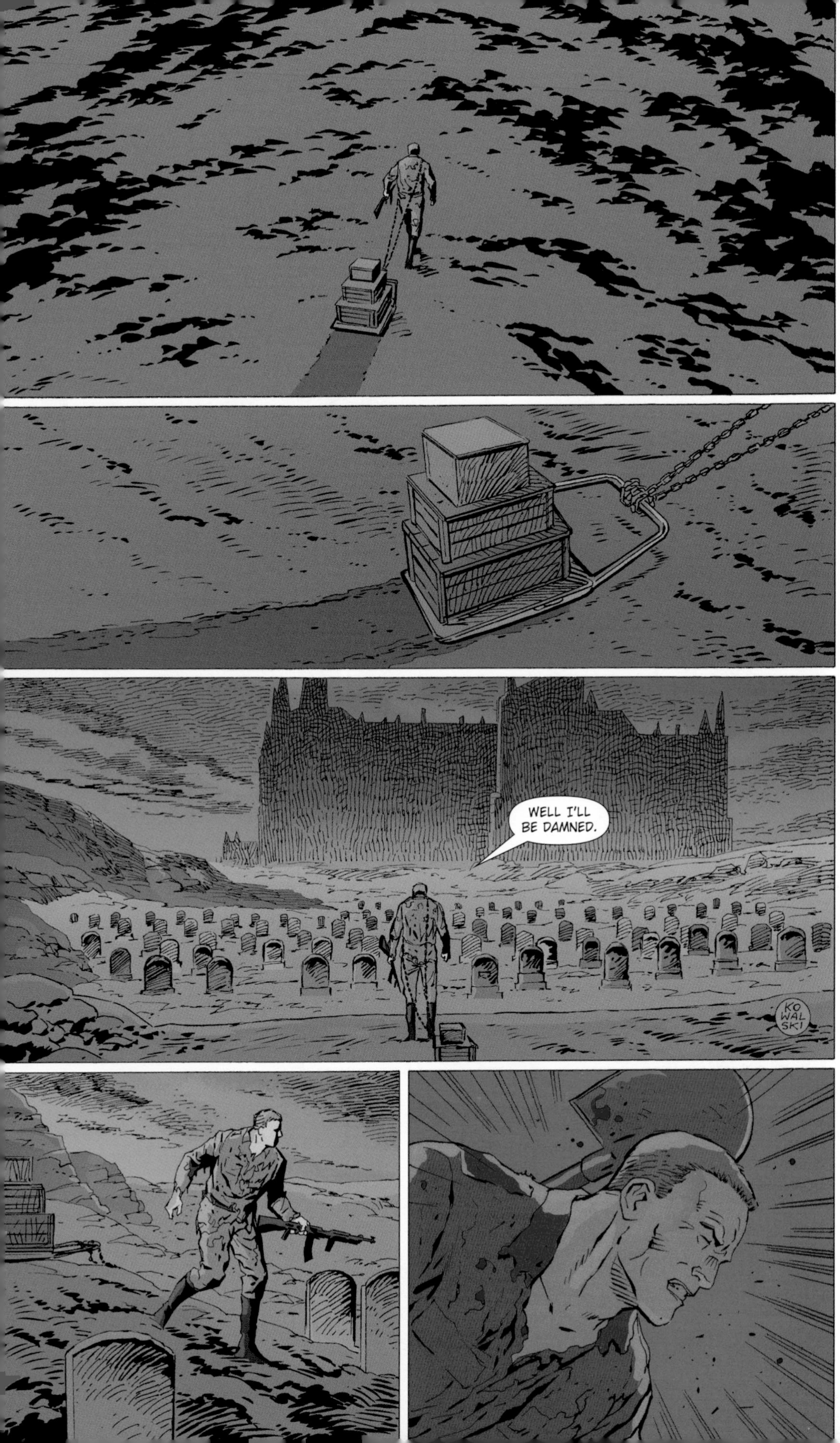
WELL I'LL BE DAMNED.
KOWALSKI

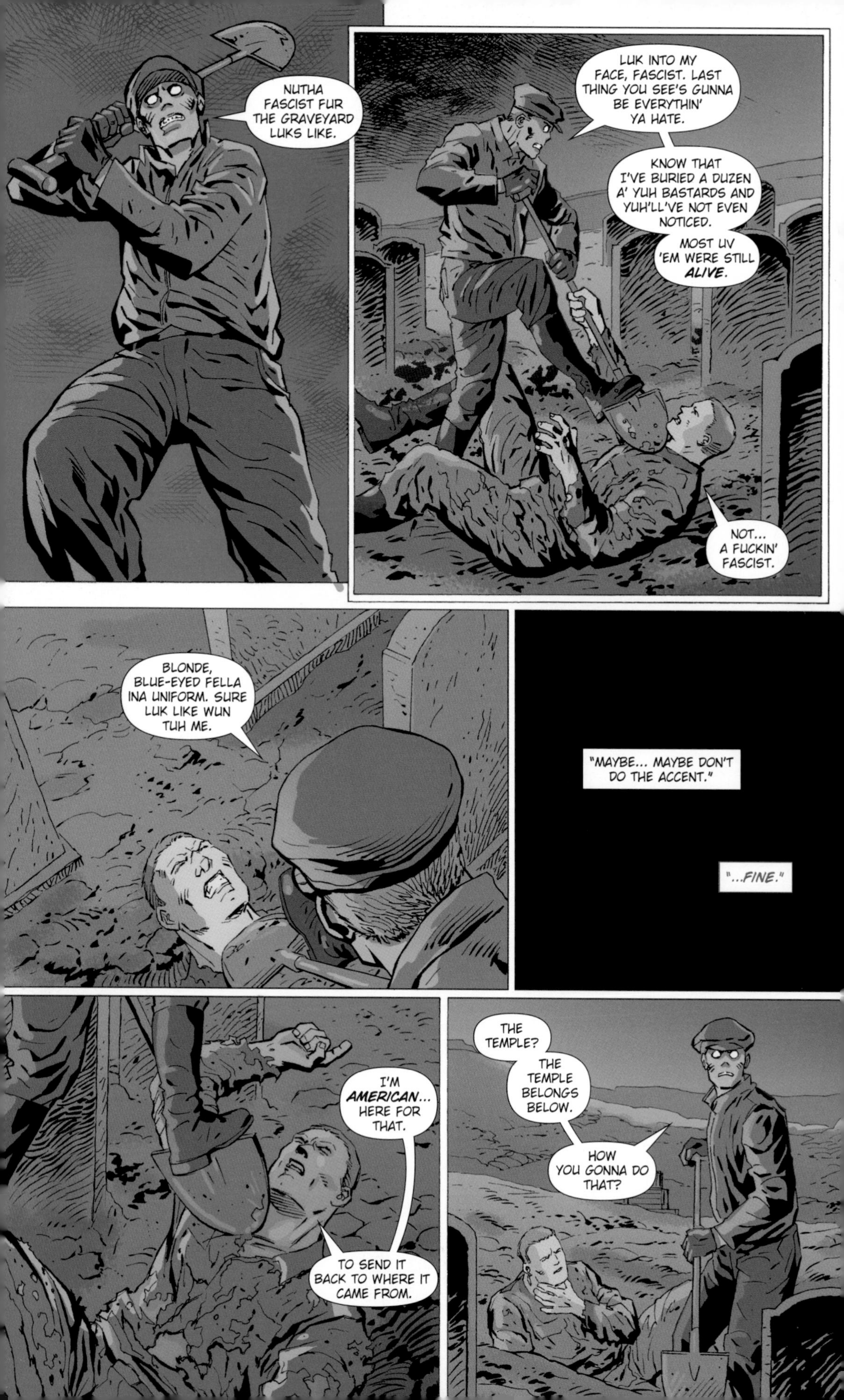
NUTHA FASCIST FUR THE GRAVEYARD LUKS LIKE.
LUK INTO MY FACE, FASCIST. LAST THING YOU SEE'S GUNNA BE EVERYTHIN' YA HATE.
KNOW THAT I'VE BURIED A DUZEN A' YUH BASTARDS AND YUH'LL'VE NOT EVEN NOTICED.
MOST UV 'EM WERE STILL ALIVE.
NOT... A FUCKIN' FASCIST.
BLONDE, BLUE-EYED FELLA INA UNIFORM. SURE LUK LIKE WUN TUH ME.
"MAYBE... MAYBE DON'T DO THE ACCENT."
"...FINE."
I'M AMERICAN... HERE FOR THAT.
TO SEND IT BACK TO WHERE IT CAME FROM.
THE TEMPLE?
THE TEMPLE BELONGS BELOW.
HOW YOU GONNA DO THAT?

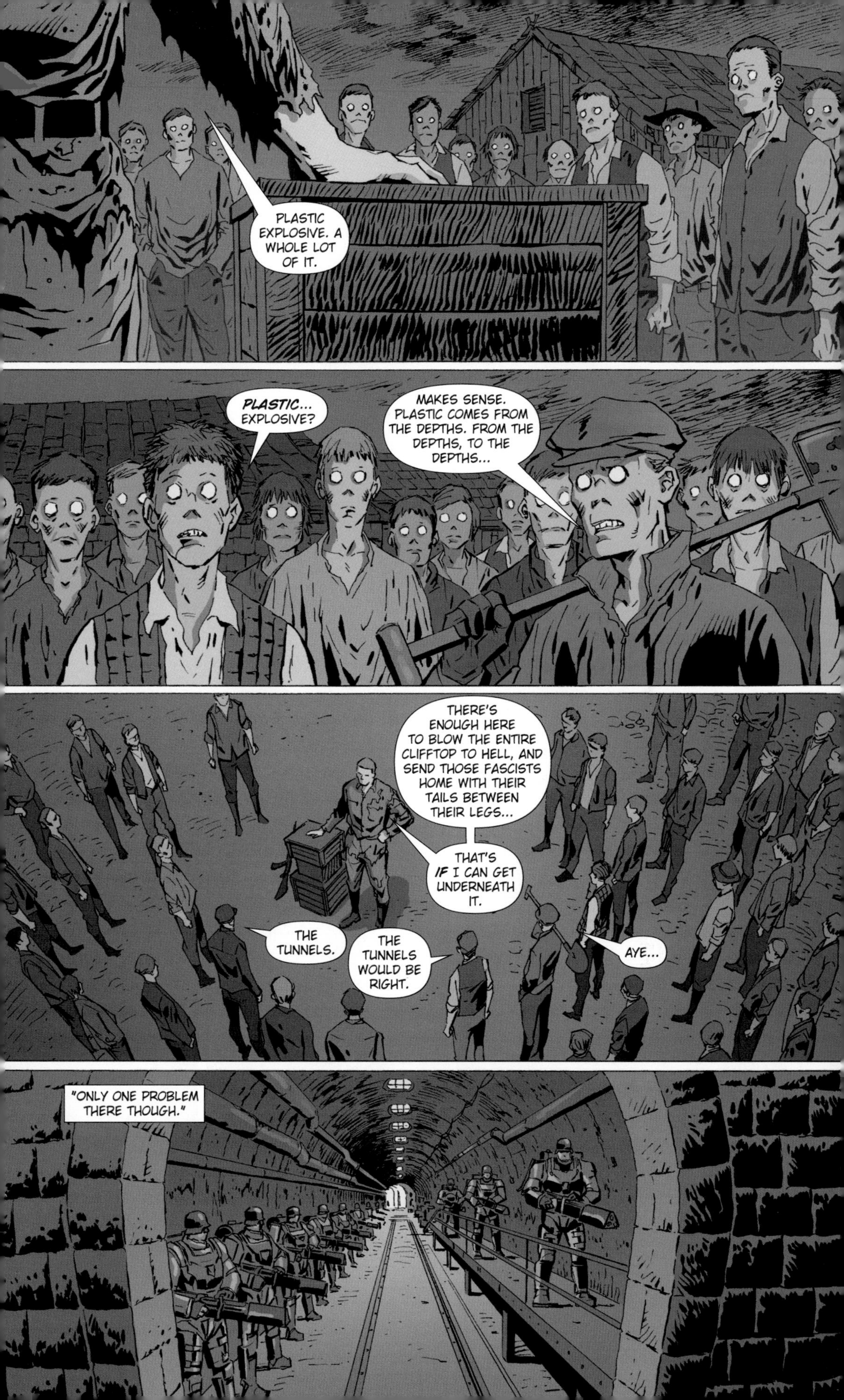
PLASTIC EXPLOSIVE. A WHOLE LOT OF IT.
PLASTIC... EXPLOSIVE?
MAKES SENSE. PLASTIC COMES FROM THE DEPTHS. FROM THE DEPTHS, TO THE DEPTHS...
THERE'S ENOUGH HERE TO BLOW THE ENTIRE CLIFFTOP TO HELL, AND SEND THOSE FASCISTS HOME WITH THEIR TAILS BETWEEN THEIR LEGS...
THAT'S IF I CAN GET UNDERNEATH IT.
THE TUNNELS.
THE TUNNELS WOULD BE RIGHT.
AYE...
"ONLY ONE PROBLEM THERE THOUGH."

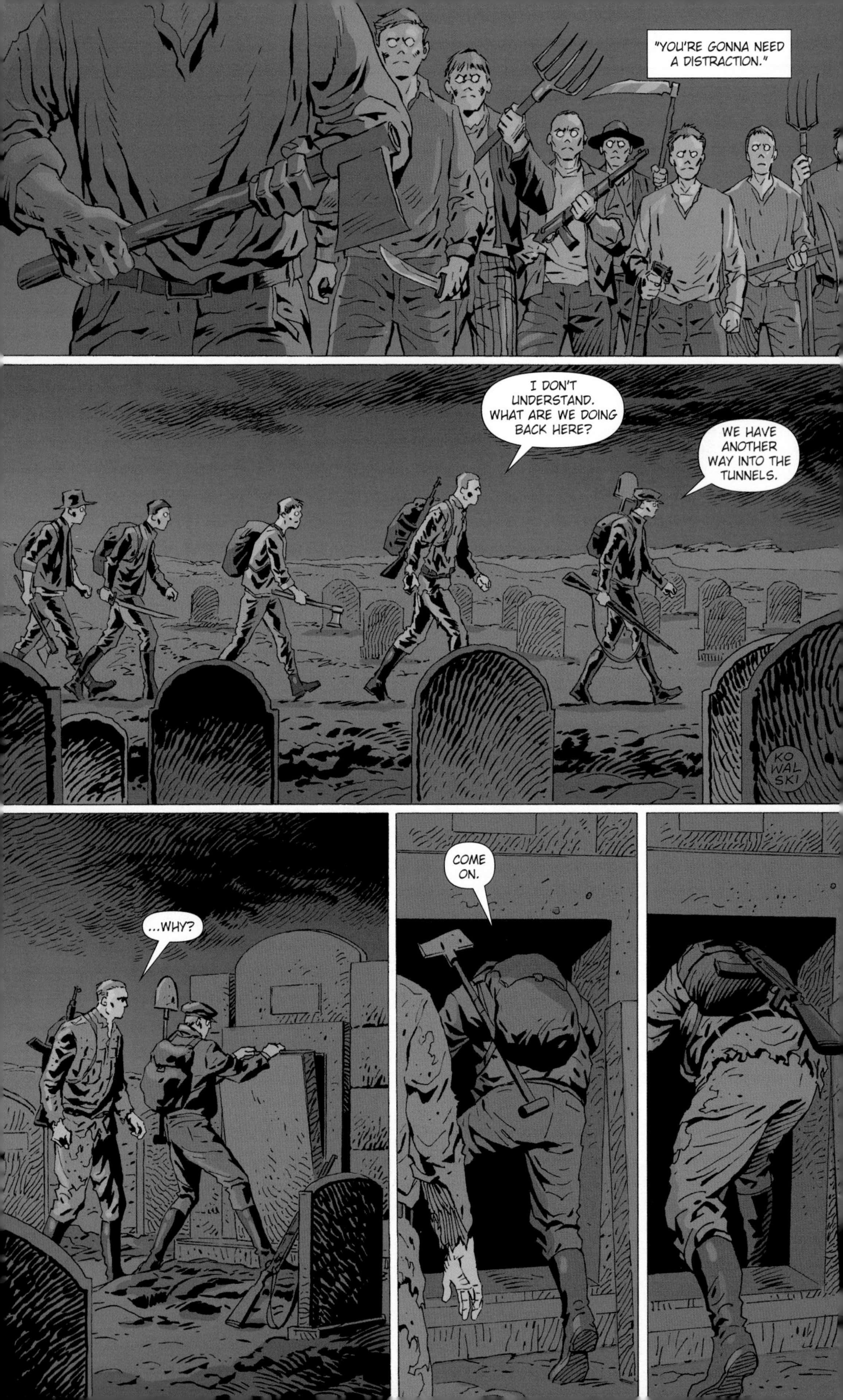
"YOU'RE GONNA NEED A DISTRACTION."
I DON'T UNDERSTAND. WHAT ARE WE DOING BACK HERE?
WE HAVE ANOTHER WAY INTO THE TUNNELS.
KOWALSKI
...WHY?
COME ON.

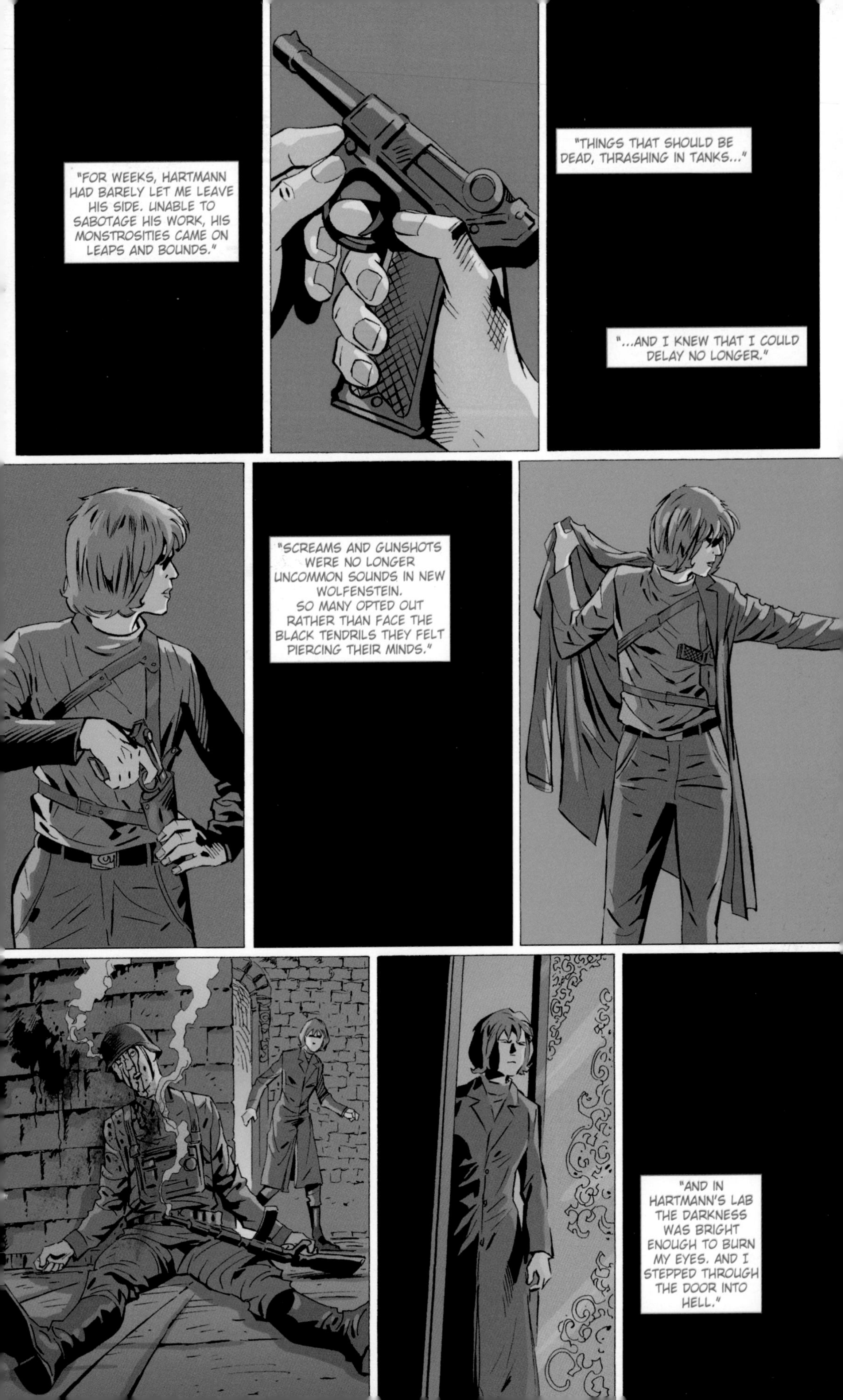
"FOR WEEKS, HARTMANN HAD BARELY LET ME LEAVE HIS SIDE. UNABLE TO SABOTAGE HIS WORK, HIS MONSTROSITIES CAME ON LEAPS AND BOUNDS."
"THINGS THAT SHOULD BE DEAD, THRASHING IN TANKS..."
"...AND I KNEW THAT I COULD DELAY NO LONGER."
"SCREAMS AND GUNSHOTS WERE NO LONGER UNCOMMON SOUNDS IN NEW WOLFENSTEIN. SO MANY OPTED OUT RATHER THAN FACE THE BLACK TENDRILS THEY FELT PIERCING THEIR MINDS."
"AND IN HARTMANN'S LAB THE DARKNESS WAS BRIGHT ENOUGH TO BURN MY EYES. AND I STEPPED THROUGH THE DOOR INTO HELL."

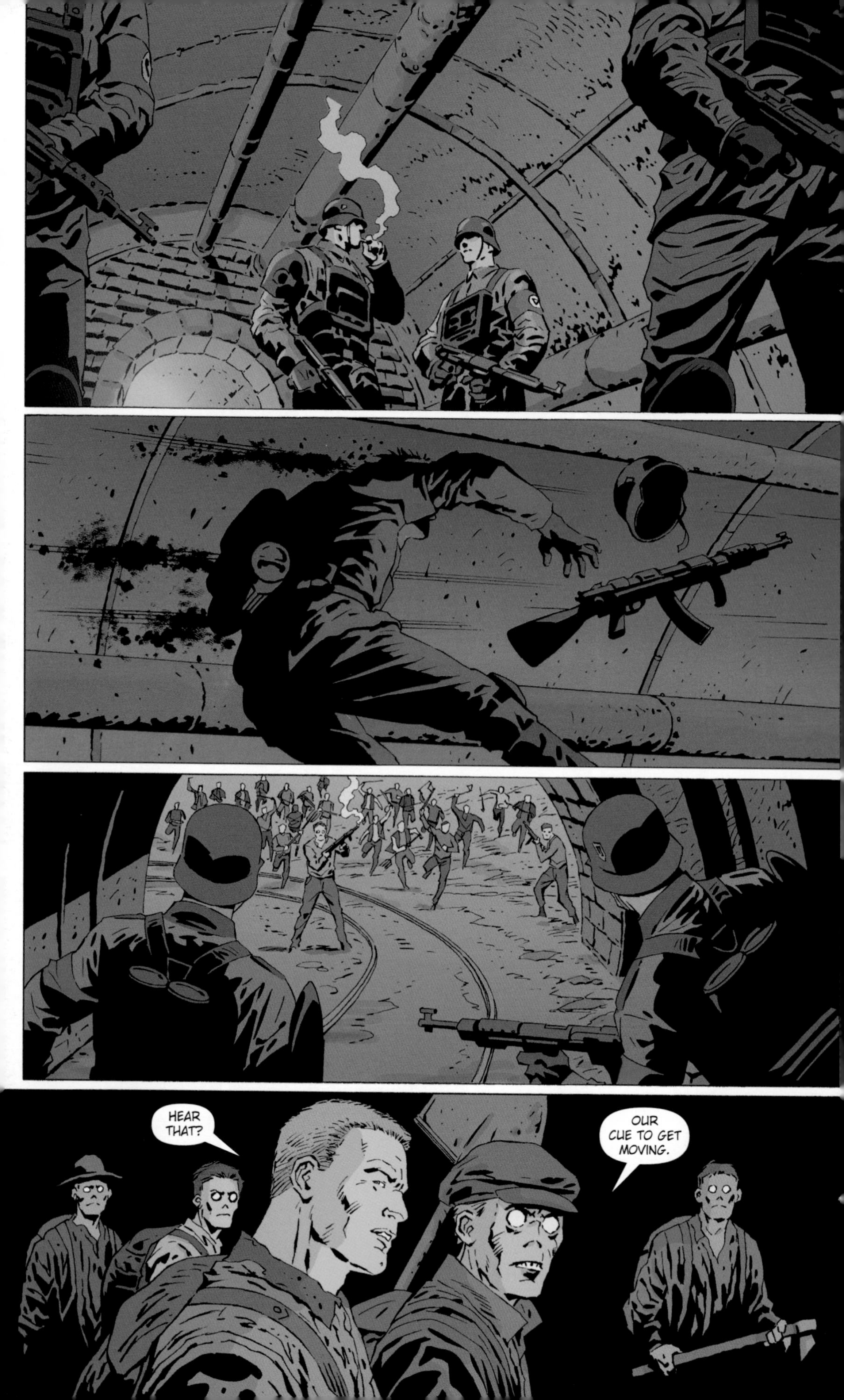
HEAR THAT?
OUR CUE TO GET MOVING.

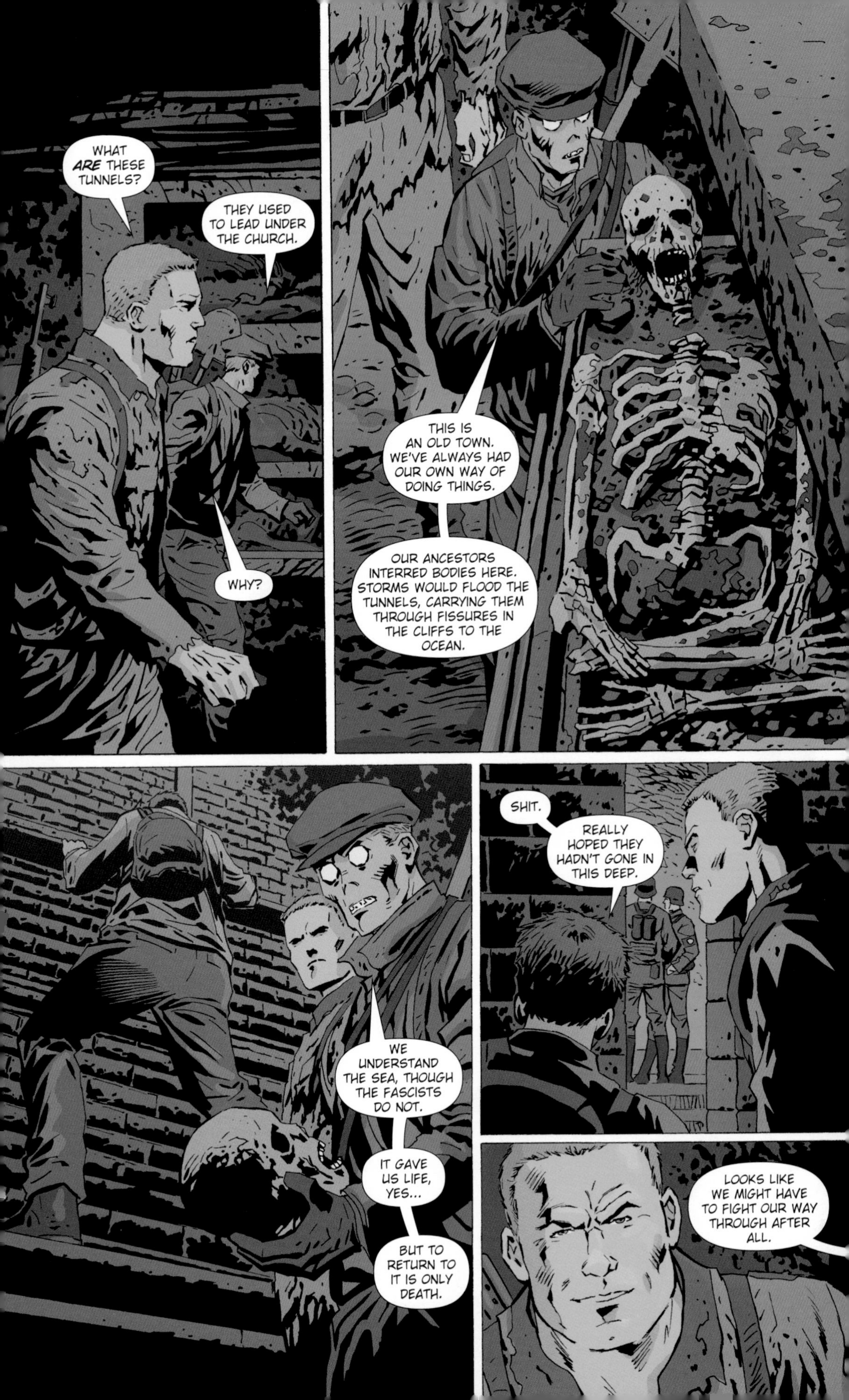
WHAT *ARE* THESE TUNNELS?
THEY USED TO LEAD UNDER THE CHURCH.
WHY?
THIS IS AN OLD TOWN. WE'VE ALWAYS HAD OUR OWN WAY OF DOING THINGS.
OUR ANCESTORS INTERRED BODIES HERE. STORMS WOULD FLOOD THE TUNNELS, CARRYING THEM THROUGH FISSURES IN THE CLIFFS TO THE OCEAN.
WE UNDERSTAND THE SEA, THOUGH THE FASCISTS DO NOT.
IT GAVE US LIFE, YES...
BUT TO RETURN TO IT IS ONLY DEATH.
SHIT.
REALLY HOPED THEY HADN'T GONE IN THIS DEEP.
LOOKS LIKE WE MIGHT HAVE TO FIGHT OUR WAY THROUGH AFTER ALL.

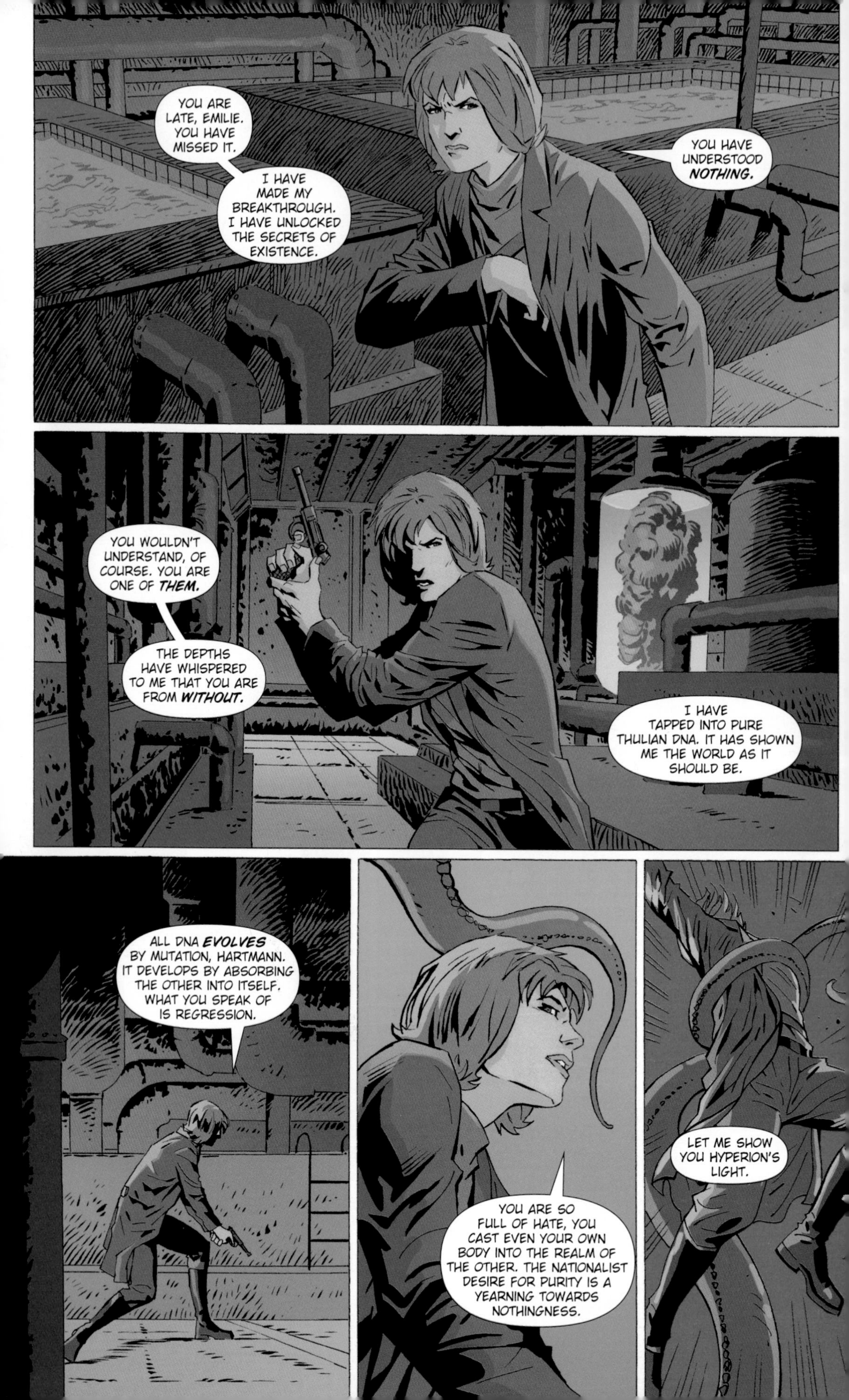
YOU ARE LATE, EMILIE. YOU HAVE MISSED IT.
I HAVE MADE MY BREAKTHROUGH. I HAVE UNLOCKED THE SECRETS OF EXISTENCE.
YOU HAVE UNDERSTOOD NOTHING.
YOU WOULDN'T UNDERSTAND, OF COURSE. YOU ARE ONE OF THEM.
THE DEPTHS HAVE WHISPERED TO ME THAT YOU ARE FROM WITHOUT.
I HAVE TAPPED INTO PURE THULIAN DNA. IT HAS SHOWN ME THE WORLD AS IT SHOULD BE.
ALL DNA EVOLVES BY MUTATION, HARTMANN. IT DEVELOPS BY ABSORBING THE OTHER INTO ITSELF. WHAT YOU SPEAK OF IS REGRESSION.
YOU ARE SO FULL OF HATE, YOU CAST EVEN YOUR OWN BODY INTO THE REALM OF THE OTHER. THE NATIONALIST DESIRE FOR PURITY IS A YEARNING TOWARDS NOTHINGNESS.
LET ME SHOW YOU HYPERION'S LIGHT.

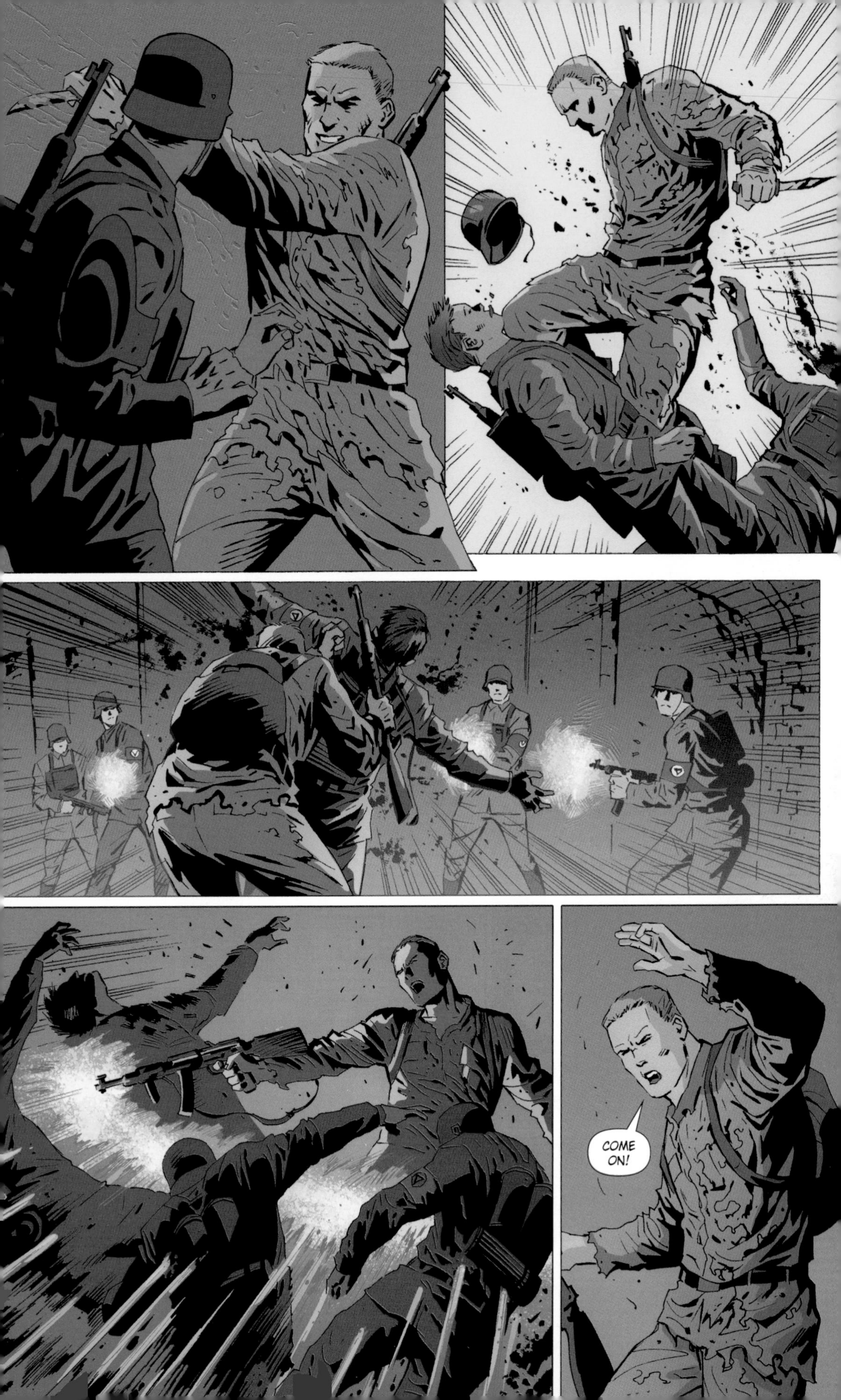
COME ON!

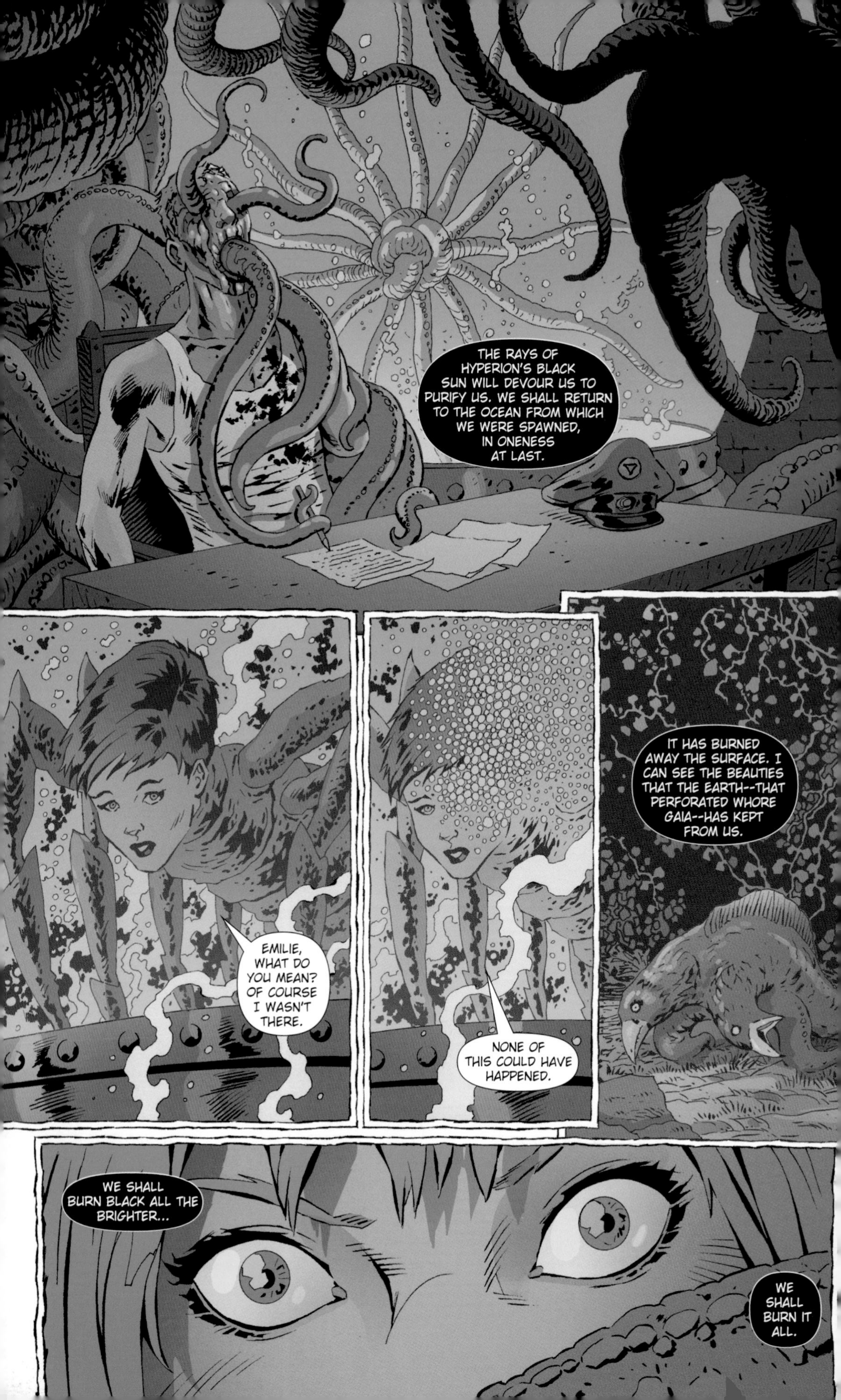

THE RAYS OF HYPERION'S BLACK SUN WILL DEVOUR US TO PURIFY US. WE SHALL RETURN TO THE OCEAN FROM WHICH WE WERE SPAWNED, IN ONENESS AT LAST.
EMILIE, WHAT DO YOU MEAN? OF COURSE I WASN'T THERE.
NONE OF THIS COULD HAVE HAPPENED.
IT HAS BURNED AWAY THE SURFACE. I CAN SEE THE BEAUTIES THAT THE EARTH--THAT PERFORATED WHORE GAIA--HAS KEPT FROM US.
WE SHALL BURN BLACK ALL THE BRIGHTER...
WE SHALL BURN IT ALL.

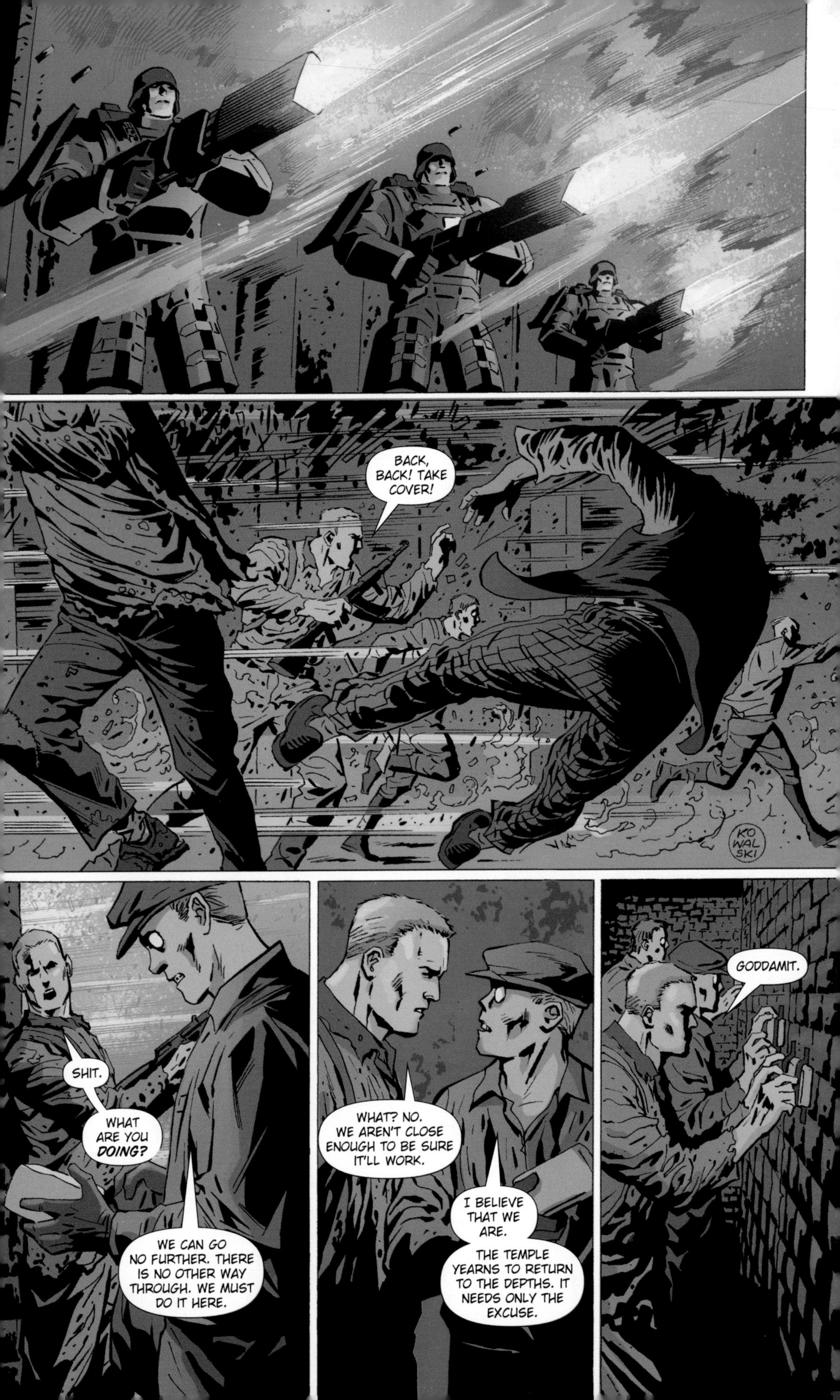

BACK, BACK! TAKE COVER!
KOWALSKI
SHIT.
WHAT ARE YOU *DOING?*
WE CAN GO NO FURTHER. THERE IS NO OTHER WAY THROUGH. WE MUST DO IT HERE.
WHAT? NO. WE AREN'T CLOSE ENOUGH TO BE SURE IT'LL WORK.
I BELIEVE THAT WE ARE.
THE TEMPLE YEARNS TO RETURN TO THE DEPTHS. IT NEEDS ONLY THE EXCUSE.
GODDAMIT.

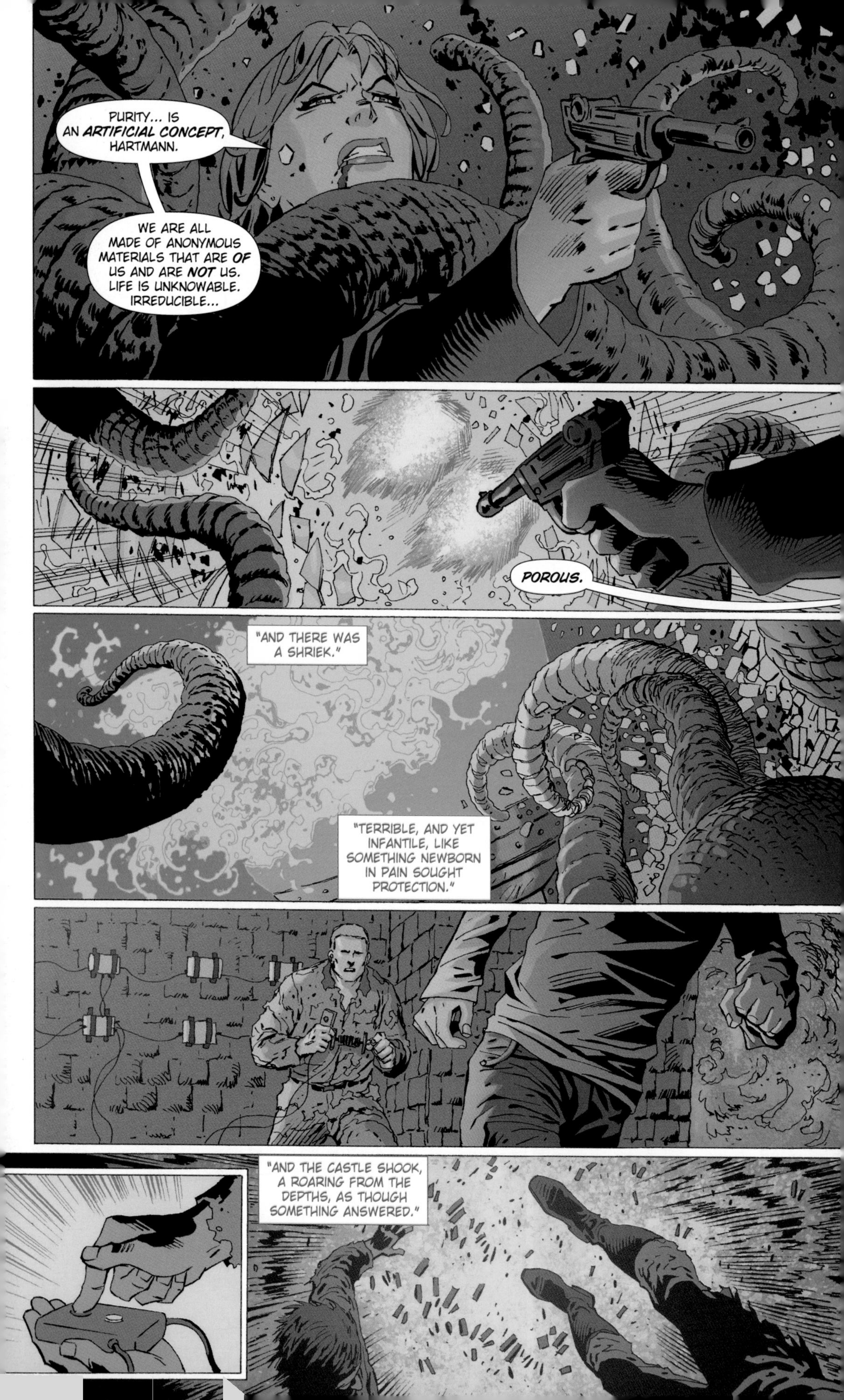
PURITY... IS AN ***ARTIFICIAL CONCEPT***, HARTMANN.
WE ARE ALL MADE OF ANONYMOUS MATERIALS THAT ARE ***OF*** US AND ARE ***NOT*** US. LIFE IS UNKNOWABLE. IRREDUCIBLE...
POROUS.
"AND THERE WAS A SHRIEK."
"TERRIBLE, AND YET INFANTILE, LIKE SOMETHING NEWBORN IN PAIN SOUGHT PROTECTION."
"AND THE CASTLE SHOOK, A ROARING FROM THE DEPTHS, AS THOUGH SOMETHING ANSWERED."

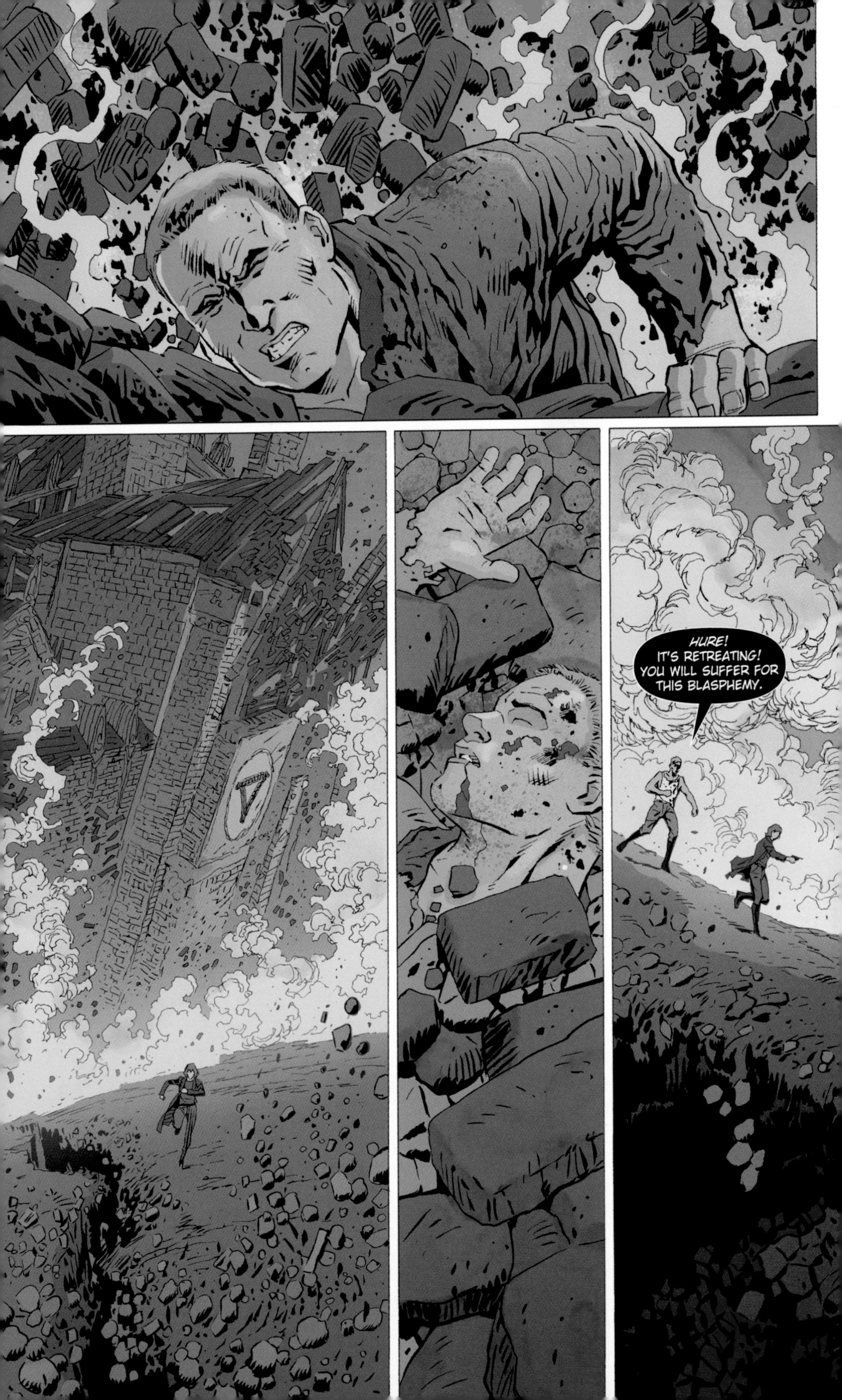
HURE! IT'S RETREATING! YOU WILL SUFFER FOR THIS BLASPHEMY.

EIGHT ROUNDS. ALL INTO THAT BEAUTIFUL BEING.

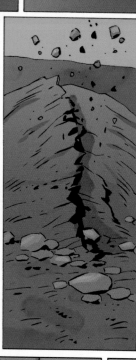

YOU'RE EMPTY.

THE SUN HAS ALWAYS DEMANDED SACRIFICE. HE HAS GIFTED ME *SIGHT*...

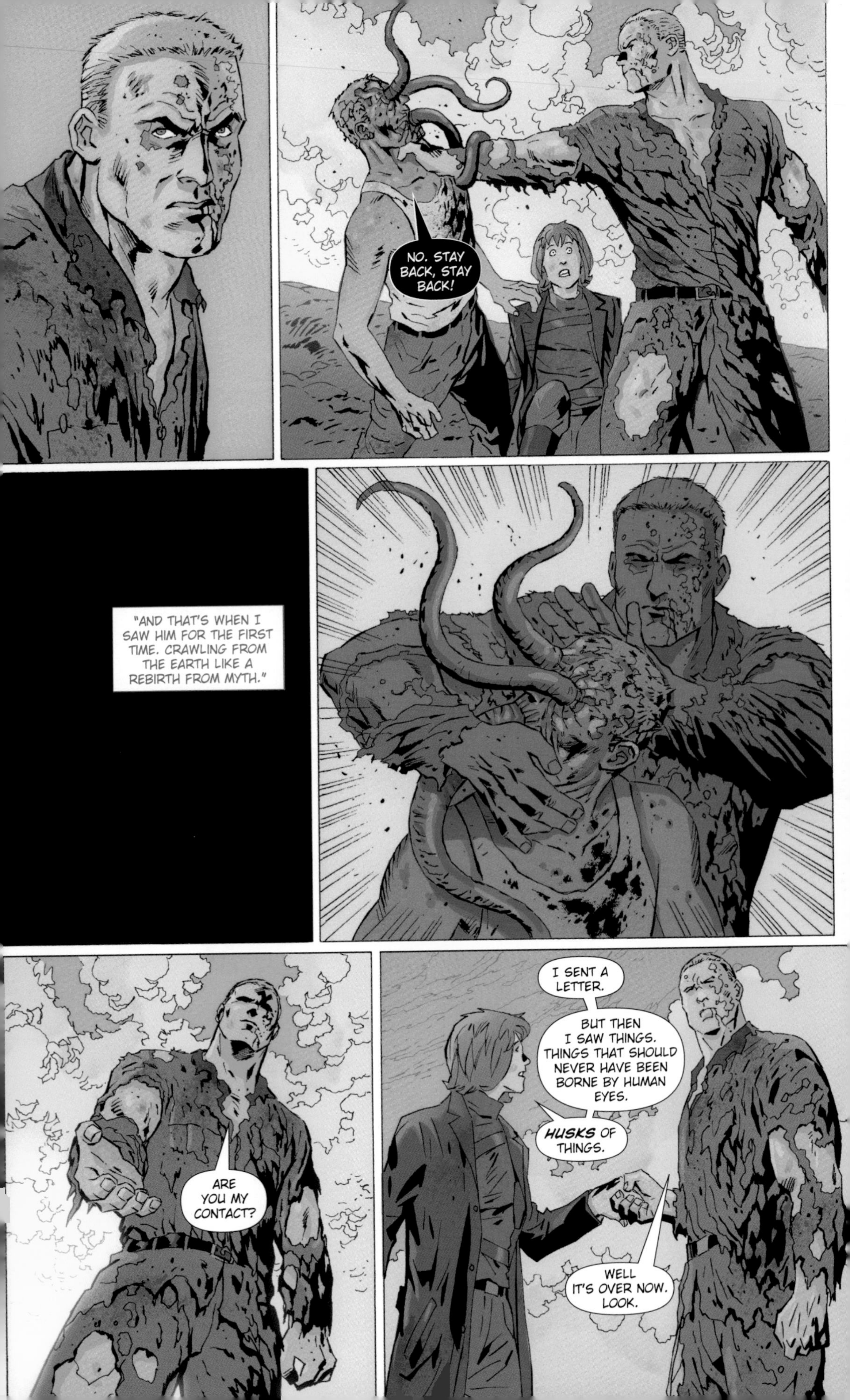
NO. STAY BACK, STAY BACK!
"AND THAT'S WHEN I SAW HIM FOR THE FIRST TIME. CRAWLING FROM THE EARTH LIKE A REBIRTH FROM MYTH."
ARE YOU MY CONTACT?
I SENT A LETTER.
BUT THEN I SAW THINGS. THINGS THAT SHOULD NEVER HAVE BEEN BORNE BY HUMAN EYES.
HUSKS OF THINGS.
WELL IT'S OVER NOW. LOOK.

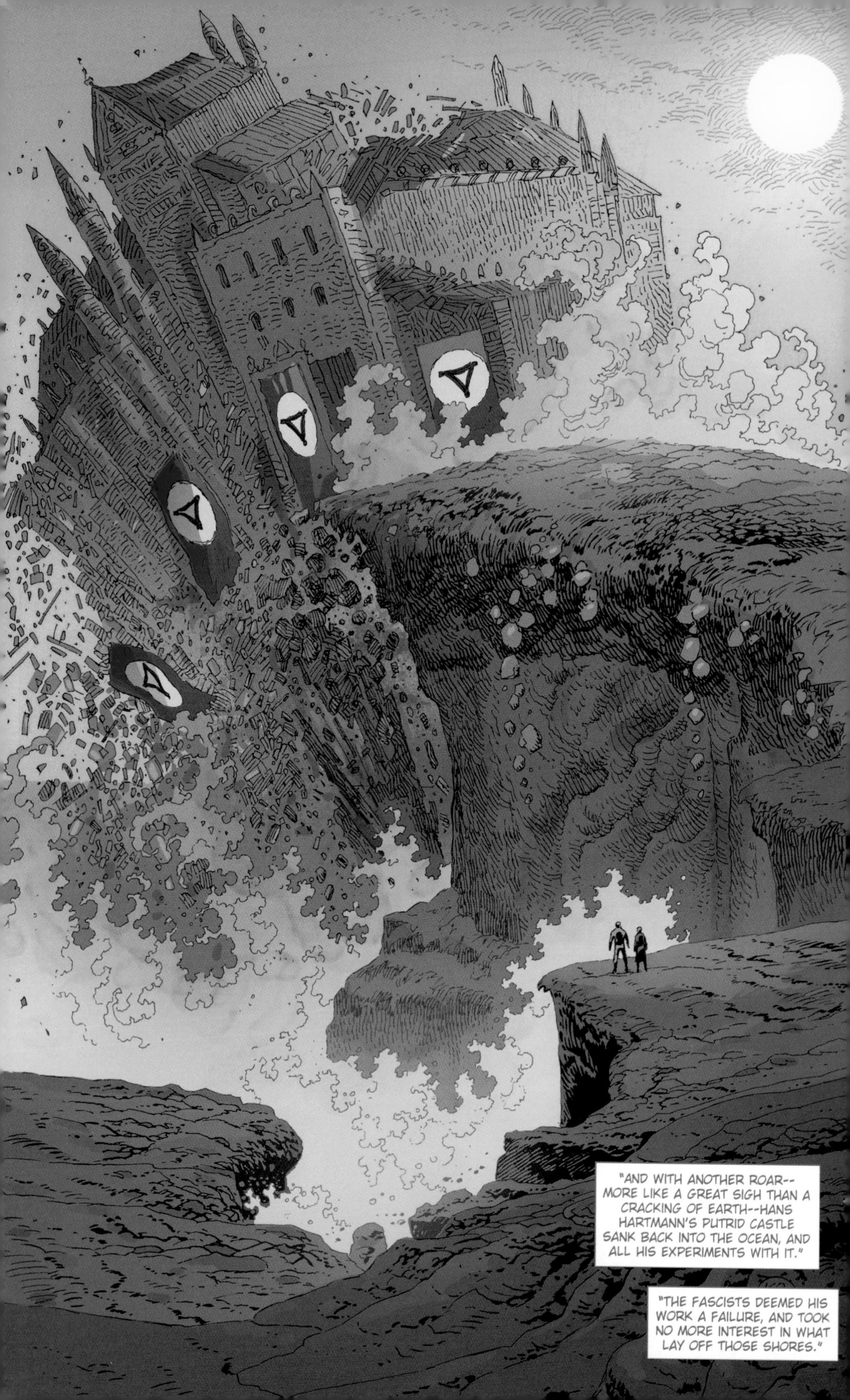
"AND WITH ANOTHER ROAR--MORE LIKE A GREAT SIGH THAN A CRACKING OF EARTH--HANS HARTMANN'S PUTRID CASTLE SANK BACK INTO THE OCEAN, AND ALL HIS EXPERIMENTS WITH IT."
"THE FASCISTS DEEMED HIS WORK A FAILURE, AND TOOK NO MORE INTEREST IN WHAT LAY OFF THOSE SHORES."

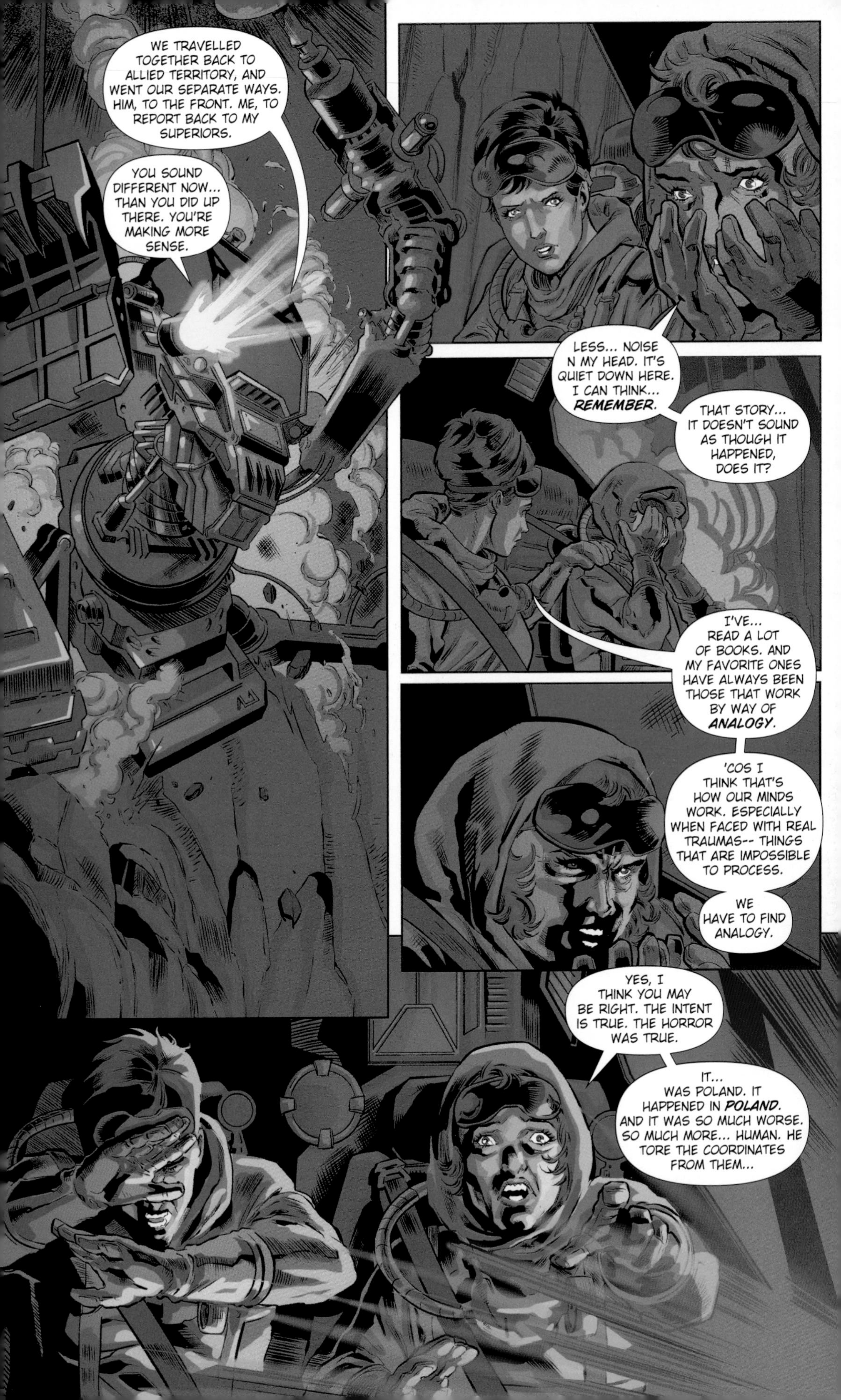

WE TRAVELLED TOGETHER BACK TO ALLIED TERRITORY, AND WENT OUR SEPARATE WAYS. HIM, TO THE FRONT. ME, TO REPORT BACK TO MY SUPERIORS.
YOU SOUND DIFFERENT NOW... THAN YOU DID UP THERE. YOU'RE MAKING MORE SENSE.
LESS... NOISE N MY HEAD. IT'S QUIET DOWN HERE. I CAN THINK... ***REMEMBER***.
THAT STORY... IT DOESN'T SOUND AS THOUGH IT HAPPENED, DOES IT?
I'VE... READ A LOT OF BOOKS. AND MY FAVORITE ONES HAVE ALWAYS BEEN THOSE THAT WORK BY WAY OF ***ANALOGY***.
'COS I THINK THAT'S HOW OUR MINDS WORK. ESPECIALLY WHEN FACED WITH REAL TRAUMAS-- THINGS THAT ARE IMPOSSIBLE TO PROCESS.
WE HAVE TO FIND ANALOGY.
YES, I THINK YOU MAY BE RIGHT. THE INTENT IS TRUE. THE HORROR WAS TRUE.
IT... WAS POLAND. IT HAPPENED IN ***POLAND***. AND IT WAS SO MUCH WORSE. SO MUCH MORE... HUMAN. HE TORE THE COORDINATES FROM THEM...

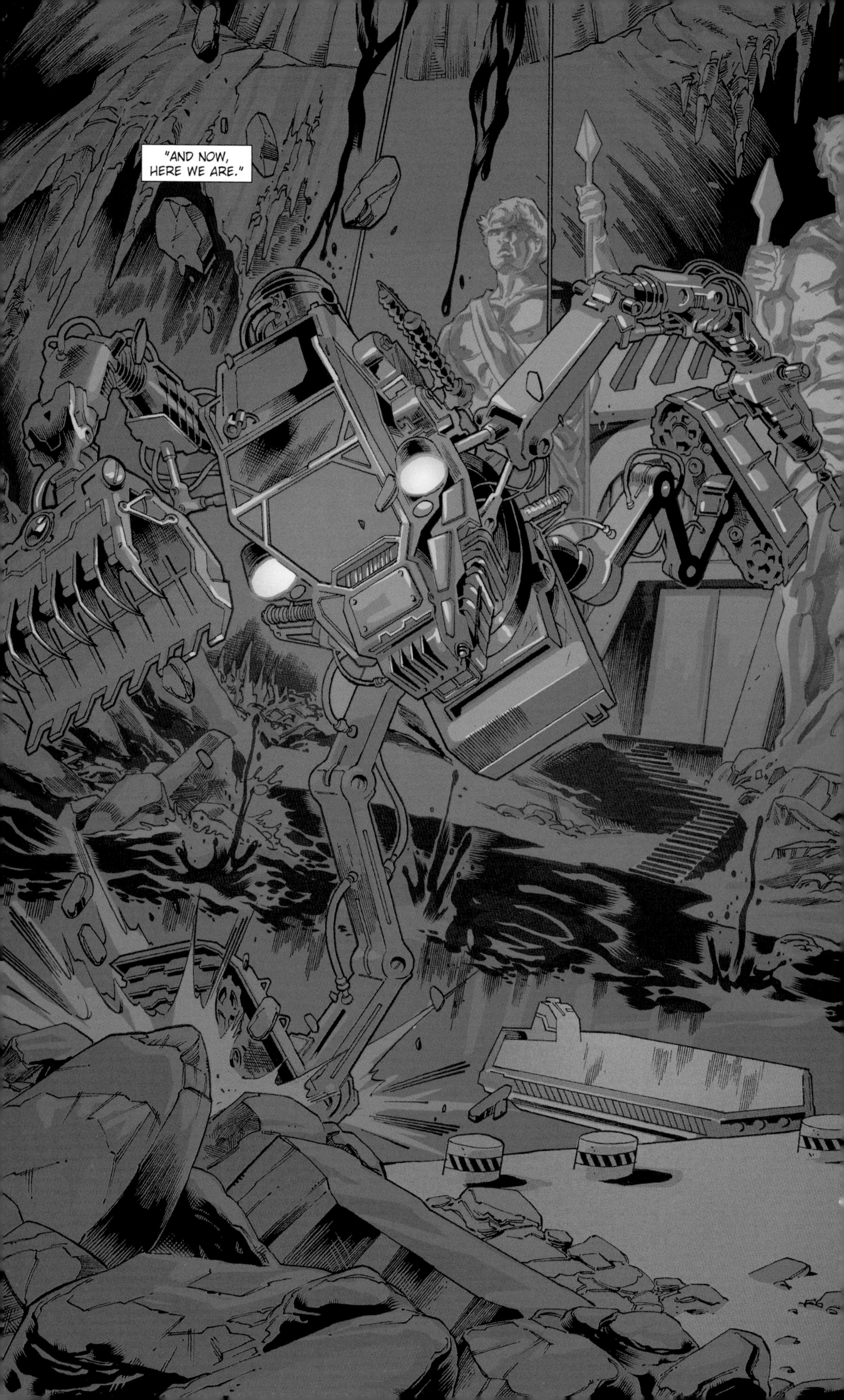
"AND NOW, HERE WE ARE."

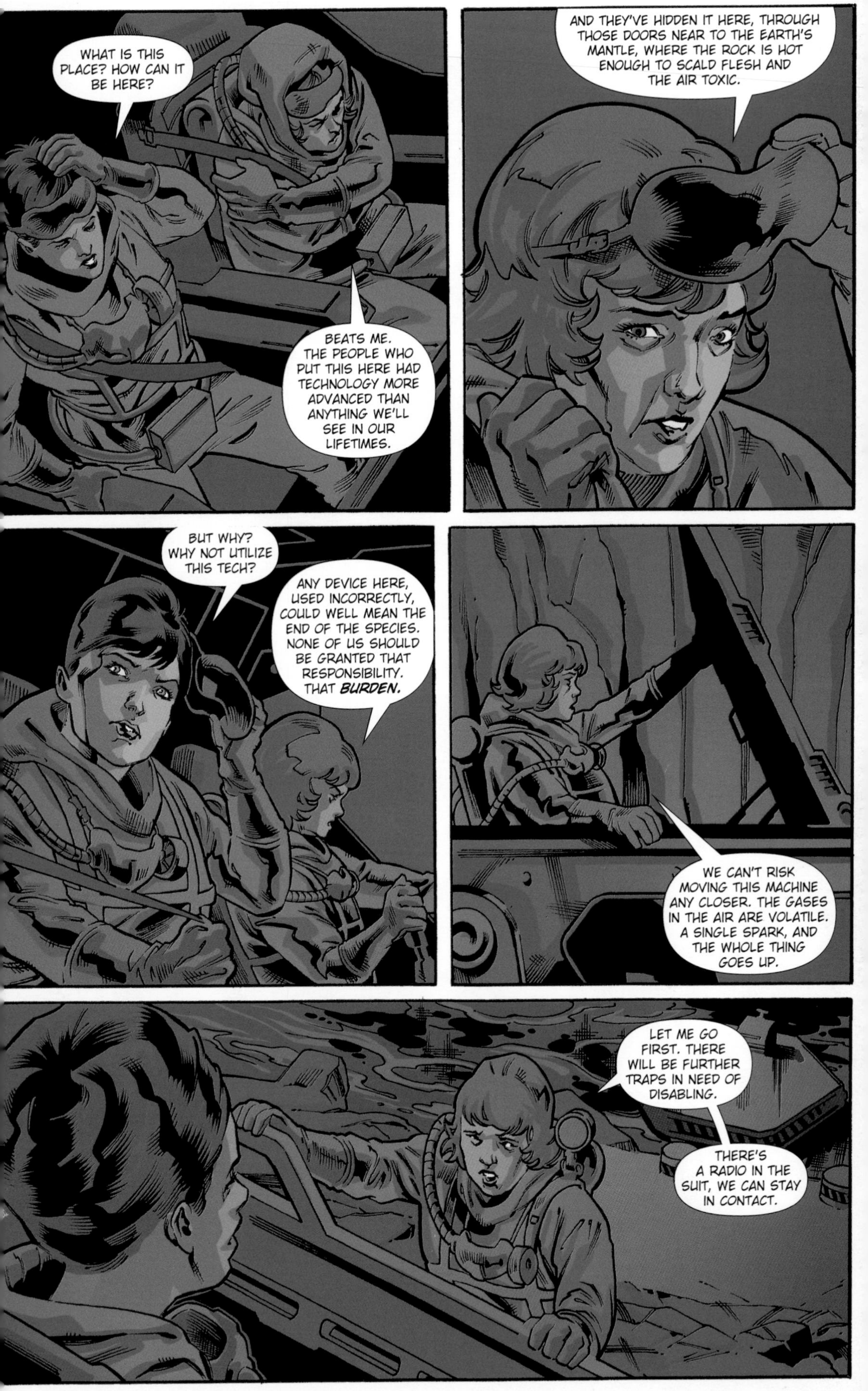
WHAT IS THIS PLACE? HOW CAN IT BE HERE?
BEATS ME. THE PEOPLE WHO PUT THIS HERE HAD TECHNOLOGY MORE ADVANCED THAN ANYTHING WE'LL SEE IN OUR LIFETIMES.
AND THEY'VE HIDDEN IT HERE, THROUGH THOSE DOORS NEAR TO THE EARTH'S MANTLE, WHERE THE ROCK IS HOT ENOUGH TO SCALD FLESH AND THE AIR TOXIC.
BUT WHY? WHY NOT UTILIZE THIS TECH?
ANY DEVICE HERE, USED INCORRECTLY, COULD WELL MEAN THE END OF THE SPECIES. NONE OF US SHOULD BE GRANTED THAT RESPONSIBILITY. THAT **BURDEN.**
WE CAN'T RISK MOVING THIS MACHINE ANY CLOSER. THE GASES IN THE AIR ARE VOLATILE. A SINGLE SPARK, AND THE WHOLE THING GOES UP.
LET ME GO FIRST. THERE WILL BE FURTHER TRAPS IN NEED OF DISABLING.
THERE'S A RADIO IN THE SUIT, WE CAN STAY IN CONTACT.

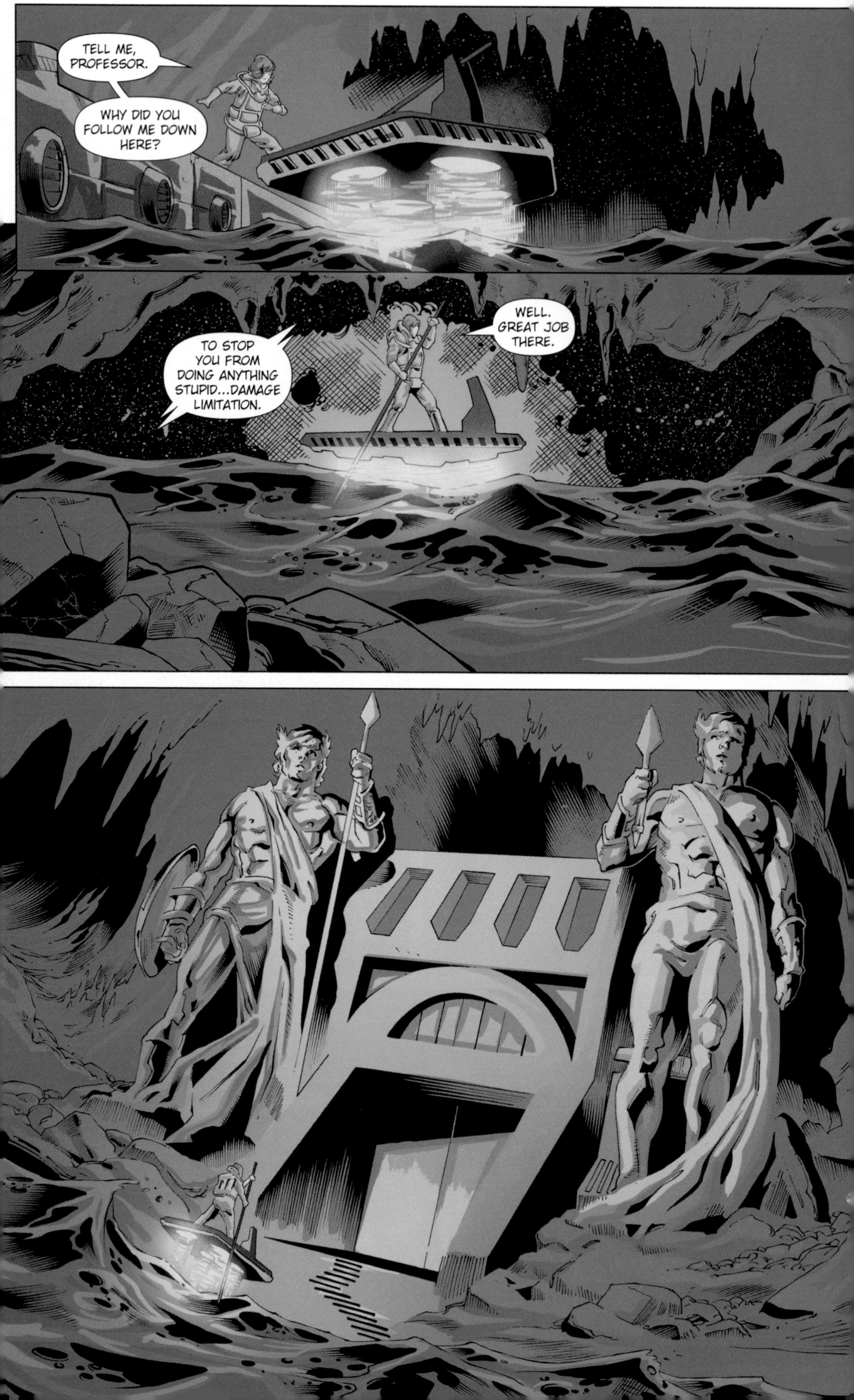
TELL ME, PROFESSOR.
WHY DID YOU FOLLOW ME DOWN HERE?
TO STOP YOU FROM DOING ANYTHING STUPID...DAMAGE LIMITATION.
WELL. GREAT JOB THERE.

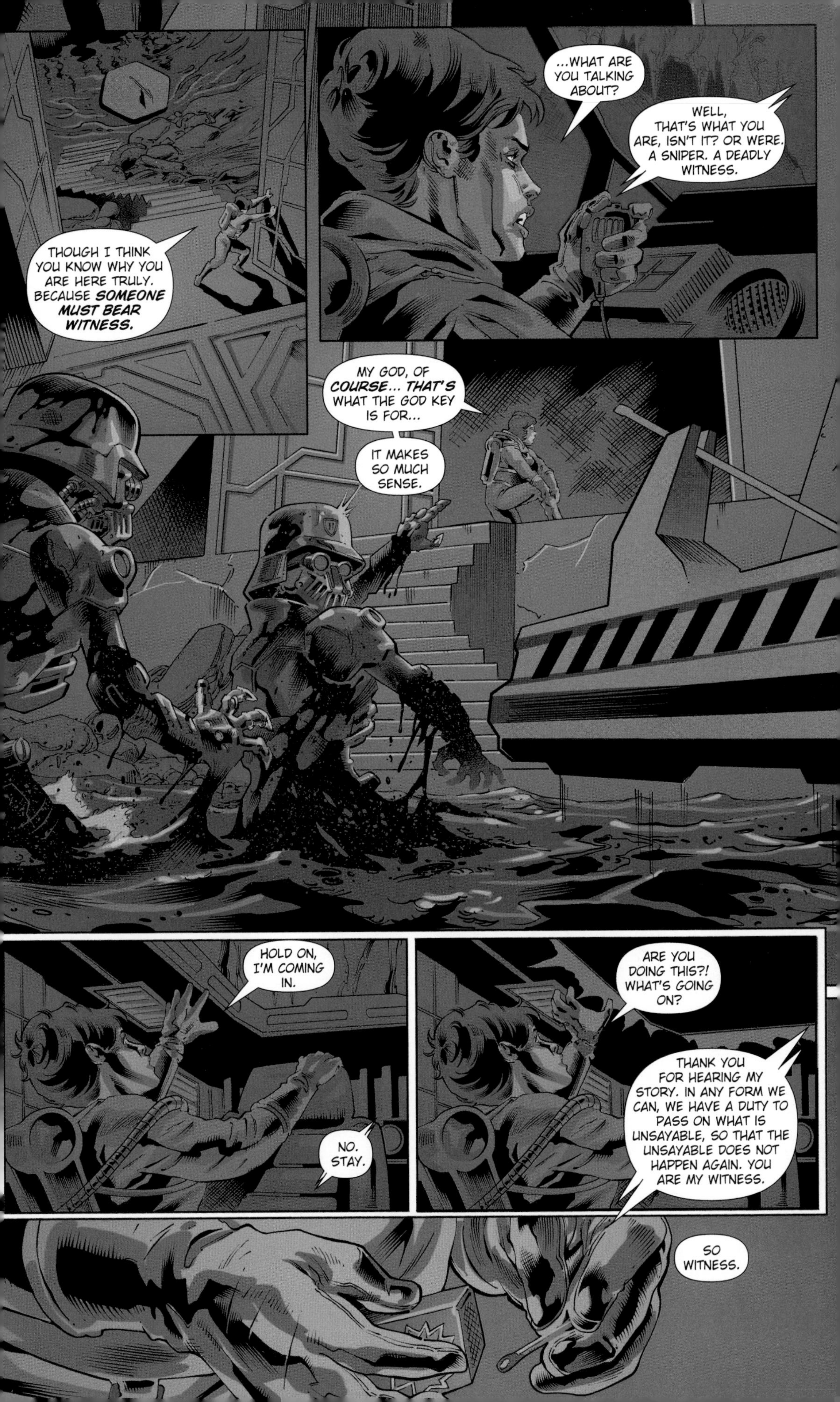
THOUGH I THINK YOU KNOW WHY YOU ARE HERE TRULY. BECAUSE **SOMEONE MUST BEAR WITNESS.**
...WHAT ARE YOU TALKING ABOUT?
WELL, THAT'S WHAT YOU ARE, ISN'T IT? OR WERE. A SNIPER. A DEADLY WITNESS.
MY GOD, OF ***COURSE*... *THAT'S*** WHAT THE GOD KEY IS FOR...
IT MAKES SO MUCH SENSE.
HOLD ON, I'M COMING IN.
NO. STAY.
ARE YOU DOING THIS?! WHAT'S GOING ON?
THANK YOU FOR HEARING MY STORY. IN ANY FORM WE CAN, WE HAVE A DUTY TO PASS ON WHAT IS UNSAYABLE, SO THAT THE UNSAYABLE DOES NOT HAPPEN AGAIN. YOU ARE MY WITNESS.
SO WITNESS.

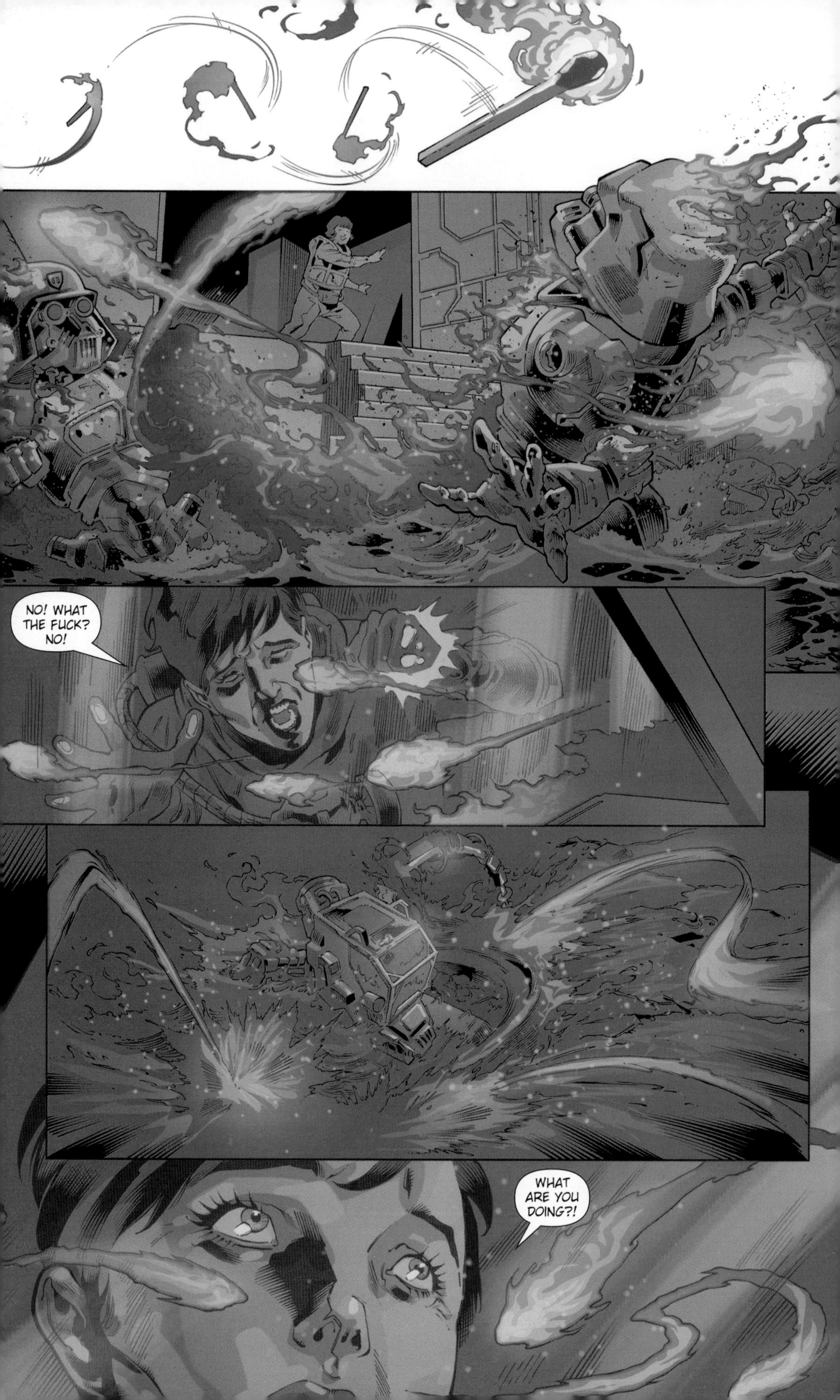
NO! WHAT THE FUCK? NO!
WHAT ARE YOU DOING?!

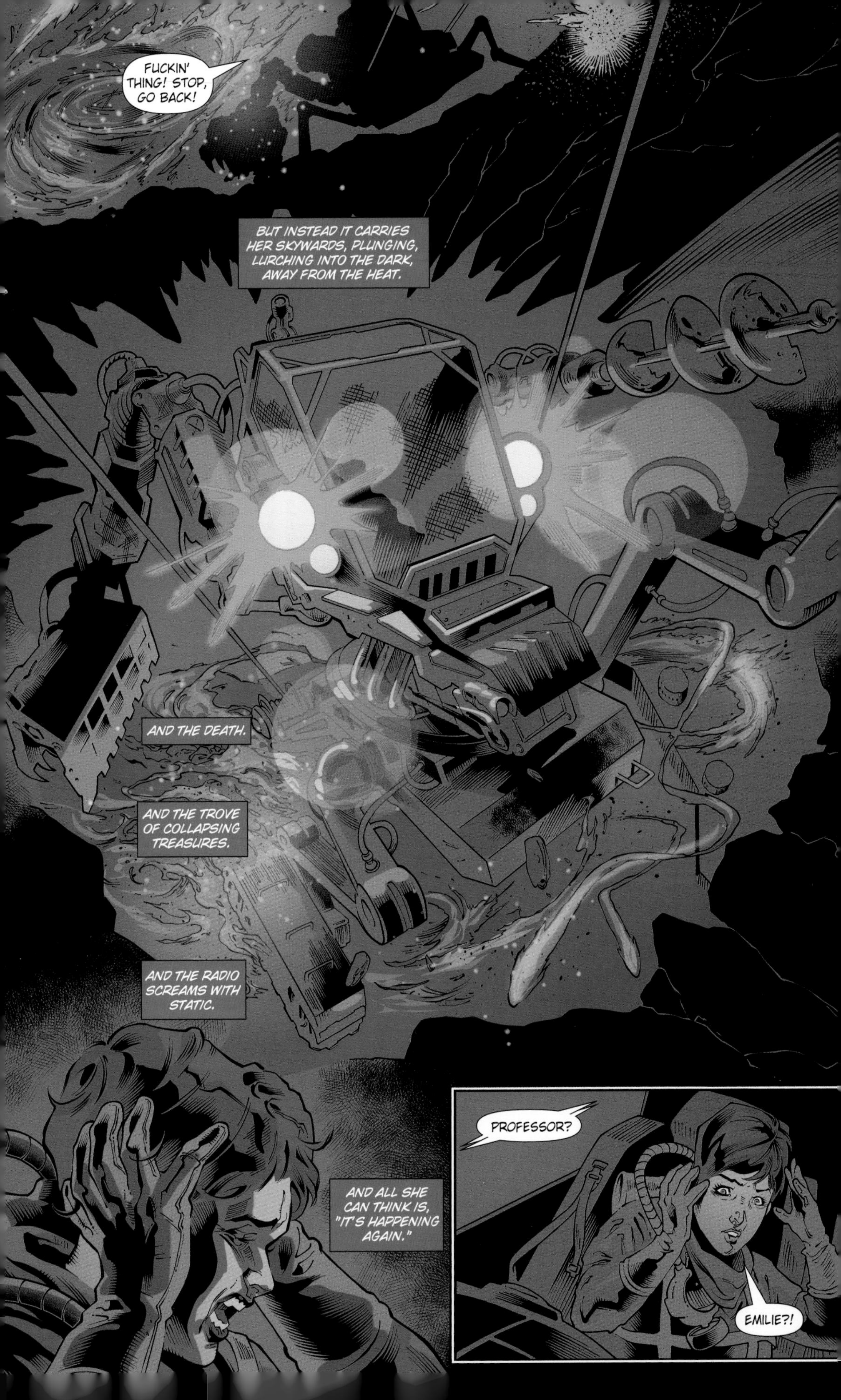
FUCKIN' THING! STOP, GO BACK!
BUT INSTEAD IT CARRIES HER SKYWARDS, PLUNGING, LURCHING INTO THE DARK, AWAY FROM THE HEAT.
AND THE DEATH.
AND THE TROVE OF COLLAPSING TREASURES.
AND THE RADIO SCREAMS WITH STATIC.
AND ALL SHE CAN THINK IS, "IT'S HAPPENING AGAIN."
PROFESSOR?
EMILIE?!

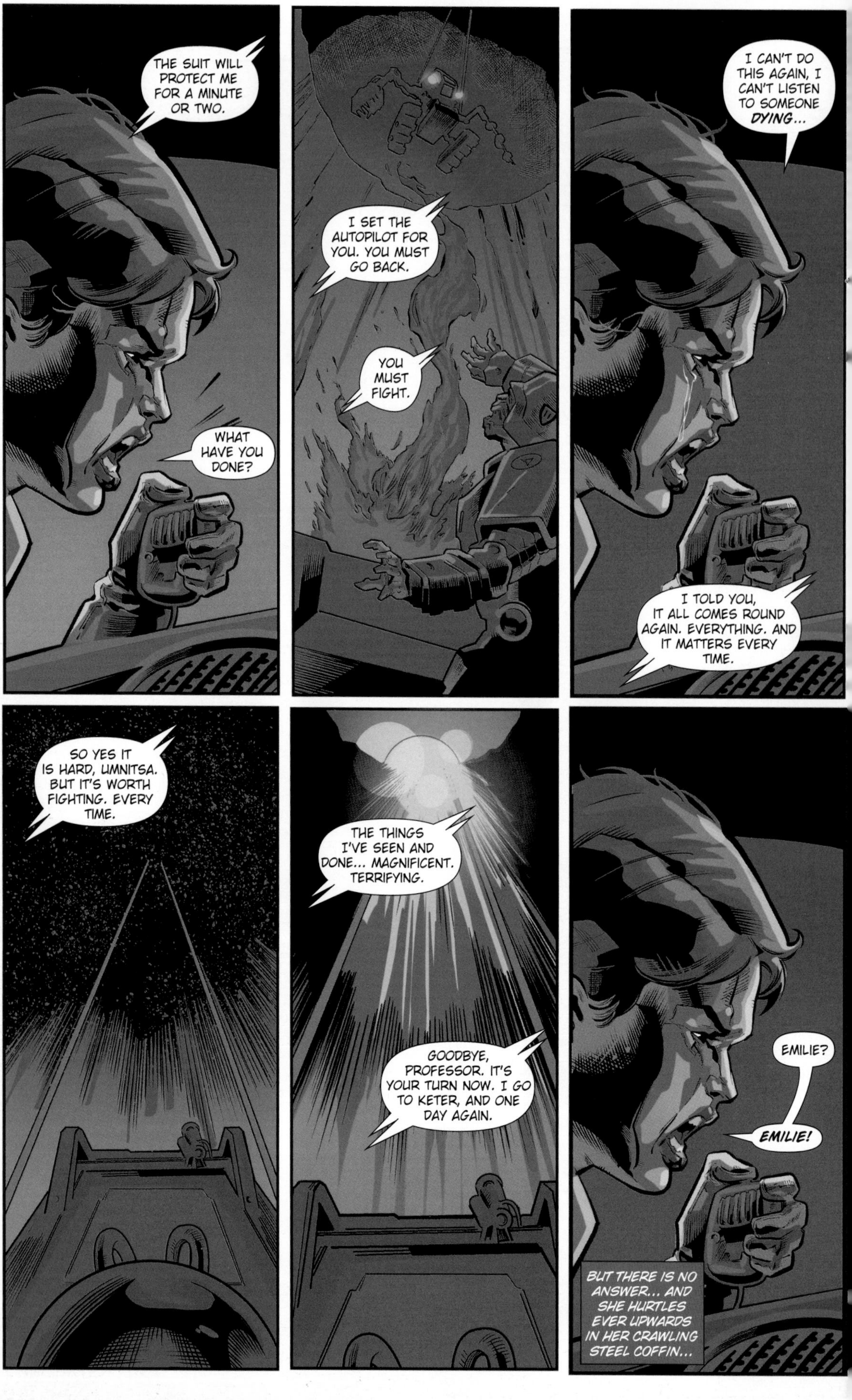
THE SUIT WILL PROTECT ME FOR A MINUTE OR TWO.
WHAT HAVE YOU DONE?
I SET THE AUTOPILOT FOR YOU. YOU MUST GO BACK.
YOU MUST FIGHT.
I CAN'T DO THIS AGAIN, I CAN'T LISTEN TO SOMEONE *DYING*...
I TOLD YOU, IT ALL COMES ROUND AGAIN. EVERYTHING. AND IT MATTERS EVERY TIME.
SO YES IT IS HARD, UMNITSA. BUT IT'S WORTH FIGHTING. EVERY TIME.
THE THINGS I'VE SEEN AND DONE... MAGNIFICENT. TERRIFYING.
GOODBYE, PROFESSOR. IT'S YOUR TURN NOW. I GO TO KETER, AND ONE DAY AGAIN.
EMILIE?
EMILIE!
BUT THERE IS NO ANSWER... AND SHE HURTLES EVER UPWARDS IN HER CRAWLING STEEL COFFIN...

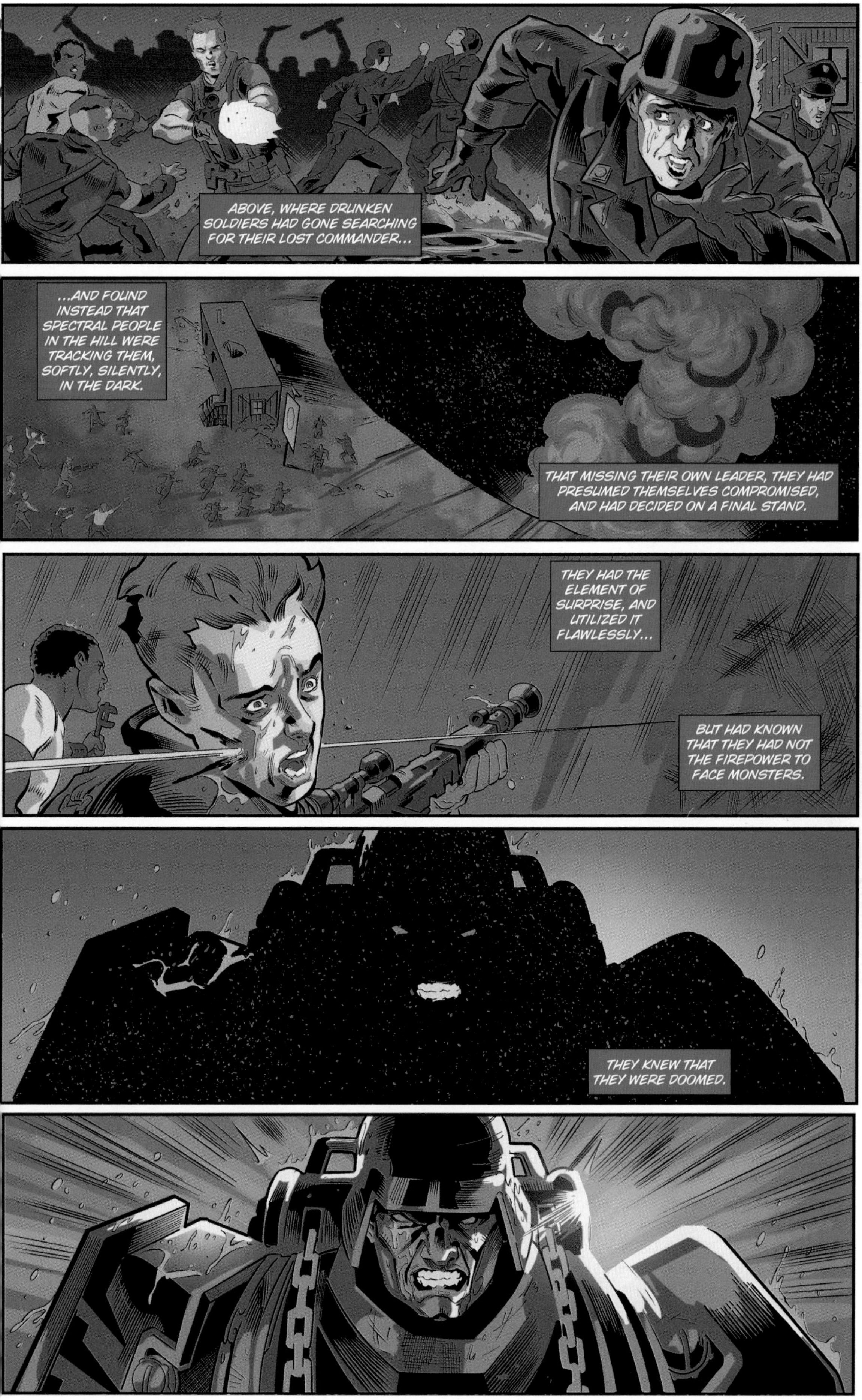
ABOVE, WHERE DRUNKEN SOLDIERS HAD GONE SEARCHING FOR THEIR LOST COMMANDER...
...AND FOUND INSTEAD THAT SPECTRAL PEOPLE IN THE HILL WERE TRACKING THEM, SOFTLY, SILENTLY, IN THE DARK.
THAT MISSING THEIR OWN LEADER, THEY HAD PRESUMED THEMSELVES COMPROMISED, AND HAD DECIDED ON A FINAL STAND.
THEY HAD THE ELEMENT OF SURPRISE, AND UTILIZED IT FLAWLESSLY...
BUT HAD KNOWN THAT THEY HAD NOT THE FIREPOWER TO FACE MONSTERS.
THEY KNEW THAT THEY WERE DOOMED.

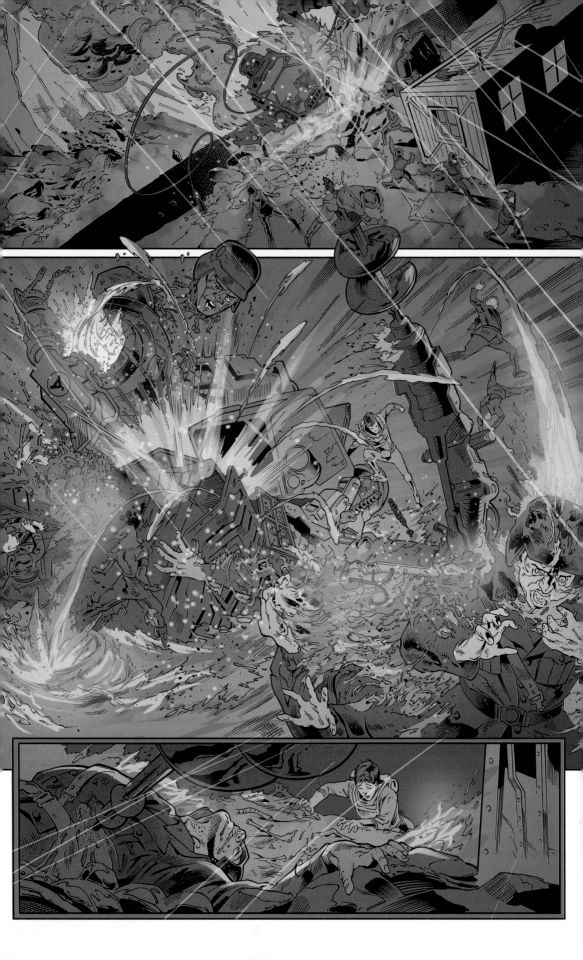

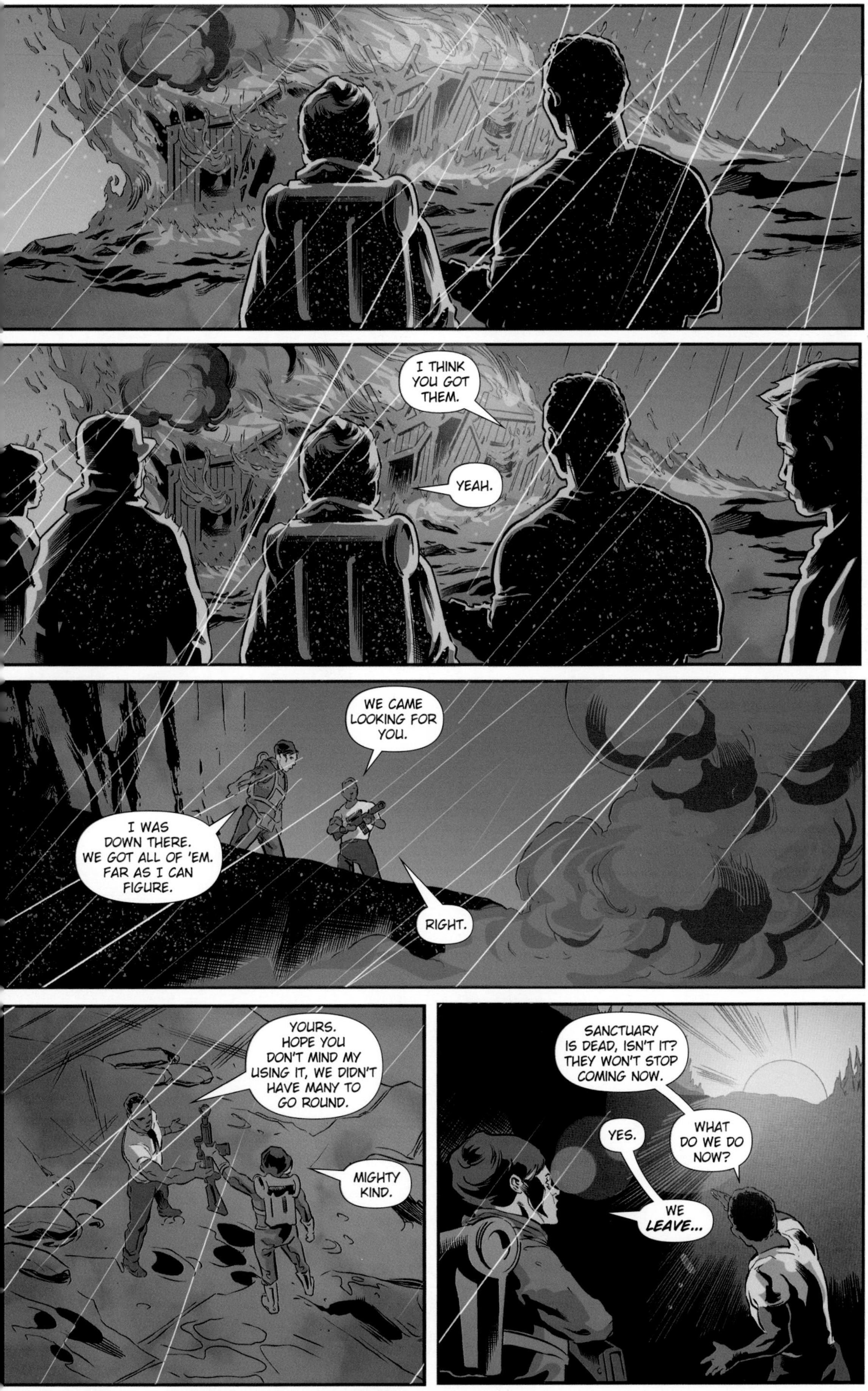
I THINK YOU GOT THEM.
YEAH.
WE CAME LOOKING FOR YOU.
I WAS DOWN THERE. WE GOT ALL OF 'EM. FAR AS I CAN FIGURE.
RIGHT.
YOURS. HOPE YOU DON'T MIND MY USING IT, WE DIDN'T HAVE MANY TO GO ROUND.
MIGHTY KIND.
SANCTUARY IS DEAD, ISN'T IT? THEY WON'T STOP COMING NOW.
YES.
WHAT DO WE DO NOW?
WE *LEAVE...*

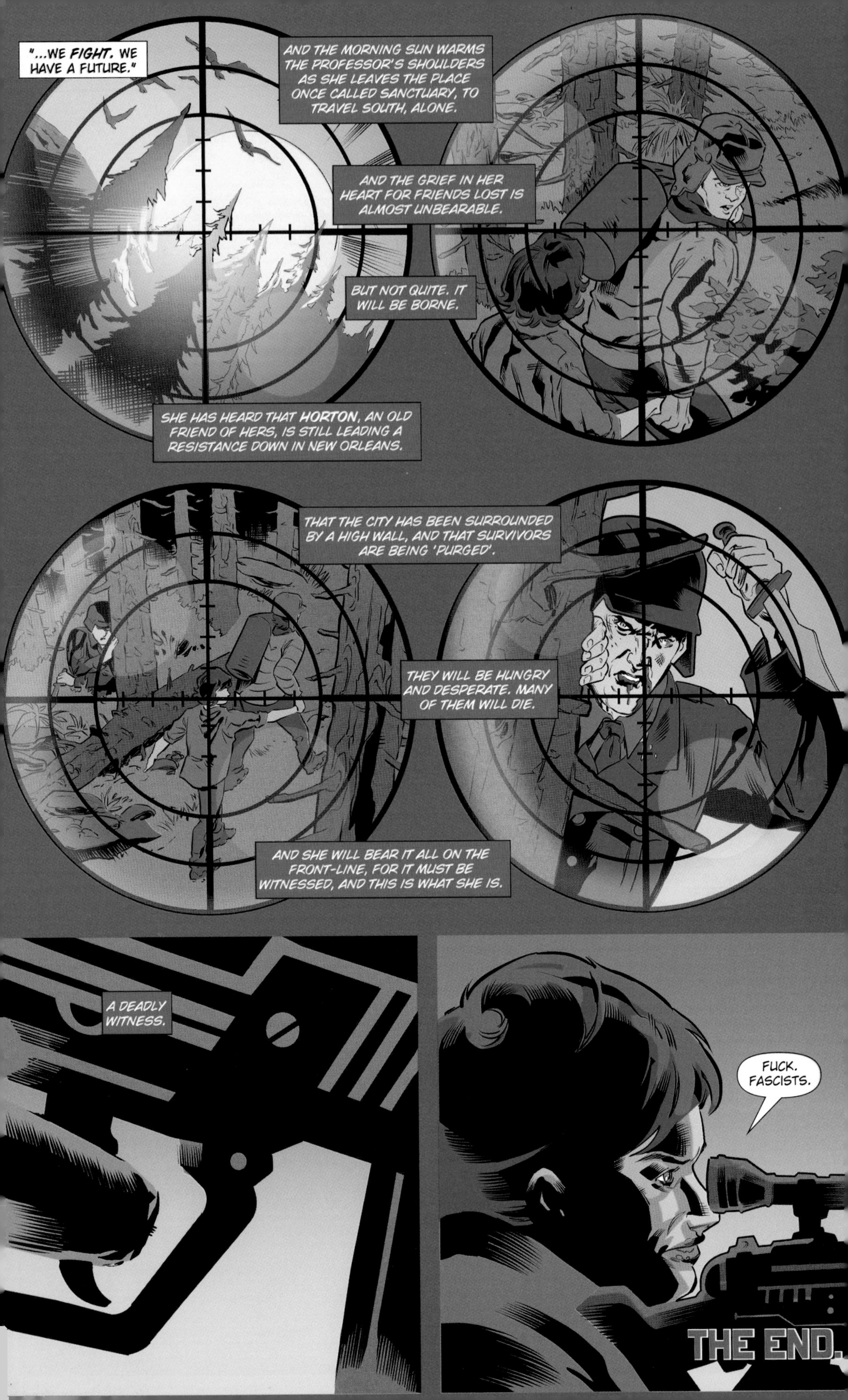
"...WE FIGHT. WE HAVE A FUTURE."
AND THE MORNING SUN WARMS THE PROFESSOR'S SHOULDERS AS SHE LEAVES THE PLACE ONCE CALLED SANCTUARY, TO TRAVEL SOUTH, ALONE.
AND THE GRIEF IN HER HEART FOR FRIENDS LOST IS ALMOST UNBEARABLE.
BUT NOT QUITE. IT WILL BE BORNE.
SHE HAS HEARD THAT HORTON, AN OLD FRIEND OF HERS, IS STILL LEADING A RESISTANCE DOWN IN NEW ORLEANS.
THAT THE CITY HAS BEEN SURROUNDED BY A HIGH WALL, AND THAT SURVIVORS ARE BEING 'PURGED'.
THEY WILL BE HUNGRY AND DESPERATE. MANY OF THEM WILL DIE.
AND SHE WILL BEAR IT ALL ON THE FRONT-LINE, FOR IT MUST BE WITNESSED, AND THIS IS WHAT SHE IS.
A DEADLY WITNESS.
FUCK. FASCISTS.
THE END.

TM

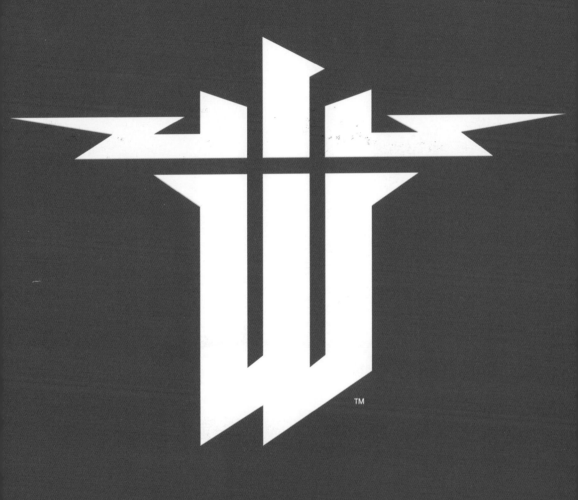

COVERS GALLERY

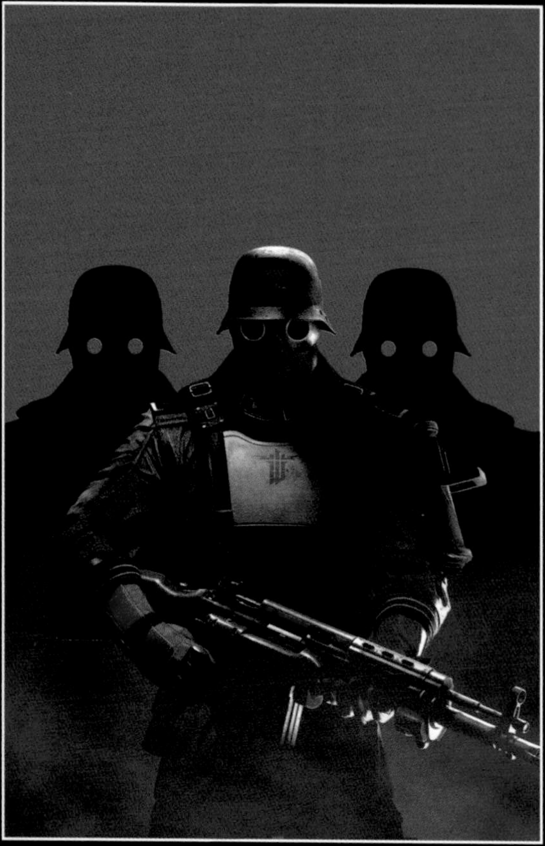

#1 COVER B: GAME ART COVER

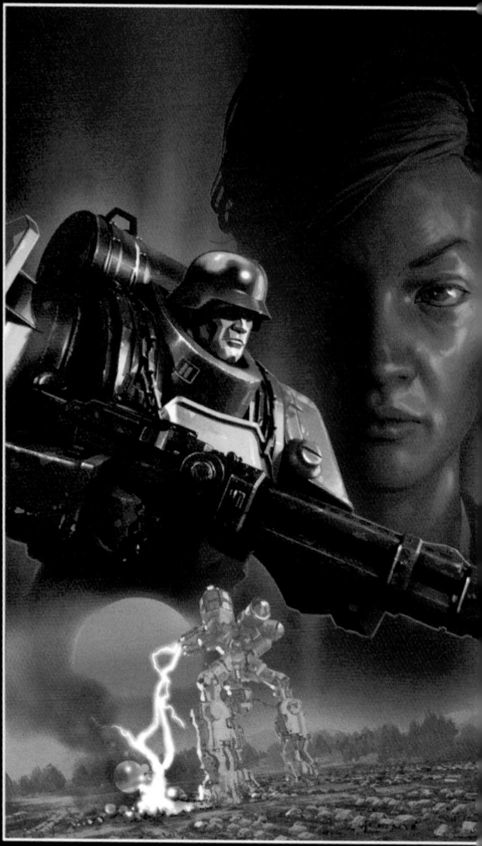

#1 COVER C: ALEX RONALD

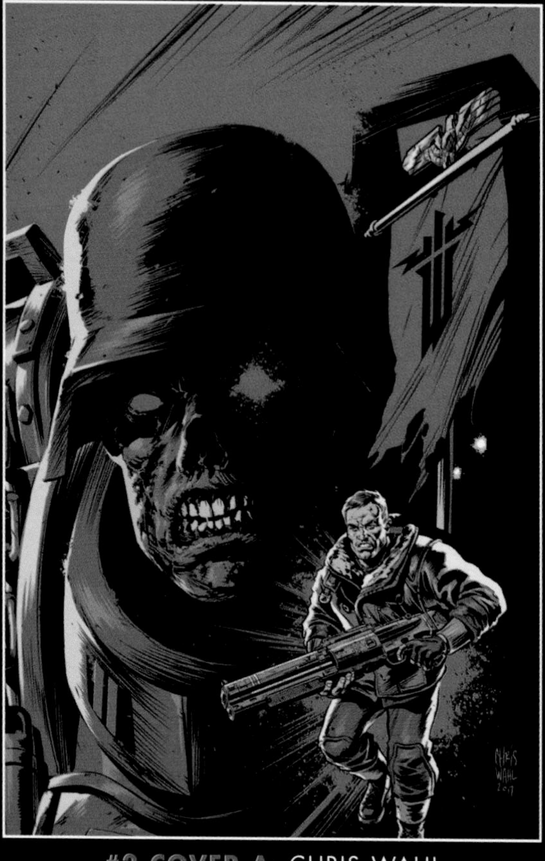

#2 COVER A: CHRIS WAHL

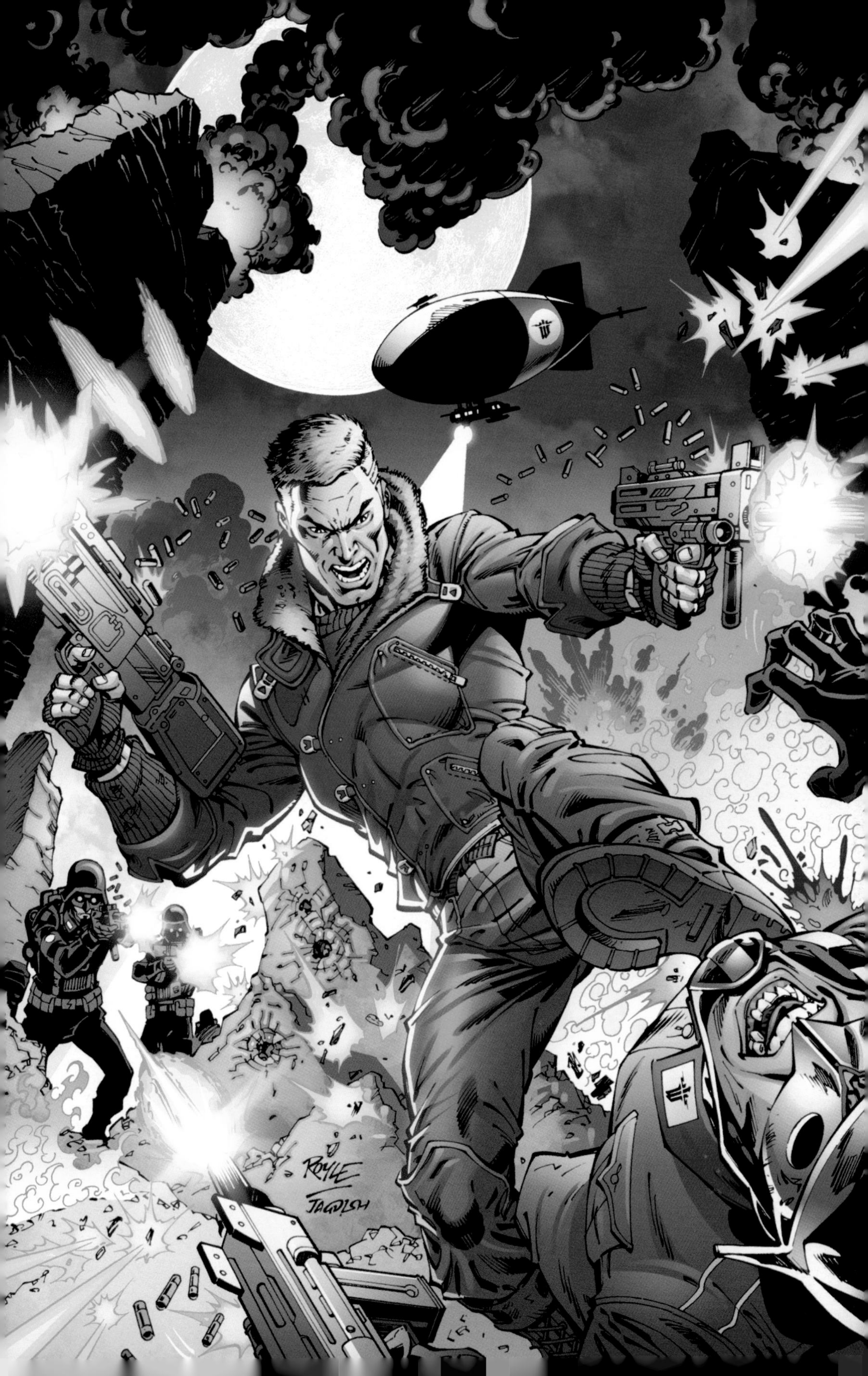
ROYLE
JAGDISH

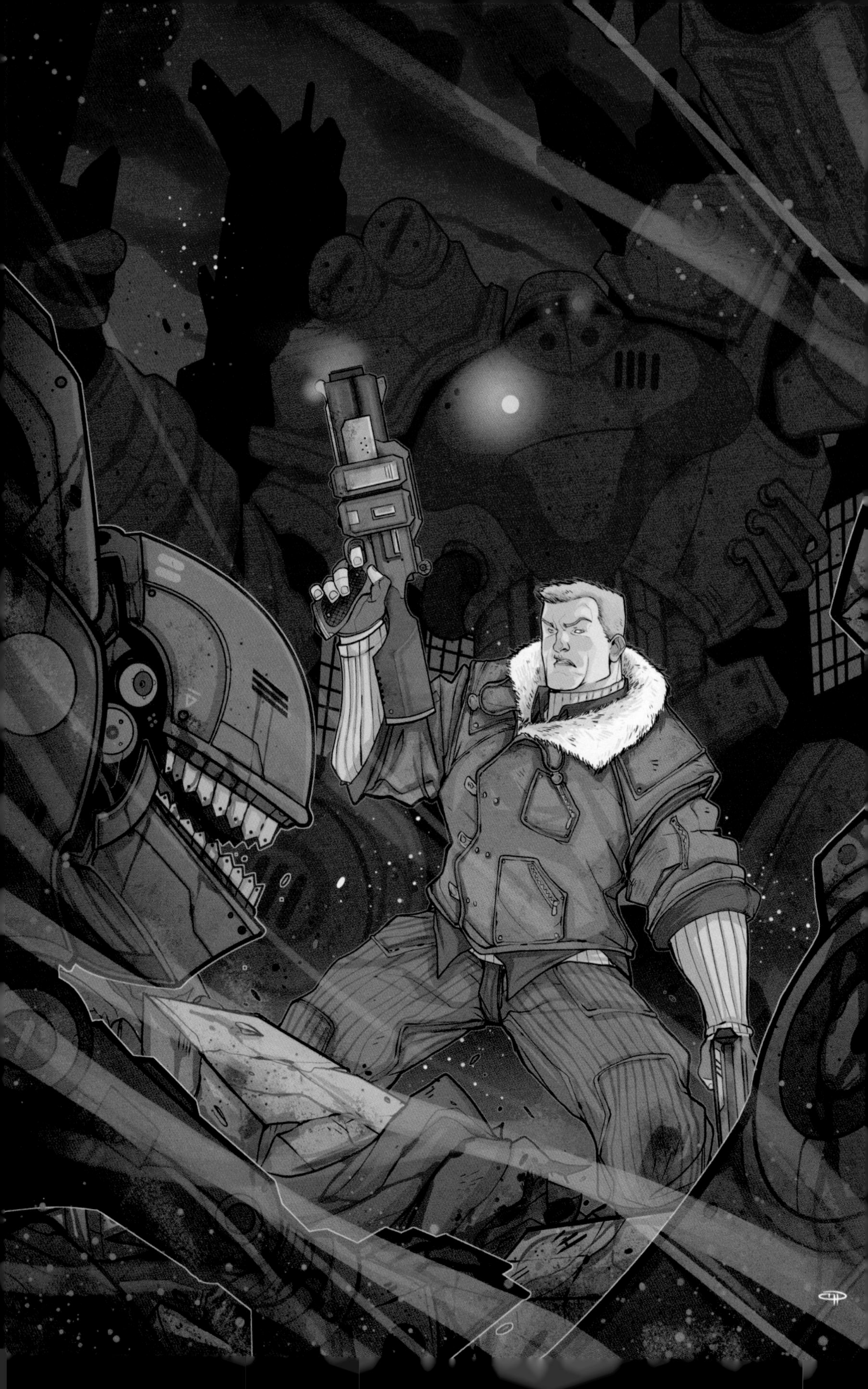

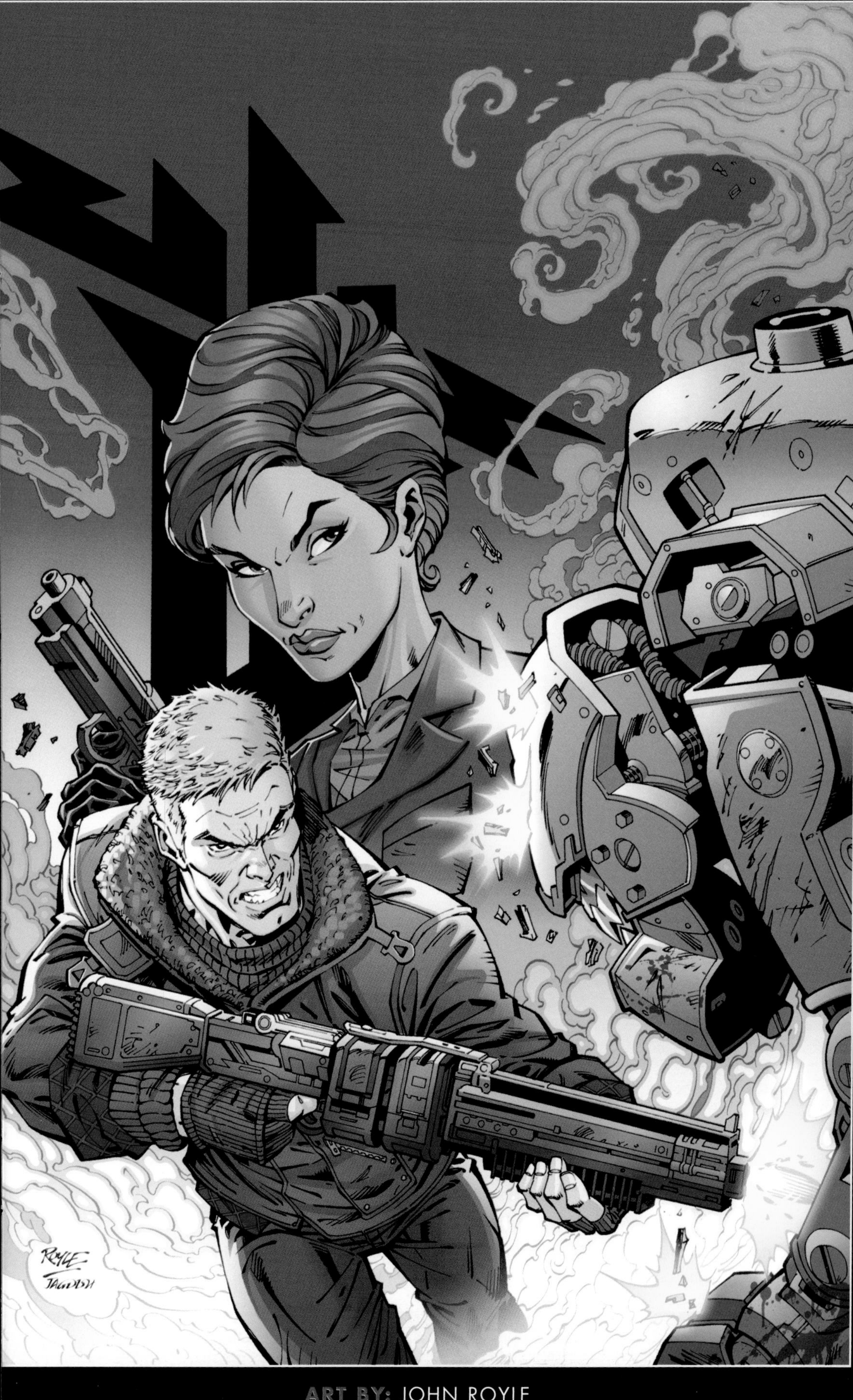
ROYLE
JAGDISH

ART BY: JOHN ROYLE

FROM TITAN COMICS

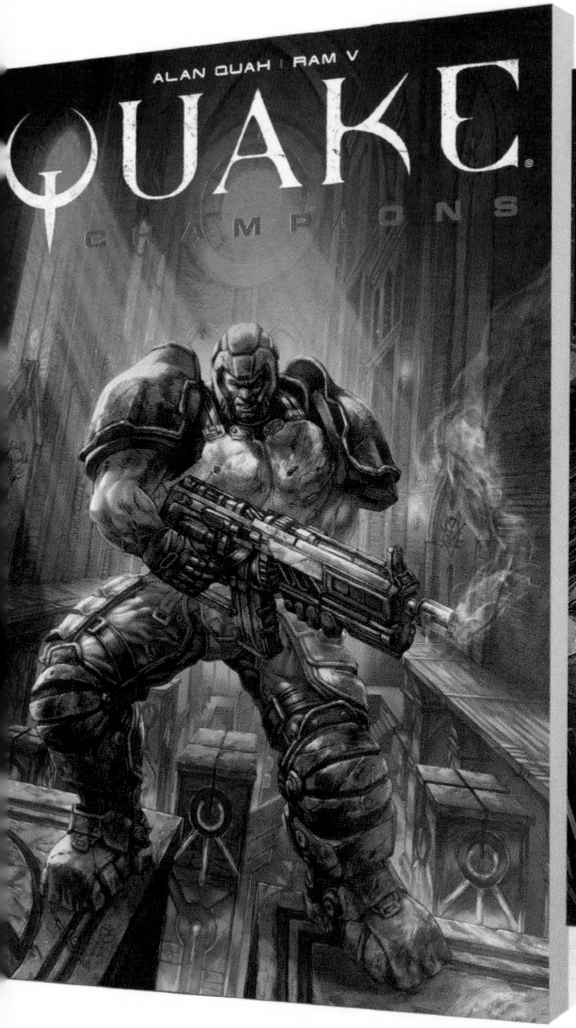
ALAN QUAH | RAM V
QUAKE
CHAMPIONS

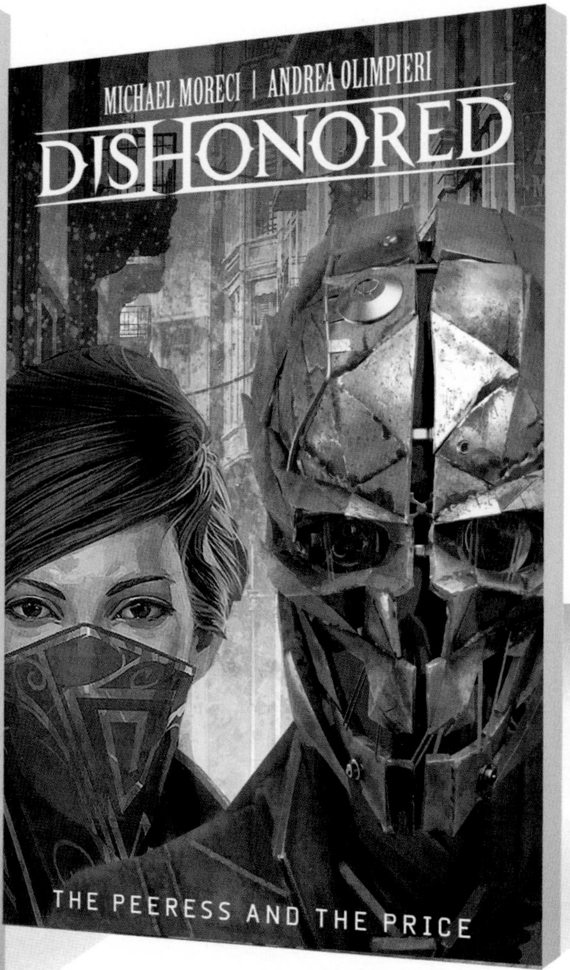
MICHAEL MORECI | ANDREA OLIMPIERI
DISHONORED
THE PEERESS AND THE PRICE

QUAKE CHAMPIONS

Hellish landscapes, brutal violence, and arcane Elder Gods collide in this brand new comic title based on Bethesda's cult first-person shooter videogame franchise.

DISHONORED: THE PEERESS AND THE PRICE

Follow the continuing adventures of Corvo Attano and Emily Kaldwin in this sequel to the highly-anticipated upcoming game Dishonored 2 as they go against brand new threats and foes.

AVAILABLE FROM ALL GOOD COMIC STORES, BOOK STORES AND DIGITAL PROVIDERS!

CREATOR BIOS

DAN WATTERS

Dan Watters is a British writer based in London. He is a founding member (along with Alex Paknadel, Ryan O'Sullivan, and Ram V) of the writing collective White Noise. His previous credits incude **Assassin's Creed: Uprising**, **Tortured Life**, and **The Shadow**. He is also the writer and co-creator of **Limbo** for Image Comics.

PIOTR KOWALSKI

Piotr Kowalski is a comic book writer and artist from Poland. His work includes **Robocop**, **Gail**, **Marvel Knights: Hulk**, **Dark Tower**, **What If? Age of Ultron** and **Dark Souls: Legends of The Flame**. He was the artist and co-creator of the critically acclaimed Image series **Sex**.

RONILSON FREIRE

Ronilson Freire is a comics artist from Brazil. He has worked on **The Green Hornet**, **The Mummy: Palimpsest**, **Justice Inc: The Avenger,** and **Vampirella: Feary Tales**.